C0-AUJ-409

THE
USE OF FORCE
IN
INTERNATIONAL
RELATIONS

STUDIES IN INTERNATIONAL POLITICS

other books in the series

International Theory and European Integration
by Charles Pentland

The Foreign Policies of the Powers
edited by F. S. Northedge

THE
USE OF FORCE
IN
INTERNATIONAL
RELATIONS

edited by
F. S. Northedge

THE FREE PRESS
A Division of Macmillan Publishing Co., Inc.
NEW YORK

Copyright © 1974 by F. S. Northedge

All rights reserved. No part of this book may be reproduced or transmitted in any form or by any means, electronic or mechanical, including photocopying, recording, or by any information storage and retrieval system, without permission in writing from the Publisher.

The Free Press
A Division of Macmillan Publishing Co., Inc.
866 Third Avenue, New York, N.Y. 10022

Library of Congress Catalog Card Number: 74-10140

Printed in the United States of America

printing number

1   2   3   4   5   6   7   8   9   10

JX
1391
. N58

Contents

7

ALMA COLLEGE
MONTEITH LIBRARY
ALMA, MICHIGAN

Preface

Despite the self-evident prominence of force and the threat of force in international relations there are relatively few published studies of this subject. In this book my colleagues, mostly research workers at the London School of Economics, and myself have tried to consider the international use of force from its various aspects, political, legal, moral and so on. It is to be assumed that so long as world politics takes the form of a number of independent states, each responsible for its own security and without a common power to keep order between them, armed force will remain, if not the last resort of kings, at least the last resort of nation-states.

It cannot be denied, however, that force in international relations is now in a state of transition, more so perhaps than at any time in the past. In the first place, war between the mightiest states, or even the use of force by the giant Powers on a limited scale, is a prospect none of them, for obvious reasons, readily contemplates. Secondly, what with the existence of the United Nations and other fora of world opinion, states resorting to force tend to meet with widespread opprobrium. Partly for this reason, the uses of force today are devious, subversion taking the place of frontal military attack, guerrilla movements doing the work of armies and fleets. In other words, the current depreciation of force, verbally at least, and the search for substitutes for it must enter into our subject. These are some of the aspects from which force in international affairs is viewed in this symposium. Our intention, however, is not to propose remedies but to inquire how and why the resort to arms in the affairs of nations takes place.

F. S. Northedge

The London School of Economics and Political Science, June 1973.

1 The Resort to Arms

Force has played and continues to play a dominant role in international relations, or so most of us generally assume. Our picture of the international scene tends to be one in which the great Powers, armed to the teeth with the most terrible weapons, are constantly threatening to use them and do from time to time use them either against one another or against weaker states. The very warning, considered to be the normal rule of international politics, *nemo me impune lacessit*,[1] implies that states not only live with one hand on the scabbard (to use our familiar anachronism) but are not afraid to unsheathe the sword on occasion, whether for attack or defence. Yet very little study is made of this commonplace instrument of international relations, force. Academic strategic studies appear to be concerned mainly with the use of, or the threat to make use of, military force as a means of achieving national security or international stability; but this is far from the study of force in all its aspects, moral and political, legal and technological. Such a study we are attempting, though in a provisional manner, in this book.

But first we must see what we take this word 'force' to mean. What precisely are we referring to when we use it? We can no doubt begin by dismissing from our minds the metaphorical use of the term 'force', as when we speak of the 'force of events' or the 'force of circumstances'. The expression *force majeure* is sometimes used to signify the compulsion of affairs or events over which we have little or no control; every politician who has had experience of office or any administrator who has had to take complicated decisions can testify to the pressure of daily facts which seem beyond the power of men or nations to modify or reverse. If there is 'force' here it is in the sense of constraints which act almost as though the responsible decision-maker was being physically moved from one position to another. This we can call the operation of metaphorical force.

[1] 'No one provokes me with impunity'.

There is an important distinction, too, between 'force' and 'power', though the two words are often used interchangeably. By 'power' – in the sense in which this term is used in political studies – we propose to mean the capability of a person or group to make his or its will felt in the decision-making process of another person or group. I can be said to have power in so far as someone else, or some institution or organization, feels that he or it must take my wishes into account when decisions are to be made. A state may be said to have power in the international system when another state recognizes that it cannot be ignored when issues have to be determined. Quite clearly, power in this sense may well reflect the capability of persons and states to apply force in the physical sense unless their will is complied with. But there are, equally clearly, many other attributes of the powerful state or person besides the capability to apply physical force; there is the ability to confer or withhold economic benefits, the attractions of an ideology, prestige or reputation for great achievements in the past, and so on. So far is power not to be precisely equated with force – in the sense of the physical impact of one body upon another – that we might almost say that force is often resorted to when power fails.

There is, however, the complication that in international relations, especially today, when we talk of states using force against one another more often than not we mean merely the threat of force. A great deal of international relations today is carried forward on the basis of deterrence, or what simply used to be called bluff. It is often pointed out today that if a state, especially a great state, has to use force, rather than the threat of force, the purpose of the operation has already broken down. The United States, for example, can never be quite one hundred per cent certain whether or not the Soviet Union will make good its threat to use nuclear weapons if its vital interests are attacked; the same applies *mutatis mutandis* to the Soviet Union, and each side knows that the other is uncertain. Yet somehow deterrence so far seems to work since neither super Power can be entirely sure that the other's bluff can be called and hence it refrains most of the time from putting the issue to the test. Here we are not speaking of force solely as a physical relation between one body and another, but of power, in the sense of a psychological relationship between one mind and another. Consequently, there is bound to be some overlap, after all, between the meaning of power and the meaning, if not of force, at least of the threat of force. Nevertheless, when we are speaking of force by itself, it is clear that we

12

have in mind an essentially physical restraint, or set of restraints, rather than the essentially psychological relationship which is power.

There is one further point to be made about force before we leave this preliminary definition. Force is often used synonymously with 'violence' and there are the obvious similarities in that both force and violence employ physical means, whether highly complicated weapons or plain fists, to achieve certain ends or fulfil certain satisfactions. But an important distinction can be drawn between the two terms in that the word 'violence' is normally applied to the use of physical force by non-governmental agencies and generally for private, rather than public, ends. The kidnapping of a child or rape of a woman for personal advantage is an act of violence; the sending of the troops of one state across the borders of another is, for our purposes here, the use of force. Hence force may be said to have a somewhat higher degree of legitimacy about it than violence; it is, relative to violence, an action sanctioned by a certain community allegedly in the public interest and for the public good. This difference is reflected in the fact that most advanced communities exact lighter penalties for 'political' crimes than for other crimes.

Obviously, it cannot always be easy to draw the line. What about so-called 'terrorists' who commit acts of violence for political ends which some states agree to be legitimate and other states deny? It was because of this disagreement that the United Nations General Assembly in the autumn of 1972 was unable to agree on the forthright condemnation of political violence. And what about states which deny that armed forces serving their political ends, such as the Chinese 'volunteers' serving on the North Korean side in the Korean War of 1950–3, are actually agents of themselves? The dividing line may be blurred but the principle of division is clear enough: the member-states of the international system organize, finance and control armed forces as instruments of their foreign policies; we wish to examine what the precise activities of these agents are and how they are related to the general political preoccupations of the state. Violence, as an incident in the everyday life of individuals, trade unions, extremist political associations, and so on, connotes quite a different form of social relationship.

Force in civil society

Many people conceive of force as though it were characteristically

13

international, or even exclusively international, whereas civil (or municipal) society is supposed to rest somehow upon consent or general will. International order accordingly reflects the ratios of armed force between the different states and their will to exploit that force in defence of an international order severally agreeable to them. Order within the frontiers of a single state, on the other hand, is looked upon as in some way the expression of a 'social will' which is in effect self-enforcing.

That no such sharp distinction can be drawn is evident in the prevalence of the symbols of force among the 'dignified parts of government' (as Walter Bagehot called them) in the constitution of all or almost all modern states. The sovereign or executive head of government in practically all states is normally visually associated with the armed forces of the state. The monarch, even the constitutional monarch, will dress, be seen and be photographed in the uniform of a high officer of one of the armed services of the state; and what president of an Asian, African, Latin American state, not to speak of many European states, is not? The monarch or president will take the salute at military parades or will have his most senior generals with him when he addresses the people from the rostrum. The ordinary citizen is deliberately impressed with the military strength of the state, not only in order to inculcate in him a proper national pride and deference towards his government and its administration, but also no doubt to bring home to him the hazards he is risking if he attempts to defy the state. The Roman lictor's rods and axes which were adopted as symbols of Fascist authority by Benito Mussolini in Italy were merely dramatic instruments for inducing in the masses the respect for government which is nurtured more unobtrusively in a parliamentary democracy.

It is interesting to observe here the use by states of the panoply of armed force which they develop mainly for external purposes as a means for inspiring respect for law and governmental authority internally. Who can say whether military parades in Moscow's Red Square on May Day, when all the terrors in the Soviet armoury are trundled out for the people to see, are intended solely to impress foreigners? French nuclear tests in the Pacific presumably have a scientific purpose and no doubt a deterrent purpose, too, but it would not be surprising if they did not succeed also in convincing some Frenchmen, at least, of the might and grandeur of France, which in turn helps to create loyalty: the distance between respect and fear is not large. The process works the other way, too: that is

14

to say, Soviet and French loyalty, which is enhanced by contemplation of the Soviet and French capacity to inflict the most frightful damage on enemies, is also an important factor in the strength of France and the Soviet Union as state-members of the international system.

There is no question, however, of deference to the state in any well-ordered community having to depend to any considerable extent on the habitual use or threat of force against the ordinary people of that community. The obvious reason why this cannot be the condition of a stable society for any length of time was stated by David Hume in the eighteenth century when he pointed out that the resources for coercion at the disposal of the state are invariably inferior to the combined force of the community to be coerced; in other words, army and police combined, even if they agree to being used for the repression of the rest of the population, cannot exceed that population in numbers. The forces of repression must always be weaker than the combined strength of the resisting mass. Consequently, as Charles Merriam has written,

> Power is not strongest when it uses violence but weakest. It is strongest when it employs the instruments of substitution and counter-attraction, of allurement, of participation, rather than of exclusion, of education rather than of annihilation.

'Rape', as Merriam puts it in another passage in the same work, 'in politics as in sex, is not an evidence of irresistible attractiveness.'[1]

Here, of course, is one of the chief differences between the use of force within the state and the use of force between states. In the intranational situation, as Merriam argues, there has to be the substitution of other means for securing compliance with the law than force or threat of force owing to the disparity of numbers between government and its agents of coercion, on one side, and the governed mass, on the other. In the international situation, on the other hand, when a whole national community organized as a state is pitted against another such community, the relations of strength are likely to be more equal. Hence, although each of these two states will no doubt use the 'instruments of substitution', as Merriam calls them, in seeking to bend the other to its will, it does not need to do so if it has a definite superiority of physical strength at its disposal. And since the 'instruments of substitution' may well take

[1] Charles Merriam, *Political Power: its composition and incidence*, McGraw-Hill, New York, 1934, p. 180.

years, possibly decades, to take effect, states in their relations with one another are more likely to try to acquire a superiority of physical strength over their most probable adversaries rather than rely upon such instruments. This is even more likely to be the case if the balance of physical strength is already moving against that state.

Needless to say, what we have stated concerning the use of force as a means of securing compliance with the law within the state may be taken as referring more particularly to the more stable states with more of a liberal democratic tradition. Unfortunately, the twentieth century has shown that a ruthless totalitarian régime can in practice keep a population in sway by methods of terror almost alone; perhaps this was the situation in many of the great empires of the ancient world. A frightened people, especially if it has recent experience of civil conflict, such as the Spanish or Greek people today, may think twice about challenging the massed force of the state, even when that state is managed by a comparatively small minority. Modern techniques of mass control have facilitated this kind of confidence trick. We should be careful nevertheless not to assume that the mass acceptance of the *status quo* in a totalitarian regime is always a matter of fear of force. Even in Nazi Germany there are reasons for thinking that a great many people acquiesced in the regime because of such factors as laziness, unwillingness to 'get involved' or to be thought unpatriotic, and the wish for a quiet life, as well as fear of the jackboot.

Force in international affairs

Force then has its role in intranational affairs even though for the most part the popular consensus on which ordered government depends recruits a wide range of psychological and other factors for its continuance, besides the use or threat of force. When that consensus breaks down or melts away, there is a condition of actual or potential civil war which resembles the normal state of affairs in the international system. Hence, force may be said to play a greater part in international than in domestic politics, and this because the conformity to law which is based on a complicated set of mental dispositions and habits within the state, other than fear of coercive sanctions, is replaced in international affairs by resistance to the attempts of the foreigner to impose either *the* law of the international system or a law of his own, if it is contrary to one's interests. In short, force in international relations tends to be more obtrusive, overt, dramatic and damaging. States, so to speak, are continuously flexing their muscles and cleaning their guns before their neighbours' windows. We have given one reason for this in this paragraph, but are there others?

The most obvious and natural answer is that in the international system each and every state is responsible for its own defence. Unless it makes provision for its own self-preservation it can depend upon it that hardly anyone else will. 'Hardly', because circumstances are conceivable and have in fact occurred in which the continued existence of one state is so vital to another that the latter virtually takes over the other's defence rather than see it overwhelmed. This occurs when one state gives a guarantee to another, as Britain did to Poland in 1939, or takes another country under its wing, as the United States did in respect of Japan in 1951. But this is not a general condition of international affairs and for obvious reasons states tend to be wary of it. Even when a state joins a collective defence organization in accordance with Article 51 of the United Nations Charter it can normally expect to take no more out of the organization by way of security than what it puts into it. As for the United Nations itself as a provider of security, a state would be fool-hardy in the extreme if it looked solely to that organization for its self-preservation. If this were not so, Article 51 would be unnecessary; it is a recognition of the fact of life that, as the world is constituted at present, states must in the last resort look to themselves for their defence.

This decentralization of self-defence which characterizes the international system has no parallel, or ought to have no parallel, in the modern well-ordered state. There the physical defence of the ordinary person against attack is provided for by special forces such as the police and the army which act on behalf of the community as a whole. The bearing of arms by the private individual is not only unnecessary; it is positively discouraged, or illegalized, or carefully controlled by licensing regulations in most ordered states; indeed in some countries, notably Britain, the bearing of arms by the police is normally highly irregular.

Public security, or, more correctly, publicly provided security, may, however, on occasion break down; the police or the armed forces may fail to do their job because they are too weak, or inefficient or corrupt. The courts and judges which are supposed to penalize attacks on the security of the general public may fail, too, to act in accordance with their responsibilities; they may fear reprisals from criminals or they may be perverted by corruption. Or the public as a whole may lack the courage or will to side with the authorities in the suppression of private breaches of law and order. In such circumstances self-defence is likely to become as decentralized as it is in the international system. The ordinary person then has to arm himself if the national machinery for providing public order either will not or cannot operate. And it is as well to remember that once this happens, as in the international system, the feeling of general insecurity grows and the desire to increase the personal holding of weapons increases with it. Nor would most people regard this as unreasonable; in fact, they may well blame as improvident those who fail to provide for the defence of themselves and their families.

The breakdown of public order which is a contingent liability within the state is a normal condition of the international system. Since 1945 there has been provision in the form of the United Nations Security Council for the centralized provision of international security, but the conditions on which this service depends – that is, the consent of all five permanent members of the Security Council – are so unlikely to be satisfied that for all practical purposes this attempt at the centralized provision of state security can for all practical purposes be written off.

Hence it has become standard practice for almost all states to provide themselves with such armed force as to deter any possible aggressor. But that qualification is a vital one. It is normally not essential for a state to provide itself with such armed force that it could effectively beat off a full-scale attack from any other state, including the most powerful states. The French proposal in the time of de Gaulle's Presidency to use their *force de frappe* for azimuthal defence, that is, to fend off an attack from any point of the globe, was unnessary and unrealistic, no matter what fine rhetoric it made. All a state needs is sufficient armed force to inflict such damage on an aggressor that it would not be worth his while to launch an aggression. The Swiss Army, for example, could not withstand a full-scale Soviet attack nor could the British so-called independent nuclear force. But both no doubt could inflict such harm on the aggressor as to make the value to the Soviet Union of acquiring a devastated Switzerland or Britain quite uneconomic.

This situation of decentralized self-defence also has its bearing on disarmament and arms-control negotiations. In theory nothing could be more sensible than the attempt to reduce the cost of mutual deterrence *pari passu* all the way round. Particularly is this true of the super Powers, the Soviet Union and the United States. These states constitute exceptions to the rule mentioned above, namely, that states will tend to provide themselves with sufficient armed force as would inflict such damage on any potential aggressor that his hypothetical gains from the aggression could not compensate for it. Since a successful attack by one of the super Powers on the other could mean that nothing less than total world power would fall into the victor's hands, each super Power tries to make its deterrent forces vastly greater than is required simply for deterrent purposes; it tends to work for 'overkill' capacity lest the other side should decide to risk almost all it has in order to gain the whole world or to prevent the other gaining the whole world. But even for lesser states it is surely a natural procedure to over-insure, rather than under-insure, against the risk of attack. If in the event less than the minimum use of force is needed to deter attack, then that is a bonus. It is better to be in that position than to be deficient in defensive resources when the moment of emergency arrives.

In these circumstances lies the great dilemma of disarmament. People often speak of the absence of 'trust' between nations as a factor responsible for the relative failure of arms control and disarmament negotiations since, say, 1945. Considering the central fact of international relations that the sovereign state is almost exclusively responsible for its own defence, it is understandable that states are hesitant to rely upon other states for ensuring that their defence is effective when the moment for putting it into operation arrives. Mutual trust is difficult enough to achieve between people belonging to the same social and cultural order; where vast moral and cultural divergencies exist, as between independent nations, mutual trust is a rare commodity indeed. But even if all the trust in the world existed between nations, the condition of decentralized defence is bound to rule out any easy disarmament agreements, even if it does not render them entirely impractical. Governments and their advisers will inevitably overstate the international risks to the security of their own countries and understate their own means of coping with those risks. Indeed, it would be a denial of elementary prudence to do otherwise.

It might be argued that in this day and age the costs and reduplication involved in decentralized defence – the more one state has of certain tanks the more its rivals must have of the same tanks – are so enormous, as are the risks of general conflict inherent in such a system, that the wiser course would be to centralize defence by handing it over to some world agency, or in other words to make the UN Security Council effective by removing the veto. Putting aside the question of whether the states of the world, and especially the five great Powers on the Council, are mentally prepared for such a great leap forward, the fact remains that force can never exist or can never be used except in relation to some fairly closely knit political philosophy. Our public armed forces in Britain, however neutral we may regard them, are in fact defending a certain social order against internal and external attack, an order which normally carries the approval of the great bulk of the British people whether they are fully conscious of giving their approval or not. The same is true of France, Italy, the United States and other countries, whatever the local differences. In the international system, too, there is a corresponding social order, consisting of 140 or so sovereign states, each responsible for its own defence. Every state, as the Second World War showed, seems prepared to use its own armed force to defend the existing system against destruction by regimes like the pre-war Nazi regime in Germany. But if one goes into greater detail about the form of this international order, to ask such questions as to whether Taiwan belongs to China or China to Taiwan, whether Israel has a right to exist, and so on, the moral rightfulness of the existing order is not only in dispute, but many millions of people would rather fight and die than accept its legitimacy. To talk of the centralization of armed force in such circumstances is to cry for the moon. The fact is that most people the world over would prefer to jog along with the existing system of decentralized power rather than approve a social order which their conscience would reject and which would have to be created in – or imposed upon – the world if a system of centralized defence were to be established.

Technology and force

The development which has made the use of force by states in their international relations a highly controversial question in the twentieth century is, of course, the harnessing of modern industry, science and technology to the manufacture of weapons and the general conduct of force in the international system. Until the First World War it almost seems that the methods of waging war had hardly advanced beyond those of the Middle Ages. With sabres, bayonets, cavalry charges, hand-to-hand combat, the men who went to war in 1914 had little that was modern at their hand, except perhaps for the internal combustion engine, a few airplanes, the machine gun and various kinds of cannon. By 1918 the European industrial revolution, which had been quietly developing in the nineteenth century since the last great war a century before, had transformed the methods of war, especially in the production of high-explosive artillery shells on a scale quite unheard of before. The Second World War ended with the application of nuclear energy to warfare and the exploitation in the service of war of a range of discoveries and inventions extending from radar to penicillin, from napalm bombs to portable concrete harbours. There is scarcely a branch of modern industry or pure and applied science which is not or could not be related to the use or threat of force in the relations between states. As the emphasis in international relations shifts from the brandishing of crude and naked force to the display of national power as a means of deterrence in all its forms, activities like space exploration as symbolizing massive state power may come to absorb more and more industrial and scientific resources.

This is a familiar story but its implications are worth examining. In the first place there is the obvious point that the more the armaments and military-service sectors of state activity become enmeshed with the total economy of the country the more the continuance of economic conditions such as full employment or a healthy balance of payments come to depend upon the state's equipment for the use of force in its international relations. Or, to put it another way, some level of political tension would seem to be not inconvenient, at least for the larger states, if it pours money into employers' and workers' pockets from the armaments industry. And conversely those whose livelihood depends on the arms business may come to think of improvements in the level of international tension as threats to their jobs; they may indeed positively fear the onset of *détente* after a period of strain and danger in international relations. Such people may fail to appreciate that there will be work for them to do and profits to earn in a peace economy as well as in a war economy. But they have a certain reason for thinking as they do in that governments and legislatures are generally more willing to vote large sums to increase the nation's capacity for using force against another nations than, say, for its educational policy. The *Report from Iron Mountain* is by no means wholly mythical.[1]

[1] *Report from Iron Mountain on the possibility and desirability of peace.* With introductory material by Leonard C. Lewin, Macdonald, London, 1968.

The mere fact that the efficiency of present-day weapons, in a world of intense arms competition, is dependent, as never before, on the highest scientific and technical skill, has added a totally new dimension to ratios of armed force between the different states. There was a time, certainly before the First World War, and possibly before the Second, too, when the level of armaments which a state chose to acquire was partly dependent upon the state's economic capacity and partly on its government's reading of the external dangers which the state had to face, and this in its turn meant the capabilities of adversary states and the hostility of their intentions. A weak state surrounded by hostile neighbours would *ceteris paribus* require – though it may not be able to provide – more capability for using force than a strong state surrounded by weak and generally friendly neighbours.

The situation today, however, is that all the major states maintain more or less substantial establishments for scientific research which spend their time inquiring into new methods of disabling the populations of their potential enemies or defending themselves against attack from those enemies. This scientific research continues at great expense from year to year in peace and war. The marvels of ingenuity produced by scientists in the last few decades lead us to believe that if scientists are set a problem – how to penetrate the defences of the other side or how to prevent his weapons reaching their targets – they will eventually solve it if they are given enough resources. And once the scientists have produced the new weapon, or anti-weapon weapon, it has been shown time and again that it is all but impossible to prevent the politicians clamouring to have it and to add it to the nation's stock of arms. 'Can we afford not to have this new weapon', governments and legislatures ask, 'if the other side already has it or is bound to have it before long?' If there is joined to those voices the pressures from thousands of entrepreneurs and millions of workers who stand to gain from the adoption of the new weapon and its manufacture in the areas where their business is carried on, the impulse to begin work on it can hardly be resisted.

Thus we may be seeing, along with the impact of pure science and technology on weapons production with all its implications, a distinct change in the sources from which the momentum behind arms races spring. Before the advent of science and technology the motivations which led a state to acquire arms derived to a large extent from a certain interpretation by that state of the dangers it had to face, principally the intentions of other states. Today, while

22

this consideration is still, of course, highly important, we have to take into account the actual availability of weapons, as rendered possible by scientific research. This means that it could be possible for the Soviet Union and the United States, for example, to be on the best of terms politically and yet to go on increasing their military capability against each other; at the same time each side may interpret an intensification of the arms race by the other, not as a result of the increased availability of weapons but of an increase in the hostility of the other towards itself. It is easy to understand, too, that an arms race motivated by the speed of scientific and techno-logical advances is harder to control and altogether more inflexible than an arms race actuated by hostile interpretations of the other side's intentions.

We may now consider yet another consequence of the increasing input of scientific and technological expertise into the production of modern armed force, though the effects of this on international relations generally are somewhat more difficult to specify. It arises from the fact that in military alliances before 1939 almost all that was required for the alliance to be effective was a legal commitment to act in the other's defence (or as the text of the treaty of alliance stipulated) when the other state was in difficulties. There might be military co-operation beforehand, as under the Anglo-French *Entente* of 1904, but this was by no means always considered neces-sary. The assumption was that when the war actually broke out and the *casus foederis* of the treaty came into effect, there would be sufficient time to co-ordinate the measures of the two or more states. Today these assumptions are no longer valid and this for two reasons. One is that the reaction time allowed before responding to the first attack, especially one delivered with nuclear weapons, would perhaps be a matter of seconds, as compared with, say, the thirty days' mobilization of fifty years ago. Hence the alliance needs to be in a state of constant war preparedness and inter-alliance diplomacy to settle inter-alliance differences – as between the NATO and Warsaw Pact states – must proceed while the two or more coalitions stand ready to fight each other at a few seconds' notice. The necessity for effective organs of consultation within the alliance which can go into operation at a moment's notice is thus clear.

But the state of permanent war preparedness which modern technology has made necessary also means that a considerable degree of continuous consultation is needed, not only to co-ordinate defence and foreign policies in a crisis, but also to ensure that the onerous economic burden of defence is shared as fairly as possible. The high rate of obsolescence of modern weapons in a state of permanent war preparedness means that defence must take a large share of the national budgets of members of the alliance. What they must ensure is that the burden of defence is fairly distributed within the state and that the state as a whole is taking care to see that its own economic contribution to the alliance is neither much below nor much above some theoretical average. None of this work can be done except within an institutionalized, even bureaucratic structure similar in many respects to that of a modern national government. It is thus easy to see how modern technology has contributed to the rigidity of structure and often the inflexibility of procedure in the present-day alliance.

Force and its human agencies

Armed force applied by a state in its relations with other states has to be administered by human agents in the form of soldiers, sailors, airmen and others, and must be approved by the population of the state applying the force, or as large a proportion of it as is relevant to governmental action in that state. As for the former, the professional ministers of force, even the most highly disciplined of troops in the most totalitarian of states, have to feel that the use of force has some legitimacy about it, in that it serves the national interest, or is likely to be successful, or is in a morally rightful cause. At one stage Russian troops in the First World War refused to fight and this led in due course to Russia's withdrawal from the war. During the Second World War the German commander, Field-Marshal Irwin Rommel, began to conspire with other officers against the Nazi regime when he realized that Germany was being asked to destroy itself in a hopeless cause. No account has ever been kept of the countless thousands, perhaps millions, of troops whose spirit or confidence in the national cause deserted them in the heat of modern international armed conflicts and who quitted the struggle.

The reasons for such failures of will on the part of members of professional forces when armed strength comes to be used are obviously as varied as human motivation as a whole. They may range from the loftiest of moral objections to the use of force, as when American soldiers have refused orders to take part in reprisal raids against villages in Vietnam, to a sheer failure of nerve, as exemplified by 'shell-shock' in the First World War. What we can say with some confidence, however, is that it seems never to have been the situation that the psychological rejection of force by the armed services of the state (even when conscripted for service) has seriously interfered with the application of force by the state as part of the normal conduct of international relations. In the First World War some of the belligerent governments seem to have feared that the shortage of physically fit men might adversely affect their war efforts; there is no record of such fears having been entertained in regard to the availability of the kind of psychological and moral qualities necessary for the use of force. But some reservations must be entered as to the psychological effects of using nuclear weapons. It is well known that some of the crew and observers in the aircraft which dropped atomic bombs on Japan in August 1945 subsequently underwent a kind of mental derangement. On the other hand, the use of nuclear force is mercifully so rare and exceptional that generalizations about the psychological prerequisites for the administration of force can hardly be based upon it.

It could also be asserted with some confidence that armed forces, even today, are no doubt less likely to recoil against the use of force when they are winning, or at least when they are not conspicuously losing. There is some significance in the fact that the German generals' plot against Hitler's life took place in July 1944 and not in July 1940, that Field-Marshal Rommel did not seem to have doubts about the Nazi regime when he was winning great victories in North Africa, that Russian armies melted away in 1917 in the face of three years of almost consistent defeat, and that American soldiers in Vietnam really began to question the whole purpose of the war when the clear-cut victories which Americans are said to prefer eluded their grasp. It is significant, too, that the contemporary widespread revulsion against international war has come at a time when survival in an all-out nuclear war has become a remote prospect for anyone. It seems that, so long as there was a chance of survival in war, and especially a chance of winning, recruitment for the armed services has been sufficient to meet the need. Even when conscription has had to be introduced, comparatively few men and women have been prepared to defy the law on grounds of moral objection to taking human life.

But more important for our purposes are the reactions of ordinary people on whose behalf the government claims to be acting when from time to time it decides to use force in its international relations. We have seen, when discussing force as a technique of government within the state, that its use is conditional upon the acquiescence of most of the people most of the time; in other words, the deviants who have to be brought to order by force must be in a minority, with the majority consenting to that use of force. Externally the same holds true in that when using force abroad government has to feel that its people are more or less behind it. One reason which may hinder that popular concurrence is that, in the external use of force, especially in wartime, they themselves are likely to be involved, even if they are not members of the armed services, whereas they tend to be more or less passive bystanders when the state employs force internally. On the other hand, the external use of force is likely to have the whole complex of emotions constituting nationalism or patriotism on its side. Certainly, before 1914 almost any external use of force by the state was likely to be supported by the people provided it was not an instantaneous failure.

This approval was generally of a moral rather than expediental character, and the same applied to the disapproval of force. Indeed, there are grounds for thinking that judgements on a government's actions within the international system tend to carry with them heavy moral, rather than pragmatic, overtones, especially as one moves from the professional policy-making élite of the country to the less concerned periphery. Approval of a government's use of force, too, will tend to be importantly governed by judgements of that government's performance in general, possibly because the ordinary person does not know enough about foreign affairs to be able to distinguish them sharply from home policy; thus, supporters of the Labour Party in Britain were more disposed to criticize Sir Anthony Eden's armed action against Egypt in 1956 than were Conservatives; moreover, both Labour and Conservative critics of that action did so rather more on moral and legal grounds than on grounds of *raison d'état*.

But, once more, it should be emphasized that a great deal will generally depend on whether the armed action was successful or not. After the Cuba missiles crisis in October 1962 President Kennedy made the penetrating remark: 'Success has a thousand fathers, failure is an orphan.' This is particularly true in respect to *ex post facto* judgements on the use of armed force; the Suez armed action of 1956 was a failure by almost any test, but this was only recognized by most people in Britain after the event, as was also the moral and legal quality of that act. Had Sir Anthony Eden's action been a conspicuous success as an international *coup de main*, no doubt many

26

of its later critics would have found reason for applauding its ethics and legality. Similarly, most of the American critics of President Nixon's heavy bombing of North Vietnam at the end of 1972 seem to have been more inspired by the doubtful effectiveness of heavy bombing than by a sense of its immorality.

This is not to say, however, that the use of force in international relations does not raise profoundly genuine moral questions which philosophers and others have debated throughout the lifetime of the international system. Can the use of force, especially against 'innocent' civilians, ever be right? Are we to judge it by its consequences or by its intrinsic quality? Does the moral status of force depend upon the number of casualties? Is the accidental killing of a single child in Vietnam morally equivalent to the destruction of many thousands in one night in an air raid on Japan? The moral dilemmas are well illustrated by the British destruction by air raid of the ill-defended and crowded city of Dresden on the night of 13 February 1945. On the face of it, could there be a more shameful act, the very quintessence of human barbarism? Yet if we look at some of the political reasons for this raid, painful questions arise which take us to the heart of the problem of force in international affairs. Was it necessary, as some apologists for the Dresden raid allege, to placate Stalin by demonstrating anti-German activity on the part of the Western Powers while Soviet forces were rolling up the Wehrmacht? Might relations between the Soviet Union and the Western Powers on which so much in the post-war world depended have changed for the worse had the Russians been unconvinced of this determination? These are terrible questions which the pressures of war raise for the human agents of force in international affairs. The choice in those affairs does not often lie simply between doing good and doing evil. It is, to a far greater extent than in internal affairs, between doing some evil and doing more evil.

The effectiveness of force

The will to use force, or to countenance its use by one's agents, is strongly influenced, as we have seen, by the prospects of success, or of the effective use of force. Where force is concerned, as perhaps in life generally, nothing succeeds like success. Hence we have contradicting judgements in the folklore of all countries. Some say 'force never achieves anything' or 'he that lives by the sword shall perish by the sword'; others that

Twice armed is he that has his quarrel just
But best of all is he that gets his blow in fust.

Discussing the effectiveness of force naturally involves the question: effective for what or for whom? We tend to think naturally of force as a means to an end; only a few out-of-date 'romantics' like Mussolini ever regarded it, after 1918, as an end in itself. Hence we have to consider what is the end that the means of force is supposed to assist. And clearly there are at least two possible answers: the international community as a whole, or the order within or the welfare of that community, on one side, and the interest of the individual state using the force, on the other. If it is assumed that the interests of individual states are all so mutually contradictory that what benefits one state cannot benefit other states in the international system, the concept of an international interest cannot be a real one. Yet, in these days, when it is hard to see how any full-scale war, for example, could benefit anybody, there is some point in saying that a certain balance of armed strength between the great military Powers *is* an international interest if it succeeds in deferring the risk of war. By the same token, a vacuum of armed strength may operate as an encouragement to war and hence by definition may militate against the international interest.

The threat of the Western Powers to use armed force in defence of West Berlin and their own rights in it in 1948–9 and 1958–61 seems to have steadied the situation there and in the international system generally; so no doubt did United Nations armed action in defence of South Korea in 1950–3 and the United States's threat to use force against Soviet missile-carrying ships in the Caribbean in October 1962. On the other hand, the reluctance of Britain and France to use force against the European dictators' breaches of international law in the 1930s, as most people would agree today, tended to encourage them in further breaches of the law and ultimately into war.

One of the essential accompaniments of the use of force in the international interest, as we may put it, is, it seems, the necessity to conciliate the opponent as soon as force or the threat of force has achieved its purpose. Force or the threat of force must be accompanied or immediately followed by an effort to reintegrate the sanctioned state into the international community, to demonstrate, so to speak, that that state's interest in a stable international community is greater than what it can hope to gain by damaging that community. Thus President Kennedy's policy of declining to triumph over the Soviet Union after Soviet vessels had responded to the President's warning and begun to turn around in 1962 has generally been recognized as an act of statesmanship. Submission to force is a harsh humiliation for any state and any government which has changed its policy as a result of force or threat of force should be rewarded and thus encouraged to go further along the road of *détente*, rather than left to be thrust out of office by a government committed to a tougher policy towards its rivals.

It is interesting to see that, if history is any guide, the policy of force or threat of force is much more likely to succeed in producing *détente* between the states concerned if immediately followed by conciliation than is the reverse policy: that is, currying favour with a state threatening force, followed by the assumption of a defensive posture against that state if conciliation fails.[1] Failure to make clear to a hostile state the borderline between what you are prepared to tolerate and what you must resist may lead to a situation in which the opponent does not know what your 'point of no return' is, or whether you will allow yourself to be pushed to it or beyond it. In these circumstances a war which perhaps neither side wanted can come about through failure of the signalling processes on either side to be co-ordinated with the other's.

But now we have to think of the effectiveness of force (by which term we include the threat of force) as an instrument of the individual state's policy. It is a curious fact that while the current abhorrence of war has been principally focused on nuclear weapons and their intercontinental carriers – conventional forces being considered almost tolerable by comparison – it is in fact nuclear weapons which have been more effective in compelling co-operation between states, at least the super Powers. There is, of course, always the possibility that the present-day structure of super-Power mutual deterrence may fail through human error and the risks of general war increase, when and if nuclear weapons spread to more than the present five states which have them. Nevertheless, it is hard to resist the conclusion that the nuclear Powers at least seem to have so frightened themselves by their stocks of infinitely varied nuclear devices that almost any use of armed force appears to them pregnant with the most awful risks. The Soviet Union's restraint in the Arab–Israeli conflict since the six-day war in 1967, the United States's reluctance to use

[1] For the defence of this procedure see Samuel Hoare (1st Viscount Templewood), 'The Double Line' (Ch. 9), *Nine Troubled Years*, Collins, London, 1954.

force when its spy-ship *Pueblo* was detained by North Korea throughout the year 1968, both seem to testify to the effect of the long shadow of nuclear arms on the attitudes toward force of the giant Powers.

It is also well known that the mere fact that the super Powers, especially the United States and the Soviet Union, have concentrated on building up their monstrous armouries of nuclear weapons and their missiles has to a large extent handicapped them in using the kind of forces which seem needed today in insurgency and counter-insurgency operations. The classic case is, of course, Vietnam. Here we have the spectacle of the greatest military Power on earth, the greatest, without doubt, in history, with a population of over 200 million, virtually having to admit defeat by the 17-million strong, economically almost undeveloped North Vietnam. All its frightening armoury of nuclear weapons has been useless. The United States, as Walter Lippmann wrote, was trying in Vietnam to kill a cloud of mosquitoes with an elephant gun.

But this is not to say that small or weak countries can no longer use force in their dealings with other small and weak countries quite effectively on occasion, and this precisely because the super Powers concentrate more and more on smoothing relations between themselves and are less and less willing to act as policemen for the rest of the world. Thus we have seen Israel in 1967 making very effective use of superior force and military skill against the Arab states and making off with considerable gains which neither the Arab states nor their backer, the Soviet Union, nor Israel's ostensible supporter, the United States, have yet been able to wrench from their grasp.[1] Again, India fought a highly successful war in 1971 against her old enemy, Pakistan, and succeeded, not only in establishing what looked like a permanent military superiority over Pakistan, but in consolidating the division of that country into two parts. All in all, it is certainly premature to conclude that the use of conventional forces in suitable circumstances cannot achieve quite considerable gains for certain countries.

As against this, it should be stated that opposite such gains in the balance sheet have to be set the inevitable costs incurred in launching and sustaining military operations on any scale. Quite apart from the obvious costs in human and financial terms of the use of force, there may well be longer-term costs of an intangible kind. Israel is now some three or four times the size it was in May 1967, when the

---

[1] Written in June 1973.

six-day war began, and her military reputation has risen accordingly; if an Arab leader paused once before challenging Israel before 1967 he must have paused many times since 1967. Nevertheless, there have been hidden adverse consequences of the war for Israel which may take years to work themselves out. Prominent among these no doubt are the internal results of having to garrison and occupy intensely hostile foreign territory in virtual perpetuity and perhaps in the process losing opportunities for a lasting settlement with the surrounding Arab territories which alone in the long run can give Israel the security it longs for and deserves. As for India, it may well be that a weak, divided and politically unsettled Pakistan could – again, in the longer term – be a worse neighbour for India even than the Pakistan of 1947–70.

But, quite apart from the profit and loss account of using force in its conventional form in the present international system, there is no doubt that all states – almost out of habit – continue to believe that force is effective, not only in deterring attack from outside, but in strengthening the state's hands in all its dealings with foreign states: in other words, it is a form of 'bargaining from strength'. There are of course certain objections to this attitude. If a country weakens itself in order to strengthen its defence forces, or if its domestic public opinion is divided as a result of an armaments drive, it may lose on the swings all, or more than all, it wins on the roundabouts. Still, it would be foolish to deny that within such limits, armed force, suitably adapted to the requirements and mood of the times, and those are vital considerations, tends to pay dividends, both in its effect on other states and in the impetus it may give to domestic cohesion.

The obsolescence of force

There is today a widespread presumption that the use of force in international relations is losing its attractiveness to states. An even more prevalent idea is that major war, in the sense of the full-scale involvement in war of the major states of the world on the model of the two World Wars, is now obsolete. Of course, the word 'obsolete' has two meanings, one of which is more appropriate to the status of force and war in practical international politics today than is the other.

One meaning is that a certain event or activity is unlikely to recur; it is a statement about the future in contradistinction to the past.

The other meaning is that it is no longer efficient as a means to a certain end. The Old Crocks' race to Brighton from Hyde Park every year is no doubt obsolete in the second but not necessarily the first meaning of the term. Feeding Christians to the lions (if it was ever actually practised in ancient Rome) is now obsolete in both senses of the word; the world is unlikely to see more of it and it neither stamps out Christianity nor amuses the spectators. We can be fairly confident that total war will not be embarked upon in future as an instrument of policy, though no one can say whether it will not occur by accident or the 'pressure of events'. We can hardly be as confident about the use of force, especially as we have seen in the previous section that under certain conditions force can have a positive value for small and weak states. But this is not to say that the use of force will not continue to be *threatened* in international relations and hence that spending on national armaments will not continue to figure prominently in the budgets of almost all countries; the effectiveness of such threats, of course, may well continue to decline with the declining likelihood of such threats ever being put into effect. Unless there is a quite remarkable shift in the historical tendencies of the last twenty or thirty years, it seems as though force, and certainly war, may give place as forms of pressure applied by one state against another to other varieties of restraints.

As for the obsolescence of force and war as effective means towards certain political ends, the technology of modern weapons and the social organization required for the full-scale use of force on a national scale have both made their contribution. These two forces have combined in the twentieth century to make the use of force on a major scale increasingly unpredictable. The First World War ended with very different results from what any of the belligerents anticipated in 1914. Hence the commonplace comparison after 1918 of war to a forest fire in a high wind, the course of which no one can predict or control.

The image applies no less to the Second World War. Who but a very few could have foreseen in 1939 that the independence of Poland, which had initially been the *casus belli*, or an important part of the *casus belli*, at the beginning of the war, would be extinguished at the end of it, even though in the end it was Poland's guarantors who won the war? Who could have foreseen that Czechoslovakia, for which the democratic Powers did *not* fight in September 1938 or March 1939, would be under foreign control, though not Germany's, at the end of a war in which the Western democracies had undertaken to liberate her? As for the impact of nuclear weapons on the massive use of force, the one thing which can be stated with certainty is that any kind of prediction about the eventual outcome of the introduction of these weapons would be utterly impossible from the moment when the war went nuclear.

Again, the social mobilization of the whole nation required for modern war makes it hard if not impossible to indicate just what the final outcome will be. Arm a modern nation with modern weapons and throw it into battle with another such nation and no one can tell what the end will be. The one thing which does seem certain is that any state which seeks by armed force to overthrow the international system, as Napoleon I's France and Hitler's Germany, will not succeed if history is any guide, though no one can say what price the defenders of the existing international order will have to pay in the process. And the same applies *pari passu* to the use of force in international relations on any smaller scale. Well has it been said, though this was long before the age of modern military technology, that war, and also other means of force, is the last resort of kings.

But in addition to improvements in weapons technology and the socialization of armed force, which has drawn practically everyone into support of the state in time of acute conflict, there have been the effects of the restraints built up since 1918 against the unilateral use of force by states in their international relations. First, there have been certain legal restraints, and these are of two kinds, the bilateral and the multilateral. As for the former, from the old non-aggression pacts of the pre-1939 period has sprung the current practice in very many bilateral treaties of today of incorporating mutual renunciations of force to change the *status quo*. In the field of multilateral conventions, since 1918 history has been filled with general treaties for the renunciation of war and force, culminating in the United Nations Charter of 1945, with its overall ban on the use of or the threat of force, with some notable exceptions, and its attempt to restrict the use of force to the organ responsible for peace and security in the international system as a whole, the Security Council.

The total effectiveness of these legal barriers to force is, of course, open to question. At one extreme, a country struggling for its survival, or the survival of its 'way of life', is not likely to pay heed to such barriers. And it has behind it, as we have seen earlier in this chapter, the justification that, in the final resort, unless it defends its own interests, practically no one else will. At the other extreme, a great state living in the public eye of the world, so to speak, is likely to consider very carefully the effect of its unilateral use of force on its standing in the international system.

One possible drawback of the attempt to illegalize various uses of force by states is that the illegalization of force tends to drive states to invent new uses of force which are not illegalized by the ban, which must be in highly specific terms if it is going to be effective. Sir Austen Chamberlain once referred to attempts to put aggression beyond the pale by defining it legally and then making an infringement of that definition the *casus foederis* of a collective security pact as 'traps for the innocent and signposts for the guilty'. There is little doubt that many forms of force practised today, such as subversion, insurgency, guerrilla warfare, the hijacking of aircraft, are not necessarily, as they would seem to be, spasmodic acts of violence by aggrieved individuals but acts of state disguised so as to avoid the stigma attaching to illegal acts committed openly in the state's own name.

Nevertheless, all this international activity since 1918 directed at the illegalization of force has served to create a world climate of opinion which is increasingly hostile to the use or threat of force. Admittedly, much of this 'world opinion' is hypocritical, biased in favour of this use of force and against that, distinctly anti-Western and pro Afro-Asia; nevertheless, the mere fact that force in international affairs is no longer applauded, as it once was, even in the state applying it, is a gain. We must concede no doubt that powerful states are not often swayed by 'world opinion', though it could be that in the United States – the 'right' kind of state for this purpose – adverse feeling against the government's Vietnam policy has been much intensified by critical world opinion. Still, there is no denying that public protest against the use of force in world politics has grown in this century. The modern statesman feels that he must say more than 'civis Romanus sum' when he orders his gunboats to shoot up a foreign port. This public reprobation of force must be added to the advancing technology of weapons production, the socialization of national force and the attempts to illegalize force as factors helping to render force more obsolete than it has even been before in the world society of states.

Conclusion

In this introductory chapter we have confined ourselves to discussing some basic questions concerning the use of force in international relations. Some of this analysis will be carried further in the chapters which follow. Our conclusion at this stage must be a mixture of resignation and hope: resignation because in a world politically constituted as it is, national policies which are based on the assumption that force can be ruled out are unrealistic and imprudent; hope because it does seem that the use of force today no longer carries the stamp of general approval. Some people, especially many of the young, even question whether the use of force can ever be justified, even in a 'good' cause. The basic difficulty in judging the role which force does and should play in international relations is in two parts: distinguishing between force used or threatened in defence of legitimate national interests and in defence of other national interests and, in the second place, distinguishing between force used or threatened in defence of national interests and force used or threatened in defence of international interests. These distinctions cannot be clear-cut in the practical flow of life; but the modern citizen should at least be aware of the principles behind them.

2 The Use of Force by the Great Powers

Why do great Powers sometimes resort to the use of military force to 'solve' a dispute involving small Powers? What factors are considered by the decision-makers before the decision to use force is made? Is force used because no other means are available or only after other means have been tried and seen to fail or because the use of force is the easiest policy, one combining a high degree of efficacy with low risk? Is a great Power likely to employ force only when it feels that a great issue is at stake?

The purpose of this chapter is to arrive at possible answers to these questions and by so doing to allow a discussion of greater issues related to great Powers' use of force. Specifically, the larger questions to be considered at the conclusion centre upon the evolving pattern of great-Power thinking involved in the decision to use force. For example, how did the establishment of a bipolar configuration in the post-war international system alter the thinking of decision-makers? What were the significant differences, if any, between the American and Soviet decisions in the cases under consideration?

These questions will be discussed in light of the evidence to be found in brief outlines of the decisions regarding the use of force made by the United States and the Soviet Union in eleven cases from 1939 to 1968. These are those involving the USSR and Finland (1939), Poland (1944–5), Yugoslavia (1948–50), Hungary (1956) and Czechoslovakia (1968); and those involving the US and North Korea (1950), Indochina (1954), Lebanon (1958), Cuba (1961), Vietnam (1961) and the Dominican Republic (1965).

It will be seen that three of these cases (Yugoslavia, Indochina and Cuba) did *not* involve the actual use of force by the great Power in question. They are included because they are cases in which the use of military force would not have been surprising or unexpected, and indeed, in other time-periods or in the context of a different international situation, would probably have involved the use of force.

36

As such, these cases help to describe more clearly the calculus of considerations which in other cases did involve the use of force.

Finally, the focus of the chapter will be on only one aspect of great Powers' use of force: the decision to use force in a dispute involving a small Power. Neglected, therefore, will be the techniques of force in these situations or the results and efficacy of the use (or non-use) of force.

The Soviet Union

The Soviet objectives which resulted in the attack on Finland in November 1939 were essentially defensive in nature: the Soviets were intent upon strengthening their western frontiers in the face of a perceived German threat – even after the Nazi–Soviet pact of August 1939. Unfortunately for the Finns, their powerful neighbour's defensive desires necessitated some sort of arrangement with Finland which the Finns were almost certain to see as involving an unacceptable infringement upon their territorial integrity and sovereignty. To the policy-makers in Moscow, numerous considerations compounded the danger as they surveyed their small neighbour to the north-west. The frontier as it existed in 1939 came perilously close to Leningrad. Furthermore, and especially in light of the threat from Germany, the Soviets saw an historical Finnish habit of looking toward Germany to offset the persistent threat posed by the Russian giant to the east. Finally, Marshal Stalin, saw a government in Helsinki which was well known to be, not surprisingly, anti-Soviet. Thus, it is difficult to imagine a Finland being more obnoxious to the USSR than was the 1939 model: a state hostile to the Soviet Union, a potential ally of the most dangerous of the potential Soviet enemies and the possessor of a strategically important territory.

The Soviet government told the world exactly what they wanted the Finns to give them and, given the precarious Soviet position and evident Soviet fears, it is not difficult in the least to understand why they wanted what they did. Soviet–Finnish talks had been going on since April 1938, but it was after Moscow completed a deal with the Germans that Marshal Stalin could turn more attention to the north and begin serious bargaining. The Soviet proposals transmitted to the Finnish government on 14 October 1939 stated the Soviet position as clearly as the Finns could have wished.[1] The Soviet

[1] Jane Degras (ed.), *Soviet Documents on Foreign Policy*, III, O.U.P., London, 1953, pp. 382–4.

government was mainly concerned, they said, with the rapid settling of two vitally important questions: the security of Leningrad and the question of 'friendly' Finnish relations with the USSR. Moscow assured their negotiating partners that 'both points are essential for the purpose of preserving against external hostile aggression the integrity of the Soviet Union coast of the Gulf of Finland and also the coast of Estonia. . . .' There then followed a demand for territorial changes which would enable the Soviets the better to defend themselves and a demand for the strengthening of a non-aggression treaty 'by including therein a paragraph according to which the Contracting Parties undertake not to join any groups or alliances directly or indirectly hostile to either of the Contracting Parties' and a demand for the suppression of fortified zones on the frontier.

The Finns refused to yield to what they saw as unjust Soviet demands on Finnish sovereignty and the Soviet government was therefore faced with the decision of whether to use force. The secret Nazi–Soviet protocol of 28 August 1939 had given the Soviets an effective free hand in dealing with both the Baltic states and Finland and thereby the Finns lost their only real hope of preventing the Soviets from doing whatever was necessary to satisfy their demands. Indeed, at this point there was little reason for the USSR not to use force to achieve most quickly and most efficiently its aims. Why, Stalin must have felt, should a country as powerful as the Soviet Union continue the unpleasant wrangling with an obviously militarily inferior Finland which lost its best hope of foreign assistance through the Nazi–Soviet understanding? The Finns hoped for Western sympathy and aid, but Stalin must have realized that there was very little chance of *effective* Western aid now that the Second World War was monopolizing Western attention and military efforts, and sympathy would not count for much on the battlefield. It is also certain that the Soviet leadership did not very much fear the power of 'world public opinion'; this had not done much to protect other small states during the 1930s and the outbreak of major war had demolished whatever slight chance there might have been of world opinion's having any effect on this occasion.

Given the probable success of military action, its simplicity and speed, and the unlikelihood of foreign intervention – probably the only hope for the Finns – it is not at all surprising that Stalin, mindful of the dangers of a continuation of the existing Finnish–Soviet relationship, decided to use military force against his little neighbour. At the end of November 1939 the Red Army attacked Finland,

and though Foreign Minister Molotov assured everyone that the responsibility for the war was entirely Finland's and that the USSR had no intention of annexing any territory,[1] when the war ended in 1940 the Soviets got what they wanted at the outset and the Soviet frontier was moved seventy miles to the west.

At the beginning of the Second World War the USSR had used force against Finland to protect itself against an enemy's use of this small state in an attack against the Soviet Union. As the war drew to a close, the Soviets were again in conflict with a state on their western border and again the issue at stake was Soviet perceptions of security.

As the end of the Second World War came near and the advancing Red Army approached the Soviet–Polish border, the Soviet leaders had several reasons for wanting to establish a post-war Poland which would be to their liking, i.e. a Poland with a 'friendly' government, preferably of Soviet choosing. Strategically, it was essential that the USSR be able to use Poland to defend itself from any future German attack, the Soviets not being slow to learn from recent history. Such defensive considerations were of especial importance as it was apparent that the post-war Soviet Union was going to be in a seriously weakened position after the terrible losses of a long war fought to a great extent on Soviet soil and at great cost. It was also important to Marshal Stalin that he control Poland as a key part of his hopes for controlling those parts of Europe immediately to the west of the USSR. Economically, control of Poland would be helpful in the post-war reconstruction of the Soviet Union. In addition, there were possibly ideological motivations behind Soviet hopes regarding Poland; it was important to the Soviets as Marxist–Leninists that the area under the sway of their ideology expand and the establishment of Socialism in another major European state would help to revive the impression that Communism was once more on the march. For these and doubtless other reasons, Stalin was intent upon the establishment of a post-war Polish government which would be amenable to Soviet wishes and therefore of Soviet choosing.

During the war, the Soviets found to their displeasure that the Polish government-in-exile in London was not willing to acquiesce in Soviet control of eastern Poland and to submit to Soviet wishes regarding post-war Polish–Soviet co-operation in the management

[1] Radio broadcast by Molotov, 29 November 1939, from Degras, op. cit., pp. 403–4.

of the territorially revised Polish state which had been agreed to by President Roosevelt and Prime Minister Churchill at Teheran in 1943. There were frequent disagreements between Moscow and the London Poles culminating in the debate about the 'Katyn massacre' which the Soviets used as a pretext for the breaking of relations with the London Polish government. So when the Red Army entered Poland on 27 July 1944, there was no legitimate Polish government to which could be entrusted the administration of the liberated territory.

Unlike the case of Finland in 1939, the case of Poland in 1944 did not present the leaders of Moscow with the question of whether to use force; there was no question of not using force in Polish territory against the retreating Germans. The question with which they were concerned was rather whether military force already being employed should also be used against groups of Poles operating in Poland against the common German enemy which were hostile to the Soviets but certainly not to the Polish government-in-exile. The decision was made much easier because Soviet forces were already operating in Poland in what was obviously a just cause, so it would not be too difficult to cover up certain unpleasant military operations against Poles in the much greater campaign against the Germans.

As was true in Finland five years earlier, the use of force in Poland to help install a 'friendly' government was obviously seen as a relatively 'easy' solution. Was it not easier to kill potential opposition than to engage in seemingly endless wrangling with the Americans, Britons and Poles? Stalin had no doubt that it was up to his armed forces to help solve potentially troublesome political problems in 'liberated' Europe. As he himself said, 'This war is not as in the past; whoever occupies a territory also imposes on it his own social system. Everyone imposes his own system as far as his army has power to do so.'[1]

And besides, what were the risks of following the easiest and most effective policy? Resistance would be no problem; the Soviets had overwhelming military superiority. The only real trouble could come from the Allies in the West. The Anglo–American leaders had a tiresome habit of pronouncing time-honoured democratic principles, but happily they did not allow these preachings to interfere with really meaningful agreements; such as the famous 'spheres of influence' arrangement between Churchill and Stalin concluded in

---

[1] Quoted in Milovan Djilas, *Conversations with Stalin*, translated by Michael B. Petrovich, Hart-Davis, London, 1962, p. 105.

October 1944. The two leaders agreed to divide spheres of influence in several East European countries on a percentage basis with the Soviets winning a 90 per cent share of post-war Poland.[1] Stalin could be forgiven for assuming that 90 per cent was so close to 100 per cent that for all reasonable purposes Poland could be considered his and that the British and Americans would probably do nothing – nothing beyond verbal protest – to stop Stalin's policies of assuring his 90 per cent. Though the British and Americans were certainly concerned about what happened to Poland, they were more concerned about other post-war contingencies, e.g. the success of the United Nations, and Stalin found their concern about Poland to be ineffective in preventing him from achieving his goals.

With the war still in progress, then, with absolutely vital Soviet interests (*inter alia*, post-war territorial security) at stake, and with minimal risks, the Soviets could proceed to have their army offer military support to the Polish Communists and, at the same time, eliminate centres of support of the London-based government controlled by the non-Communist Polish underground. The most notorious example of such Soviet assistance was provided by their refusal to attempt to offer support to the members of the underground taking part in the Warsaw uprising just prior to the entry of the Red Army into the Polish capital.

By 1948, four years after the use of the Red Army to help install a Communist government in Warsaw, Moscow exercised effective control over most of Eastern Europe. But in that year developed a dispute that would call into question the solidarity of the bloc.

In June 1948 the Yugoslavs were formally expelled from the Cominform, a formal organization of European Communist parties. Tito's party's independent policies had been annoying Moscow since the Second World War and Stalin undoubtedly thought that the Cominform expulsion would serve to bring the errant Slavs into line. The Soviety Party leader may have been surprised that the announcement of his displeasure did not immediately cause Tito to apologize and agree to mend his ways or cause the loyal (to Moscow) Communists in Belgrade to overthrow the obviously undesirable Tito, but he was probably certain that some other more concrete measures would serve the same purpose.

Determined to force the recalcitrant Yugoslavs to surrender to the higher purposes of the Socialist Fatherland, the Soviets exerted over a long period one kind of pressure after another – always short of

[1] The Americans voiced strong disapproval of this agreement.

41

actual military force – against Yugoslavia. The USSR and its East European satellites denounced a series of post-war treaties concluded with Yugoslavia, conducted an intense propaganda campaign in an effort to get the Yugoslav people themselves to see the error of their leaders' ways and the bloc instituted a total economic boycott of Yugoslavia. In addition, the Soviets established *émigré* organizations of anti-Tito Yugoslavs in several East European states, massed troops on Yugoslavia's borders and caused numerous border incidents. An impressive array of coercive devices by anyone's standards, but, though they did cause considerable inconvenience – especially the economic measures – they did not bring to an end Yugoslavia's independence.

This policy failure was the cause of consternation in the Kremlin. The continued Yugoslav resistance in the face of so much pressure from both the Soviet Union and its allies was not the sort of example which Stalin wished to be presented to his unhappy East Europeans; such a policy might prove not only attractive, but also infectious. To make matters even worse, Tito was developing his own ideology of independent Communism which also might be attractive to some restive leaders in the bloc. These ideological pretentions added an offensive character to what had previously been a purely defensive struggle on the part of the Yugoslavs.

There were strategic considerations for Stalin to consider as well. As Tito's relations with the United States and Great Britain began to improve from 1949 onwards and these two Cold War enemies of the USSR began to reciprocate with economic and later military aid to Tito, the consequences of continued Yugoslav recalcitrance must have appeared even more dangerous in Moscow. There seemed the real possibility that the Anglo–Americans might soon acquire a forward position in the heart of the Balkans, and, at the same time, demonstrate to the rest of the world that the onward march of Communism was not unstoppable, not to mention irreversible.

To these concrete considerations of Cold War losses must be added Stalin's sense of personal pique at being defied by the ruler– a one-time Comintern flunkey in Moscow – of a weak country so recently under his thumb (as it no doubt seemed to him).

Why then, when all else failed, did the Soviets not use armed force and attack Yugoslavia? The answer seems to involve three interrelated factors: necessity, time and the West. Stalin seems to have thought that an invasion was not necessary; all the other tools at his command were certain to bring such an insignificant country as

Yugoslavia to heel. But, as we have seen, all the tools at Stalin's command did *not* bring the Yugoslavs to heel. The important thing, however, is that it took several years to bring Stalin to this unwelcome conclusion. Had this failure been apparent by the end of 1948, the USSR might have intervened, but by the end of 1949 and the start of 1950 the question of the Western reaction had to be considered more seriously. In the summer of 1948 a Red Army-forced downfall of the remarkably irritable Tito might well have secretly pleased many Western policy-makers. American intervention then would have been almost inconceivable, but by the start of 1950 things had changed. In a rare case of foreign policy foresight and wisdom, the Americans and the British had decided to support the Yugoslav heretics by providing economic and military aid. The outbreak of war in Korea frightened the Yugoslavs who felt they too might soon be the victims of an attack and they drew even closer to the formerly vilified capitalists. By 1954 they had formed an alliance with Greece and Turkey, both firm members of the Western team in the Cold War. In addition, the United States developed a much firmer policy *vis-à-vis* the USSR during the period of Soviet pressure against Belgrade. With the Marshall Plan, the Truman Doctrine, the formation of NATO and the response to the North Koreans, it must have appeared obvious to Moscow that any use of military force could very easily involve an armed confrontation with a much stronger enemy.

It would seem then, that the decision of the Soviet Union not to use force against Yugoslavia was forced upon the Soviet policy-makers by a fear of involving themselves with an adversary much more powerful than Yugoslavia alone would have been.[1] The Soviets found themselves in a position in which either answer to the question of whether or not to use force presented grave consequences because they overestimated the efficacy of the policy options short of the use of force.

In the mid 1950s, it was important to the Soviet Union that, in dealing with the West and with the increasingly obstreperous

---

[1] No doubt the Soviets did consider the possibility of a guerrilla resistance to Soviet occupation of Yugoslavia. They certainly remembered the activities of Tito's partisans against the Germans during the Second World War and the military problems this would pose for the Red Army would not be slight. Though the possibility of resistance was not considered to be great in 1948, by the time the use of force was seriously considered, the solidarity of the Yugoslavs with their government, and with it the chances of armed resistance, was apparent.

43

Chinese as well as with the various leaders of the East European states and their many problems, there could be no question of any of the bloc countries following a policy so independent as to be at variance with the desires of Moscow. In effect, this meant East European states firmly controlled by the various Communist parties which, at the very least, were expected to contain unpredictable forces of (revolutionary) change, Yet the *rapprochement* with Belgrade (1955) and the start of 'deStalinization' (1956), processes which Moscow had hoped would give a greater measure of independence to the Socialist states, seemed to be resulting in changes in Eastern Europe which could easily lead to revolt and the chance of dissolution of Moscow's control of the Warsaw Pact states.

Political and social unrest in the summer of 1956 reached a climax in Poland in June when riots erupted in Poznan. Fearing the spread of disturbances, the Soviet leadership moved in and rearranged the Polish Party hierarchy, bringing the popular Wladislaw Gomulka back into the top position of the Party power structure. With broad public support, the moderate Gomulka was able to contain the most violent expressions of unrest and allay Soviet fears which might have led them to take an even more active part in Polish affairs. Unfortunately, in Hungary the forces of change seemed to be outrunning the ability of the Hungarian Communists to control.

On 18 July 1956 the Hungarian Party leader Rakosi resigned at the instigation of the Soviets and was replaced by Ernö Gerö, also the choice of Moscow.[1] The resignation was the result of Rakosi's inability to deal satisfactorily with obvious signs of discontent with his hard-line rule in Budapest. By this change in the Hungarian power structure the Communist Party of the Soviet Union hoped to control the evident forces of change which, it was apparent to Moscow, could easily run out of control and result in changes in both domestic and foreign policies in Hungary which would be detrimental to Soviet goals of stability and gradual change in Eastern Europe. As it was, existing dissension in the bloc was causing alarm in the Kremlin and *Pravda*, the organ of the CPSU, warned those 'who will rise to the bait about national Communism, about the fact that the international bonds among Communist parties have become "superfluous"'.

Despite Soviet warnings and the change of rulers in Budapest,

[1] This section is based largely on Ferenc A. Vali, *Rift and Revolt in Hungary: Nationalism versus Communism*, O.U.P., London, 1961, pp. 234 ff.

demonstrations which started in the Hungarian capital on 23 October were followed by an increase in violent public reaction to what were seen as government provocations. The Soviets promptly reacted by sending in Soviet troops on 24 October to contain the disturbances and prevent the dissolution of Communist rule. This first military intervention was a political and military failure as it increased feelings of nationalism among the populace and did not decisively defeat the 'freedom fighters'. A cease-fire was announced on 28 October and the Soviet forces withdrew.

The Soviets had long talks with Premier Nagy (elected on the night of 23 October), hoping to arrive at some form of compromise balancing Hungarian nationalism with Soviet fears regarding the possible dissolution of Communist rule and consequent effects on the rest of Eastern Europe. But these Soviet hopes failed, and Moscow now witnessed what they most feared. The new Hungarian government suggested in a Central Committee meeting of 26 October the election of a new National government and decided to negotiate with the USSR 'on the basis of independence, complete equality, and non-interference in one another's internal affairs'. To make matters worse, on 30 October the Nagy government announced the restoration of the multiparty system and declared that the time was ripe to prepare for free elections.

The USSR had excellent reasons for deciding to intervene a second time, this time to bring down the 'unco-operative' Hungarian government. The events in Hungary were (it must have appeared from Moscow) beyond the ability of the Nagy government to control. The Soviets felt that the propaganda effect of a successful ignoring of Soviet wishes would be too disastrous in its consequences to be allowed. It was not unlikely in the volatile situation then existing in the bloc that the sight of one state enacting sweeping political reforms in the face of Soviet opposition would lead to similar uprisings and hopes for rapid change in other states in Eastern Europe. And the dominoes would tumble one after another. If only the Nagy government had been able to control the forces of change, as the Gomulka government had been able to do in Poland earlier that same year, the Soviets would not have felt themselves forced to unleash the forces of order, in the form of military force.[1]

---

[1] It is most unlikely that Hungary's 1 November decision to leave the Warsaw Pact was influential in Soviet thinking. See, for example, Vali, op. cit., p. 359 and Adam B. Ulam, *Expansion and Coexistence: The History of Soviet Foreign Policy, 1917–67*, Secker & Warburg, London, 1968, p. 597.

There were possible negative factors for Moscow to consider before deciding to intervene. First, there was the chance that violent Hungarian resistance would itself lead to revolution elsewhere in the bloc. But it was *more* likely that inaction would produce the same dreaded result, and besides, the other East European governments themselves were concerned about the spread of unchecked revolt in Hungary. Secondly, there was world public opinion to be considered, but what was a brief expression of public condemnation when compared with such tangible gains as the preservation of East European order – especially so when public opinion in the West was preoccupied with the Suez affair. Probably the most important consideration was that of possible Western reaction in the tangible military form. Even had the West been willing to take the obvious risks of intervention or even threats of action, however, they were most unlikely to do so at the time of the Suez distraction and the Soviets could see no signs of Western military action which could presage any threat or move regarding Hungary. Finally, of course, the chance of *effective* military resistance to Soviet military force on the part of the Hungarians themselves was nil. There had been trouble at the time of the first invasion, but the second would involve such an overwhelming preponderance of force as to make effective resistance impossible.

With so many good reasons to intervene and with each possible negative consequence offset by a positive consideration of at least equal weight, the decision was probably not a difficult one.

In 1968, the USSR again saw trouble in Eastern Europe in the form of a potentially dangerous demonstration of independence by one of the bloc members. The reform movement in Czechoslovakia which reached its peak in August 1968 and led to the Soviet invasion in the same month must be seen against the background of growing Soviet fears regarding the solidarity of the East European Socialist states. These fears, resulting partially from the liberalizing reforms in a number of the states of Eastern Europe, were exacerbated by the Sino–Soviet dispute and China's apparent efforts to win European converts to its position and by West Germany's *Ostpolitik* with its moves to improve relations with the Soviet Union and Eastern Europe. Any reforms in the Warsaw Pact states which suggested the possibility of a diminution of the control exercised by the Communist parties in any field of domestic or foreign policy were seen as endangering the strength of the bloc as a whole and, consequently, the Soviet Union itself.

Thus it is not surprising that, to Moscow, the rapidly increasing pace of reform in Czechoslovakia in 1967 and 1968 was viewed with increasing alarm. In Czechoslovakia itself, the Soviet leaders were probably alarmed primarily by the appearance of a reform movement which was moving too far in front of the Party and was in danger of outrunning the ability of the Party to control. (Memories of a similar breakdown of control in Hungary in 1956 must have been in the minds of the decision-makers in the USSR.) Moreover, drastic changes in traditional methods of government in Eastern Europe, such as the ending of censorship of the media, were certain to place in jeopardy the continuity of Communist rule, i.e. Communist rule as favoured by Moscow. Finally, given the above-noted Soviet concerns about outside pressures (especially from China and the German Federal Republic) it was natural for Soviet leaders to see the Czechoslovak reforms in internal matters being followed by dangerous changes in Czechoslovak foreign policy.

Then there were Soviet worries about the reforms unconnected with the internal consequences in Czechoslovakia alone. First there was the country's strategic location to consider, bordering on West Germany and located in the heart of East Europe. Then there was the possible deleterious effect of the reforms upon Czechoslovak relations with the Soviet Union and the Warsaw Pact; reliance on popular support for popular policies might cause the Czechoslovak leadership to turn to far-reaching revisions of national alignments of which Moscow approved. In addition, Czechoslovak reforms could very easily spread to other states of the bloc where public pressure for a similar liberalization were thought, quite rightly, to exist. Such a spread of debilitating forces of reform could very easily result in a fatal (for Soviet interests) weakening of bloc solidarity in the face of increasing and devisive pressures from the outside. The Soviet leaders also had to be mindful of criticism from those of influence in world Communism who were even more fearful than the Soviets of the possible effects of the Czechoslovak developments. Concerns about the contagious nature of the reforms expressed in Poland and East Germany were bound to influence Moscow. Finally there were economic considerations. Czechoslovakia was an economic keystone of Eastern Europe and any lessening of its contribution to its fellow Socialist states would weaken all of Eastern Europe and the Soviet Union itself.

Given the obvious Soviet distress about the course of events in Czechoslovakia, what could Moscow do to demonstrate to their allies in Prague the error of their ways? Certainly at that point force would have been out of the question; the effects on Soviet relations with China, the West and progressive regimes in Eastern Europe would have been disastrous. So while the use of armed force at this stage would have been the simple answer, its use was overruled and less drastic, though more tedious and as it turned out less successful, methods of pressure were resorted to. From March 1968 onwards the Soviet Union and her allies in the Warsaw Pact increased their pressure on the Prague leadership in efforts to get the Czechoslovaks to moderate the potentially dangerous reform movement. Meetings were held with the Czechoslovak leaders to try to persuade them of the danger inherent in their course. Military manoeuvres of the Warsaw Pact were held in Czechoslovakia in May and June and after the June exercises there was a long delay before the foreign troops were withdrawn from Czechoslovak territory. The extremely hostile press campaigns in the German Democratic Republic and Poland as well as in the USSR pointed out to the Czechoslovaks precisely what they were doing wrong, leaving no doubt in their minds – the leaders in East Berlin, Warsaw and Moscow must have hoped – about what was to be done. *Pravda*, for instance, warned of the 'attack on the Socialist foundation of Czechoslovakia' and the aim of 'rightist, anti-Socialist forces' to restore capitalism and undermine Czechoslovakia's 'friendship with the USSR and other Socialist countries'. *Pravda* rather ominously warned the Czechoslovaks of the similarity of developments in their country in 1968 with those in Hungary in 1956.[1] *Kommunist* likewise expressed the Soviet Party's concern with the obvious desires and efforts of the 'revanchists of West Germany' to support the Czechoslovak reforms.[2] Finally, in the middle of July, five Warsaw Pact states sent a letter to the Czechoslovak leaders stating bluntly that whereas a 'counter-revolutionary situation' existed in their country, the Party leadership under Dubček had lost control of the situation and the situation in their country represented a danger to the whole 'Socialist commonwealth'. The 'healthy forces' in Prague, the letter went on, must bring the situation under control and could count on outside aid in doing so.[3]

It was only after six months of pressure of various kinds and the clearest possible exposition of Soviet concerns about the Czechoslovak

---

[1] *Pravda*, 11 July 1968, from Robin Alison Remington (ed.), *Winter in Prague: Documents on Czechoslovak Communism in Crisis*, M.I.T. Press, Cambridge, Mass., 1969, pp. 203–7.

[2] *Kommunist*, July 1968, ibid., p. 208.

[3] As published by *Pravda*, 18 July 1968, ibid., p. 224.

situation that it was decided to send in the military forces of the USSR and some of its Warsaw Pact allies. While the dangers of such action still existed, as they had when it was first felt necessary to do something about Czechoslovakia, it was obviously decided in August that the dangers of a runaway reform movement were so great that, since all else had seemingly failed, force, the only alternative left, would have to be resorted to.

The United States

In 1950 the Cold War was at its height and for American policy-makers the outlook was not encouraging. It must have seemed in Washington that, save for a few minor setbacks here and there, the USSR and its expansionist ideology were not to be stopped – and especially not in Asia. Since the end of the Second World War 'International Communism' had scored a number of apparent triumphs against the defensive legions of the 'free world'. Eastern Europe had 'fallen' to the Soviet imperialists at the close of the war. With the apparent permanency of the division of Germany, the Soviet zone was added to the list of satellites, and in February 1948 a *coup d'état* in Prague delivered Czechoslovakia into Soviet hands. Of course by 1950 it seemed certain that the Soviets had 'lost' Yugoslavia and were not about to regain her, but at that time, the significance of the Yugoslav–Soviet break was not as apparent as it was later to become to numerous Western writers. In Europe, the American policy of containment was a success in that it appeared to stop the onrush of the relentless 'red tide'. Marshall Plan aid had helped to restore stability in Western Europe and had hopefully taken the minds of the Europeans off the lures of the Communist parties, which were especially strong in Italy and France. And the Truman Doctrine had caused the threats of Communist-inspired subversion to evaporate in Greece and Turkey. Finally, the establishment of NATO in 1949 seemed to augur well for the future of a Europe willing and able to defend itself. Unfortunately, in Asia things were not so promising.

Despite half-hearted US efforts to prevent it, China had been 'lost' to the Communists and was, it seems, subservient to Moscow. The sudden 'fall' of 'democratic' China seemed to suggest that the Soviets were turning to Asia – a weak link in the Western chain of defence? – to renew the offensive which had stalled in Europe because of US resolution, money and military force.

South Korea was definitely a weak link in the defensive chain. The division of Korea, effected in 1945, was at first expected to be only temporary but as Soviet–American relations worsened at the start of the Cold War it became effectively permanent and South Korea became to all intents an American protectorate. Nevertheless, the Americans had seemingly made it clear that while they wished the South Koreans the best, they were unwilling and/or unable to include yet another small state among those which the US was committed to defend. The Joint Chiefs of Staff policy regarding Asia stated bluntly that 'under no circumstances would the United States engage in the military defence of the Korean peninsula.'[1] In addition, American defence planners saw no reason to defend South Korea in any event. As General Ridgway wrote, 'By 1949, we were completely committed to the theory that the next war involving the United States would be a global war, in which Korea would be of relatively minor importance and, in any event, indefensible. . . . The concept of 'limited warfare' never entered our councils.'[2] With American planners thinking in terms of an all-out war, the defence of South Korea was seen to be both impossible and unnecessary.

Still, the North Korean attack on 24 June 1950 took Washington completely by surprise and US policy-makers had to face immediately the question of whether to meet force with force. The question was made all the more difficult because the US was militarily unprepared to meet such a challenge. The only troops in the vicinity were performing occupation duty in Japan and were not prepared for combat duty and besides there were very few of them even if they were to be committed to Korea. President Truman later outlined the considerations in his mind at the time the decision to use force in Korea was made in Washington on 25 and 26 June 1950.[3] The President's careful study of recent history had shown him, he said, that appeasement had invariably encouraged further aggression and he saw in the Communists the images of Hitler, Mussolini and the Japanese. He was certain that if the Communists were permitted to swallow South Korea, they would proceed to topple the other free

[1] As quoted in Soon Sung Cho, *Korea in World Politics 1940–1950: An Evaluation of American Responsibility*, University of California Press, Berkeley, 1967, p. 245.

[2] Matthew B. Ridgway, *The War in Korea*, Barrie & Rockliff, London, 1968, p. 11.

[3] Harry S. Truman, *Years of Trial and Hope, 1946–1953*, Hodder & Stoughton, London, 1956. President Truman must have been flattered by subsequent Presidents' imitation of his thinking when they were faced with what they thought were replicas of the Korean situation.

nations of Asia – not unlike a row of dominoes. Furthermore, the example of South Korea's fall would be a lesson to other small countries faced with a Communist threat and they would certainly not have the courage to resist if they had reason to know that the US would acquiesce in their demise. Also at stake were the principles of the United Nations, according to which President Truman was determined to act. Besides UN principles, there were American principles at stake; the US response in Korea would be seen as the acid test of five years of talk about collective security and America's allies would judge her harshly if she failed to back up talk with action. There were also important strategic considerations to weigh. If Korea were to fall, Japan would be vulnerable to attack and both Okinawa and Formosa would be faced with Communist might from two sides. Finally, in the United States itself, Senator McCarthy and his associates were starting to question the sincerity of the administration's anti-Communism and an unequivocal response in Korea would demonstrate their resolve after China's 'fall' the previous year.

All these considerations argued for a swift US reaction to North Korea's attack; yet there were factors suggesting caution. First, of course, was the lack of adequate forces to be really effective in Korea. More important was the possible effect on the USSR of the use of American military force. As was mentioned above, American planners had considered the possibility of a major war with the Soviet Union as the probable outcome of the use of force on the borders of the rival spheres of influence and so the Korean situation must have appeared to Washington as a terrible dilemma: either the US had to allow South Korea to fall or it must take a chance on a total war with the USSR. President Truman decided, for the reasons he outlined, that the risks of not acting forcefully in this situation outweighed the chance of war with the Soviets and he ordered US naval and air forces into action in Korea.

The outlook for the United States in 1954 was somewhat brighter than it had been in 1950. President Eisenhower had prudently given up his hopes and promises of 'rolling back' the Communists but, since the 'loss' of China in 1949, the Soviet Union, conceived at that time as the one true centre of Communism, had not made any more gains at the expense of the 'free world'. The stopping of the Communist advance in Korea was thought to have been a salutary lesson to Moscow that the West would not sit idly by while small nations were taken over through outside intervention. But in Indochina the

French were experiencing great difficulty in preventing the take-over of their colony by the Communist Vietminh.

It would have been folly, so it must have seemed in Washington, to have halted the Communists' advance in Korea only to allow its expansion in Indochina. In February 1950, before the start of fighting in Korea, the US had decided to aid the French in their efforts by supplying them with military assistance, thereby hoping to stop the spread of Communism from the newly transformed China. After the Korean War, aid to the French was increased. A National Security Council policy statement in early 1952 succinctly expressed the rationale for the then continuing aid to France. The US objectives were 'To prevent the countries of South-East Asia from passing into the Communist orbit, and to assist them to resist Communism from within and without and to contribute to the strengthening of the free world'.[1] As French fortunes fared worse in 1953 the Americans sharply increased their aid which was expected to help cause the resounding defeat of the Vietminh by 1955.

Of course, increased American aid led to no such thing and in 1954 the Eisenhower administration was faced with the growing probability of imminent French, i.e. 'free world', defeat and Vietminh, i.e. Soviet International Communist, victory. As intervention had succeeded, if not brilliantly at least adequately, in Korea, it might have seemed logical that it might work in Indochina. Thus in the spring of 1954, the US was faced with the decision of whether to intervene with American military force to prevent the almost certain defeat of the French in Indochina.

The administration was not reticent about the importance of South-East Asia to the United States. Secretary of State Dulles said in March 1954 that 'Under the conditions of today, the imposition on South-East Asia of the political system of Communist Russia or its Chinese ally, by *whatever* means, would be a grave threat to the whole free community.'[2] The question of intervention was discussed and seriously considered throughout the spring of 1954 and again after the fall of Dien Bien Phu at the end of June. Indeed, the administration hinted twice in the spring of 1954 that the US was not adverse to intervening to help the French. President Eisenhower felt there were three solid reasons for the use of American force to

---

[1] Neil Sheehan *et al.*, *The Pentagon Papers*, Quadrangle, New York (Routledge & Kegan Paul and Bantam, London), 1971, p. 27.

[2] Quoted in John W. Spanier, *American Foreign Policy Since World War II*, 2nd edn., Pall Mall Press, London, 1962, p. 109.

prevent the French defeat: the strategic importance of Indochina for the defence of the rest of the region, the possibility of Indochina's being the first in a row of dominoes falling one after the other, and the danger inherent in Chinese Communist support for Ho Chi Minh, leader of the Vietminh.[1] Secretary of State Dulles was adamant that the US force the Communists to realize that they were facing a Power which would compel them to halt efforts for the expansion of Chinese control in South-East Asia.

Given the legitimate reasons for US involvement in the war, the President listed three basic requirements for such participation: the legal right for intervention, in the form of a French 'invitation', 'free world opinion' favourable to US aims in the form of a coalition involving Great Britain and 'free' Asian states as well as the US, and favourable action by Congress. (Congress seemed to be unwilling to favour intervention unless America's allies supported the action.) However, President Eisenhower felt that there were already enough ground forces in Indochina to do whatever could be done and that air strikes against the Vietminh would probably not be very effective. Besides, the military was less than enthusiastic about an operation in Indochina. Admiral Radford, Chairman of the Joint Chiefs of Staff wrote to the Secretary of Defence pointing out the Joint Chiefs' 'belief that, from the point of view of the United States, with reference to the Far East as a whole, Indochina is devoid of decisive military objectives and the allocation of more than token US armed forces in Indochina would be a serious diversion of limited US capabilities'.[2] In addition, at the time, the size of the army was being reduced and its existing strength was probably insufficient to become involved in fighting in Indochina. Furthermore, a US Army report (the Ridgway Report) indicated that American involvement would have meant a very substantial commitment with heavy losses.[3] Also, US intervention would comprise an act of war with its risks of leading to a wider conflict and might show the world the spectacle of America's having intervened and lost.

So, despite Secretary Dulles's assurances that American force would not precipitate a wider war, the decision was made in April not to use military force to prevent a Vietminh victory, which soon

[1] Dwight D. Eisenhower, *The White House Years: Mandate For Change, 1953–1956*, Heinemann, London, 1963, pp. 340 ff.

[2] Sheehan, op. cit., p. 44.

[3] Melvin Gurtov, *The First Vietnam Crisis: Chinese Communist Strategy and United States Involvement, 1953–1954*, Columbia U.P., New York, 1967, pp. 125–6.

materialized. After the débâcle of Dien-Bien-Phu, however, the administration again considered the wisdom of the use of American forces and again decided against intervention. President Eisenhower suggested two consequences which might follow intervention. US intelligence estimated that intervention entailed a 50 per cent chance of causing Chinese involvement in the fighting, and all were well aware of the results of Chinese involvement in Korea. Secondly, intervening without Great Britain (the President had been unable to persuade the British to join him) would cause a weakening of close British–American relations which were so important for the defence of Europe, certainly a more important consideration than South-East Asia. In addition to these two primary considerations there was the moral stature of the US to be kept in mind; the traditional US policy of anti-colonialism would probably be damaged. Finally, it was incumbent on the administration to be wary of damaging its domestic political prospects by involving the nation in a repeat of the unpleasant Korean episode.

Thus, the Americans decided not to use military force to prevent the victory of a Communist force in a situation which, at least superficially, bore resemblances to the Korean situation of four years earlier, and allowed the conclusion of a compromise solution in Indochina.

After the Suez crisis in 1956, the United States became increasingly concerned with what Washington saw as the possibility of a Communist-dominated Middle East. This concern, which existed largely because of the perceived role of the region as a prize in the larger East–West conflict and as a region of strategic importance both because of its location and for its major natural resource, oil, was made concrete with the establishment at the beginning of 1957 of the Eisenhower Doctrine, a Presidential policy given official status in a joint Congressional resolution which announced the importance of the continued independence and integrity of states in the Middle East to the security of the US. In light of this link, the Doctrine declared that America was prepared to use force to aid any state in the region which 'requested assistance against armed aggression from any country controlled by international Communism'.[1]

Despite such manifestations of US interest in a stable, non-revolutionary and pro-West Middle East, by the summer of 1958 the region appeared to US policy-makers to be falling apart. In April

[1] Paul E. Zinner (ed.), *Documents on American Foreign Relations, 1957*, Council on Foreign Relations, New York, 1958, p. 206.

1957 the US Sixth Fleet had been sent to the eastern Mediterranean when revolution in Jordan threatened to end that state's pro-Western policies and in August of that year, a successful *coup d'état* in Syria did bring about such a realignment. The nadir of US fortunes came with the revolt in Iraq in July 1958, which brought to power an anti-Western revolutionary government which eliminated Iraq as a keystone of the Baghdad Pact, a Western alliance formed in 1955 as a Middle Eastern bulwark against the Communist Power to the north. To make matters worse for American planners, the new Iraqi government promptly formed an alliance with Nasser's United Arab Republic which, since 1956, was seen by Washington as the centre of a subversive network in the Arab world which was intent upon fomenting revolution throughout the region. With probably the strategically most important state lost, the US, with its ally Great Britain, lost no time in attempting to salvage what remained of Western influence in the Middle East and they turned their attention to Lebanon and Jordan, both of which still remained pro-Western but which appeared to be struggling not to succumb to the spread of Nasserite revolution.[1]

The violent domestic troubles in Lebanon which started before the revolution in Iraq, seem to have been of the domestic variety. What started as a revolt against Lebanese President Chamoun's plan to retain his office beyond the expiration of his term soon came to involve anti-Western Arab nationalists supported by arms and men from like-thinking Arabs in Syria. (As if to drive home to the US their intense feelings regarding the West, the revolutionaries destroyed United States Information Agency libraries in both Beirut and Tripoli.) Thus, with Lebanon on the brink of destruction, at least the destruction of the kind of Lebanon desired in Washington, Secretary Dulles let it be known on 20 May 1958 that, even though there was little evidence that Lebanon was suffering from 'armed aggression from any country controlled by international Communism', he was not about to allow such hazy language in the Congressional resolution on the Middle East (the Eisenhower Doctrine) stand in the way of the invocation of this same Doctrine. Surely, the Secretary must have felt, any country which was even friendly with the Soviet Union was as good as controlled by International Communism anyway and there was no denying that Syria and other Arab states were friendly with the USSR. In any event, putting aside such academic

[1] Only the case of Lebanon will be considered here as the Jordanian half of the 'rescue operation' was taken care of by the British.

quibbling, Secretary Dulles said that if the Lebanese government were to ask for aid, the Doctrine would be considered broad enough to allow a positive response to the request. After a period of waiting and watching in both Beirut and Washington, the revolution in Iraq ended any doubt that American aid was necessary to prevent a similar untoward occurrence in Lebanon and President Chamoun sent an urgent request for President Eisenhower to send in US troops to allow his government to survive.

In a statement to the public explaining his decision to intervene in the Lebanese situation, President Eisenhower said that he had ordered the Marines ashore that day, 15 July 1958, in answer to the request of President Chamoun. The troops were in Lebanon, he said 'to protect American lives and by their presence there to encourage the Lebanese government in its defence of Lebanese sovereignty and integrity'.[1] In a message to Congress the same day, the President emphasized that the revolt in Lebanon was backed by radio broadcasts from Cairo, Damascus and the Soviet Union. In addition, arms and money used in the uprising were supplied by Syria. The Congress was told that all these hostile forces both within and without Lebanon were intent upon destroying the Lebanese government and installing a government which would be subordinate to the UAR. Finally, the President stressed that the situation had been drastically altered by the revolt in Iraq, also backed by Nasser.[2]

Yet there were also to be considered factors which argued against the use of armed force. Primarily there was the possibility that the Soviet Union itself might intervene to counter US force, as indeed Moscow had intimated might very well happen. Secretary Dulles, however, made little of this possibility, suggesting that the Soviets would probably make threatening gestures but would not act because of the respect for US power which would be used against them in the general war which could follow a great-Power confrontation. The Secretary of State seemed to agree that intervention might damage US standing in the Arab world, and lead to problems with oil supplies and the US use of the Suez Canal. But these considerations were of secondary importance. Finally, some Congressional leaders told their President that intervention would cause an unfavourable reaction in world public opinion.[3]

---

[1] Paul E. Zinner, *Documents on American Foreign Relations, 1958*, Council on Foreign Relations, New York, 1959, p. 303.
[2] Ibid., pp. 304–6.
[3] Eisenhower, op. cit., pp. 271 ff.

In the end, of course, President Eisenhower decided to use military force and he himself fairly summed up his reasoning. 'This was a country we were counting on heavily as a bulwark of stability and progress in the region. . . . This sombre turn of events could, without vigorous response on our part, result in a complete elimination of Western influence in the Middle East.'[1]

With the intervention in Lebanon apparently stopping the spread of International Communism, the United States was then faced in Cuba shortly thereafter with this same menace in its own neighbourhood. After having preserved the Western hemisphere for so long as an exclusively US-controlled hemisphere, it is not surprising that the advent to power of a self-styled Marxist-Leninist in Cuba should have caused such consternation in Cuba's great neighbour to the north. The revolution (the Castro government gained power on New Year's Day 1959) soon acquired a marked anti-American character which in itself was enough to convince many in America of dyed-in-the-wool Communism. Then the Cuban leadership began to align the country with the Soviet Union both in its pronouncements and in its diplomatic, military and economic intercourse. The Cubans established diplomatic relations with all Communist states save the German Democratic Republic; they received both military supplies and advisers from the Soviet Union; and they signed economic agreements with some of the Communist states, serving to transfer the bulk of Cuban trade from the Western hemisphere to Eastern Europe and the Soviet Union. Two years of what Washington saw as provocative anti-American activity on the part of the Cubans finally led in January 1961 to the severing by the US of diplomatic relations with Cuba.

As the new Kennedy administration took office at the start of 1961 it was immediately faced with what appeared to many in the US government as a dangerous threat to the American hemisphere. There seemed to be no doubt that the revolutionary Cubans would continue their virulent anti-US policy and, indeed, attempt to spread their poisonous doctrines to some of the other Latin American 'democracies'. Obviously, something had to be done. The Eisenhower government had not been sleeping during its last months in office and had set in motion the planning and preparations for an amphibious landing in Cuba by a force of anti-Castro Cuban refugees which was seriously expected to cause an uprising among the

[1] Ibid., p. 269.

discontented Cubans still on the island. When President Kennedy assumed office he was therefore faced with two crucial decisions regarding this scheme which the outgoing administration had set in motion: (1) should the contemplated invasion go ahead as planned? and (2) if it was decided to proceed with the invasion, should the US contribute any of its own armed forces to the venture?

It seemed self-evident that something had to be done to rid the hemisphere of the possibility of the spread of revolution emanating from Castro's Cuba and it was undoubtedly a relief to the new President that something was being done. Arthur Schlesinger, Jr., a close personal adviser of President Kennedy, later summarized the reasoning which lay behind the President's decision to allow the 'invasion' to proceed in a slightly truncated version.[1] President Kennedy felt that during his few months in office he had scaled down the scope of the invasion to what he considered to be only an exercise in 'mass infiltration', thus reducing the penalties for failure to a lower level. In addition, he saw the dumping of 800 troublesome refugees in Cuba as a policy preferable to dumping them in the US. He also believed that the refugees had a strong commitment to the return of a 'free Cuba'; in any event there was little sense in protecting Castro by stopping these patriots. Furthermore, the President was assured that, even without direct American participation, the invasion would succeed. Finally, like President Truman in 1950, President Kennedy in 1961 had to consider his political opposition. A failure to act decisively would be treated by many Republicans as a display of weakness.[2] 'More generally, the decision resulted from the fact that he had been in office only seventy-seven days' and did not feel himself to be in a position which would allow him to flout the 'massed authority of senior officials'. As President Kennedy himself said after the Bay of Pigs débâcle, 'You always assume that the military and intelligence people have some secret skill not available to ordinary mortals.'[3]

[1] Arthur M. Schlesinger, Jr., *A Thousand Days: John F. Kennedy in the White House*, Deutsch, London, 1965, pp. 257–8.

[2] Roger Hilsman, *To Move A Nation: The Politics of Foreign Policy in the Administration of John F. Kennedy*, Doubleday, New York, 1967, pp. 30–3.

[3] Quoted in Schlesinger, op. cit., p. 258. Roger Hilsman (op. cit., pp. 30–3) echoed Kennedy's self-criticism when he emphasized the new President's failure completely to understand the emotional nature of the commitment to the plan of his advisers. 'President Kennedy failed in trusting too much the judgement of experts whose expertise was inevitably parochial.'

Given his decision to proceed with this adventure, why did the President not decide to use US forces, if not to ensure success, at least to make the probability of failure less likely? The Joint Chiefs of Staff tried unsuccessfully to impress upon the new President the necessity of some degree of US military involvement in the Cuban invasion if it was to have any chance of success. Though President Kennedy was quite willing to supply and train the refugee force then in Guatemala, he never deviated from his firm belief that it would be impolitic to commit US military force to this adventure. This belief seems to have been based upon two considerations. His primary consideration was his insistence that the landing should not involve an unacceptable political risk to the US. Reaction to a successful landing involving American support would be unpleasant and damaging to the country's reputation; but an unsuccessful landing involving American support would compound the failure, making the US appear not only immoral but also incompetent. Secondly, he was determined to have an invasion staged by and for Cubans and to have it seen by the world as such. This, too, would protect America's reputation for fair-dealing and non-interference.

In sum, President Kennedy was determined not to involve US prestige and influence on a venture of dubious value for the United States and Cuba and one which involved the risk of seriously damaging US interests even in the unlikely event of success.

At the same time as the Kennedy administration was making its way toward the Bay of Pigs failure, it was becoming increasingly concerned with the possibility of another failure for the West in Indochina. Even though President Eisenhower had, in 1954, decided not to commit US military forces to defend the newly created South Vietnam, America had, by 1961 and the start of the Kennedy administration, assumed an effective commitment to the South Vietnamese government to prevent Communist domination of their country. Without continued US aid, it was doubtful whether South Vietnam could be prevented from coming under the control of South Vietnamese Communists, dependent upon the already Communist North Vietnam. Gradually, the nature of the Kennedy-assumed commitment to the South, the rationale for which had not changed significantly since 1954, was drastically altered with the introduction of large numbers of 'advisers' and, perhaps more importantly, the assumption of a combat role by these troops by the start of 1962. How was it that a low-level involvement inherited by the new administration in January 1961 was qualitatively transformed by the introduction of American force into combat situations within the space of one year?

Basically, once the decision had been taken to prevent Communist control of the South, a decision which apparently had been made by the previous administration, it was 'only logical' to do whatever was necessary to achieve this noble end. Probably the most significant aspect of this increasing US commitment of force during the first year of the Kennedy administration to defend what it saw as its interests in South-East Asia was the gradual nature of the involvement. Indeed, it would be difficult to say that, unlike the other cases we have examined, the commitment of US forces was the result of *a* decision. Rather, each step into what became the Vietnamese morass was seen as just a small step, and moreover a logical extension of the previous one. Each step was, therefore, taken, it now appears, to make the previous ones succeed.

In retrospect, it would appear that there were two decisions taken by President Kennedy (who 'was convinced that the techniques of "revolutionary warfare" constituted a special kind of threat')[1] in 1961 which significantly altered the nature of the US commitment. In May, 500 US troops were ordered into South Vietnam to assist the South Vietnamese themselves defeat the Vietcong; and in November the decision was taken to again increase the numbers of US forces in Indochina and for the first time to allow these forces to become involved actively in combat with the Vietcong.

Since, as was noted above, these decisions were not felt by decision-makers in Washington to be major changes in US policy since 1945 but rather necessary tactics in the pursuit of eternal Cold War goals, we should concentrate here on the reasoning that persuaded the Kennedy administration to continue this commitment so many years – and so many world political developments – after it was made. The reasons given in the various memoranda contained in *The Pentagon Papers* appear to fall into six interrelated categories.[2] First, it was necessary to deny South Vietnam to the Communists. President Kennedy was concerned about possible Soviet intentions to make use of 'wars of national liberation'. He was particularly impressed by Premier Khrushchev's 6 January speech indicating Soviet support for such revolutionary wars and he had it studied by the members of his new administration.[3] Second, it was an American duty to assist the South Vietnamese to establish 'a viable and

[1] Ibid., p. 415.   [2] Sheehan, op. cit., pp. 125–30, 139–53.
[3] Hilsman, op. cit., p. 414.

increasingly democratic society'. Third, there was the strategic importance of a 'free' South-East Asia to the rest of Asia and to American interests in the Pacific (Vice-President Johnson reported to his President after returning from Vietnam in May that US failure to fight the Communists in Vietnam would result in grave setbacks for the US in the Pacific). Fourth, US resolve would demonstrate to America's adversaries her seriousness of purpose, her credibility. Fifth, the US had to intervene to demonstrate to her friends and allies that America kept her promises, thus ensuring continued confidence in the US as the defender of freedom, i.e. US interests abroad. And sixth, American decisiveness would prevent domestic controversy in the US resulting from the 'loss' of Vietnam. Joseph McCarthy's song was over but his melody lingered on.

One cannot escape the impression that this non-decision series of decisions was made because, if for no other reason, it was the easiest policy to follow; if President Kennedy followed the advice of the military and his close advisers in the Administration it was not necessary to counter their laudable reasons for favouring American force being used in Vietnam. As in the Bay of Pigs fiasco, to continue what seemed to be a policy of the *status quo* was the simplest 'decision' to make – or perhaps to avoid making.

With the Indochinese imbroglio seeming to be moving on its own accord – a self-propelled foreign policy – the United States was faced in 1965 with what appeared, to some, to be the imminent formation of a 'second Cuba'. The Kennedy administration's concern in Latin America was not solely the prevention of the spread of Communist revolution via Castro's Cuba. It was also hoped to further the cause of inter-American concord by helping Latin Americans to develop their economies and improve their societies and governments. The spectre of revolution emanating from Cuba meant that Washington came increasingly to view its Latin American policy primarily in terms of how best to prevent a 'second Cuba' from springing up elsewhere in the hemisphere. To the policy-makers in the US the Dominican Republic appeared to be a ripe target for the messianic Cubans. Hence, soon after the Bay of Pigs 'invasion' President Kennedy approved a contingency plan for landing US troops in the Republic. The President stressed that the United States could not afford and would not permit the imposition in the Republic of a pro-Castro or a pro-Communist regime.[1]

[1] Abraham F. Lowenthal, *The Dominican Intervention*, Harvard U.P., Cambridge, Mass., 1972, p. 26.

American policy *vis-à-vis* the Dominican Republic, then, was shaped from the outset of the Democratic administrations of Presidents Kennedy and Johnson by the single-minded desire to prevent the Republic from becoming the dreaded 'second Cuba'.

The internal political development of the Dominican Republic from the death of Trujillo in May 1961 until the arrival of the US Marine Corps in April 1965 followed a bewildering course with faction following faction as the government of the country. Suffice it to say that at the time of the intervention, the government was in the hands of a military group which had vowed to return the state to a 'rightist' course from which it had been taken by the 'leftist' Juan Bosch, from whom the soldiers now in charge had taken the government seven months earlier. Suffice it also to say that on 28 April 1965 President Johnson ordered the Marines to land in the Republic for reasons which seemed to alter as days passed and the situation 'cleared'. What were the fears in Washington which led to President Johnson's decision and what was the reasoning which the administration gradually developed to explain the intervention after it had occurred?

In his statement to the public on the landing of the troops, President Johnson stated directly that the Marines were sent in 'in order to protect American lives'. This, he emphasized, was no longer possible for the Dominican authorities to do adequately.[1] Two days later, on 30 April, the American President again said that the troops were in the Dominican Republic 'in an effort to protect the lives of Americans and the nationals of other countries in the face of increasing violence and disorder'. But, he added, 'there are increasing signs that people trained outside the Dominican Republic are seeking to gain control. Thus the legitimate aspirations of the Dominican people and most of their leaders for progress, democracy and social justice are threatened and so are the principles of the inter-American system.'[2]

Then on 2 May President Johnson issued yet another statement clarifying the reasons for the Marines' presence in the Republic. He again mentioned the need to protect the lives of foreign nationals and Americans and then explained precisely what he apparently had meant in his statement of 30 April.

The revolutionary movement took a tragic turn. Communist

[1] Richard Stebbins (ed.), *Documents on American Foreign Relations 1965*, Council on Foreign Relations, New York, 1966, p. 234.
[2] Ibid., p. 237.

leaders, many of them trained in Cuba, seeing a chance to increase disorder, to gain a foothold, joined the revolution. They took increasing control. And what began as a popular democratic revolution, committed to democracy and social justice, very shortly moved and was taken over and really seized and placed into the hands of a band of communist conspirators.

Finally, President Johnson emphasized that 'The American nations cannot, must not, and will not permit the establishment of another Communist government in the Western hemisphere.'[1]

Two key words in the 2 May statement sum up what was undoubtedly the reason for the American intervention in the Dominican Republic. They are, of course, 'Communist' and 'Cuba'. Because of their concern with the spread of Communism from Cuba to other Latin American countries, the policy-makers in Washington apparently decided, without conclusive evidence, that since there were almost no negative factors to hold them back – save bad public relations, which would quickly pass – to avoid possible danger it was best to act immediately and develop reasons for the actions at their leisure after the situation had been brought under control.

Conclusion

In all five cases involving the USSR, the Soviet leaders felt that national security was threatened, either immediately or as the result of a continuation of the existing situation. Finland and Poland were not to be permitted to be used by greater Powers, in both cases Germany, in order to attack the territory of the Soviet Union. In the cases of Yugoslavia (perhaps less so than the others), Hungary and Czechoslovakia, Moscow thought that failure to stem uncontrolled changes in the *status quo* could easily lead to a threat to the USSR itself. Thus, to a great extent, the Soviet response in all five cases (and again, to a less degree, in the Yugoslav case) was seen by Moscow as being essentially defensive. Steps had to be taken to *prevent* the establishment or continuation of a situation antithetical to vital Soviet interests.

It is important to stress that these Soviet concerns which were instrumental in the decision to use force in four of the cases and to consider seriously the possibility of using force in the fifth were seen to be of an extremely vital nature. Soviet objectives in these instances

[1] Ibid., pp. 241–5.

were seen by Moscow to be of the 'eternal' nature, i.e. involving concerns of survival and security rather than involving more ephemeral objectives such as the conquering of territory, populations or mens' minds or the increasing of the state's prestige.[1] Moscow felt that if extreme steps were not taken in these instances, the very existence of the USSR would be in peril. The fact that the pursuit of these eternal objectives involved of necessity the obtaining of the more 'wordly' objectives should not obscure the larger motives for for the Soviet actions. The use of force by the USSR in these cases was motivated by considerations of Soviet national interest of the most fundamental kind.

The first two cases both involved the Soviet fear of military attack from the West; Finland and Poland could be used by Germany to launch an attack on the USSR. As time went on, however, it was not so much the West which was feared because it could attack the Soviet Union via Eastern Europe, but rather it became fear of the 'infection' of heretical ideas, of the consequences of success of the forces of change. If the Yugoslavs were permitted to be successful in their independence or if the Hungarians or Czechoslovaks were allowed to continue their rampaging reforms, the 'principles' of these 'anti-Socialist' practices would be seized upon by other Soviet allies and a dissolution of the bloc, with all its attendant consequences for the USSR, would follow. In all five cases an ounce of prevention was seen as being preferable to a pound of cure, especially as the disease could easily kill the doctor.

Like the Soviet Union, the United States saw the cases in which it used force as involving questions of defence of the US itself, as the defence of the US was inextricably bound up with the defence of the entire 'free world'.[2] A hole in the dike would inundate the West. Thus in all six cases under discussion the fear of the spread of Com-

[1] See Raymond Aron, *Peace and War: A Theory of International Relations*, translated by Richard Howard and Annette Baker Fox, Weidenfelt & Nicolson, London, 1967, pp. 72–4. Similarly see F. S. Northedge's discussion of the 'hierarchy of interests' in his *The Foreign Policies of the Powers*, Faber, London, 1968, pp. 16–18 and K. J. Holsti's discussion of goals and interests in his *International Politics: A Framework for Analysis*, 2nd edn., Englewood Cliffs, N.J., 1972, pp. 136–42. Northedge lists as the primary interests of a state its self-preservation and integrity and Holsti likewise includes self-preservation and defence of strategically vital areas among the 'core' interests and values of a state.

[2] The cases involving the US did not, of course, involve such direct challenges to its vital interests as did those involving the USSR, but the essential point is that it was thought, equally in Washington and Moscow, that the defence of respective national interests was at stake.

munism was felt to be crucial in the decision-making process (even when it was decided not to use force, this fear was a great incentive to do so) and was signified as being such by the decision-makers in question. The 'lessons of Munich and appeasement' were applied again and again as was the 'lesson of Korea'.

Likewise, America also became increasingly concerned about the infectious nature of forces of change within its own area of influence. Cuba and the Dominican Republic were seen as the possible fountainheads of a revolution which could spread 'a foreign creed' throughout the hemisphere. But farther away from the US itself, on the borders of the 'free world', in Korea, Indochina and Lebanon, it was the necessity of preventing the fall of the dominoes which actuated America's use of military force.

In each case under review, probably the primary consideration in each capital was the possible effect on other Powers of a decision to use force; particularly, was there a chance of counter-intervention?[1] However, only the case of Yugoslavia presented the Soviet rulers with the real possibility of *effective* Western intervention to counter the use of force and only the case of Yugoslavia presented them with the real possibility of *effective* national resistance (the Finns surprised them).

It may seem, therefore, that the use of force in the other four cases represented an 'easy option', one involving little risk and great efficacy. But it would appear that this was the situation only in the Finnish case,[2] which, significantly, was the case of the five in which Soviet security was most imperilled. It was both dangerous and unnecessary to dally with the Finns, but in the cases of Yugoslavia, Hungary and Czechoslovakia the Soviets tried other means of persuasion before giving up the fight or deciding to use force. As there was no doubt in 1956 and 1968 that force would be successful, the conclusion must be that Moscow was worried about the detrimental effect of outraged opinion both within and without its sphere of influence. Thus, except in the wartime cases of Finland and perhaps Poland, the Soviets did not take the 'easy option' of force

[1] F. S. Northedge and M. D. Donelan point out that, in the disputes they considered, 'If a state went so far as to intervene with its own forces, rival states were unlikely to do the same. The danger of war outweighed their interest. What the intervening state had most to fear was that its rivals would respond with arm's-length assistance to the other side. . . .' (*International Disputes: The Political Aspects*, Europa, London, 1971, p. 131.)

[2] The case of Poland is somewhat special in that, as noted above, Soviet troops had to be in Poland whether or not they were to be used to help install a 'friendly' government in Warsaw.

but made their decision only after other means had been tried and had been seen to fail.

That it was possible that Soviet intervention would be one result of American intervention in Korea the US policy-makers knew. Similarly in Indochina in 1954, the spectre of a Korea-like Chinese involvement was a factor considered by President Eisenhower and advisers when they decided not to send US forces. But in the other instances, the chances of actual military involvement on the the Soviets or Chinese, while not dismissed out of hand, were idered serious. In Korea, Indochina and Vietnam there was be resistance to any US military force as wars were already and the Americans would enter the fighting on one side. sistance could also be expected, though this possibility ar to be a major consideration in Washington. But in the Dominican Republic any significant resistance was the question.

case which involved the greatest risk, Korea, was an instance, not unlike the Soviet problems apropos Finland, in which the US felt it had to act as this was possibly its last chance to stop the onward rush of the USSR. More than in any other case, then, US policy-makers saw vital US interests of security – and perhaps survival – at stake. While these questions were certainly considered in the other decisions there was never again this 'do-or-die' aspect.

Unfortunately, it is difficult to generalize about the question of the use of force as an 'easy option' when talking about the United States experience. In Korea, the use of force was felt to be the *only* 'option'. In Indochina and Vietnam, other methods of 'persuasion' were tried' though, since wars were in progress, they were predominantly military in nature and were but logical predecessors to the eventual use of the US military from 1961. Likewise, in Cuba, many other forms of pressure were applied before the Bay of Pigs invasion. Only in the cases of Lebanon and the Dominican Republic did the US choose the use of force because it was quick and clean.

The reasons for the Soviet decision to refrain from using force against Yugoslavia have been considered above. But what can be said about the American decisions not to use force in Indochina in 1954 and against Cuba in 1961? Whereas the predominant Soviet fear about using force against Yugoslavia was probably the fear of Western counter-action, the Eisenhower administration in 1954 seems to have been motivated primarily by the belief that the use of force would not be efficacious and could not be employed without harming other more important American interests. Chinese intervention was felt to be a possibility (the Joint Chiefs of Staff said the chances were 50–50) but was not one of the more important considerations. It is difficult to perceive in the Indochinese situation factors which were radically different from those which in other situations did result in the use of force and the conclusion presents itself that the key variable was perhaps the nature of the men in office.

In the case of Cuba, on the other hand, there was a situation that was again not very different from the other cases. Yet force was not used when its use would probably have been successful. The arguments presented by President Kennedy both to go ahead with the invasion and to forbid the use of American forces could have been similarly applied in some of the other examples.

It seems, therefore, that whereas the Yugoslav case had features quite different from the other cases of Soviet decision-making, the cases of Indochina and Cuba are puzzling because they are not so different from the other US cases. It can be concluded only that in the several American cases, in different time periods similar – though not identical – evidence was given different weight from what it might have been given at another time by other decision-makers. As one political scientist wrote, 'If some governments operate to fulfil a series of logically consistent goals, many more do not seem to be working toward the achievement of any specific objective or, at best, improvise policies to meet specific domestic or external crises or commitments.'[1]

Two of the most important changes in the international system which have occurred during the thirty-year period under discussion have been the emergence, and more recently the decline, of a bipolar configuration of power and the advent and rise to a dominant position of nuclear weapons. With regard to the decisions of the Soviet Union and the United States to use force in disputes involving small Powers, the emergence of bipolarity has accentuated the over-riding importance of the conflict-finding character of the spheres of influence of each of the two great Powers and the paramountcy of the expected reaction of the bipolar rival to any use of force. Though the United States's decisions invariably involved the perceived intent of 'the other side' to expand the borders of its sphere of influence, only the Yugoslav case of the three post-war Soviet examples involved a similar Soviet perception of Western aggression – in its

---

[1] Holsti, op. cit., p. 132.

various forms. However, the Soviet cases did involve a Soviet belief that failure to act to bolster the defences of the USSR's sphere could lead to an effective Western victory. Raymond Aron noted in theory what we have seen in the actual behaviour of the USSR and the US in the cases examined above when he wrote that 'The leaders of the coalition [in a bipolar system] must simultaneously be on guard to prevent the growth of the other great Power or coalition and to maintain the cohesion of their own.'[1]

In addition to guarding the integrity of the boundaries of its sphere of influence, each great Power, as was noted above, was extremely concerned with the possible reactions of its rival to its own use of force. As Andrew Scott suggested, 'The most important rule to be followed by a nation that is intervening in its own sphere of influence is to act in such a way as to minimize the danger of a direct conflict with the other great Power and to facilitate the other Power's acceptance of the action.' Furthermore, Scott suggests that interbloc intervention is out of the question if war is to be avoided.[2]

The primary effect of the advent of nuclear weapons on the great Powers' use of force was succinctly put in Chapter 1 of this volume: '. . . it is hard to resist the conclusion that the nuclear Powers at least seem to have so frightened themselves by their stocks of infinitely varied nuclear devices that almost any use of armed forces appears to them pregnant with the most awful risks.' This fear of the 'awful risks' associated with any use of force caused both the USSR and the US to act with great caution when contemplating the use of force and has emphasized the supreme importance of possible rival perception and response in pre-use of force calculation. In the cases discussed, the question of escalation resulting from counter-action by the rival great Power had always to be considered. And the basic caution or conservatism of both Moscow and Washington was evident in their calculations – especially so after Korea and the Soviet acquisition of destructive capabilities closer in magnitude to those of the US. Such great-Power conservatism, born of nuclear fears, was especially evident in the location of the use of force. All Soviet examples were unquestionably within the Soviet sphere of influence and all American examples involved areas of demonstrated Western concern and intention. The actual use of force in several

[1] Aron, op. cit., p. 136.
[2] Andrew M. Scott, 'Military Intervention by the Great Powers: The Rules of the Game', I. William Zartman, *Czechoslovakia: Intervention and Impact*, University of London Press, London, 1970, pp. 89–90, 92.

cases may have surprised the rivals, but the location of the use of force should not have.[1]

Both of these developments, bipolarity and nuclear weapons, have been causes of the increasing importance of the political (rather than a strictly military) aspect of the decision to use force. The United States has been criticized for its pursuit of a strictly military victory in the Second World War when the USSR was simultaneously fighting a political war. Yet, since the rise of the two nuclear super Powers, the significance of what Morton Halperin has called the 'political-effects objectives' of the use of force has been marked in the behaviour of both the USSR and the US.[2] Both Moscow and Washington, perhaps the latter to a greater degree, were eager to demonstrate to all concerned the limits of their patience in dealing with threats to their security. Military success was, of course, important, but the political messages transmitted and the political demonstration effect were more important.

[1] Northedge and Donelan, op. cit., p. 164, have noted the propensity for great Powers to establish a doctrine of 'limited sovereignty' with regard to near-by states, but during the period under discussion, the area of application of this type of policy was enlarged to include what each Power took to be its sphere of influence, the US's being much vaster.

[2] Morton H. Halperin, 'Limited War', Robert L. Pfaltzgraff, Jr. (ed.), *Politics and the International System*, Lippincott, Philadelphia, P.A., 1969, p. 217.

3 The Regional Use of Force

A marked development of international society since 1945 has been an increasing resort by states to regional arrangements as a means of threatening or using force. What is meant by the rather vague expression 'regional arrangements'? Primarily it refers to the formal alliances created in the Cold War. These alliances have tended to take the form of coalitions at a regional level. The reasons for this are examined later in this chapter. There are also less important formal treaties which have sought to dispose of force on a regional scale, such as the five-Power agreement by which Britain, Malaysia, Singapore, Australia and New Zealand have shared an ill-defined common security interest in the general area of the Malayan Peninsula.

On the other hand, there are informal agreements. These include groups of formal bilateral treaties which together have the effect of multilateral alliances. Thus France retains an 'active interest in the external and internal security' of her former colonies in West Africa,[1] controlling to a large extent the regional balance of power. For it is not through the multilateral but moribund French Community so much as through a series of bilateral treaties that French influence is expressed. Britain has, or had, similar agreements in East Africa. These led to her intervention in army mutinies in Tanganyika, Kenya and Uganda in 1964 to 'stabilize' the new governments there. But some informal arrangements are more in the nature of tacit understandings. A vague but important understanding developed between the United States and Britain which helped to define their roles in Asia. Britain could ill afford to keep a militarily significant presence East of Suez, and a strong case can be made for the argument that she had no business there, strategically or politically. A major reason given for the presence was that in order to

[1] Herbert Tint, *French Foreign Policy since the Second World War*, Weidenfeld & Nicolson, London, 1972, p. 202.

'earn' the 'special relationship' with America special responsibilities had to be undertaken, even at considerable expense. Hence Britain, as a *quid pro quo*, 'defended' the Indian Ocean. In return America underwrote not so much British investments to the east and north of Malaya as the 'special relationship' itself.[1] A more precise agreement can be seen to be operating between the three white Powers of Southern Africa: Portugal, Rhodesia and South Africa co-operate regionally against black guerrillas.

There are therefore two main classes of regional arrangements: those bound by formal and those bound by informal agreements. Some or most of these are involved in other business, which may concern political or cultural ties, economic co-operation or the quasi-force of aid and military assistance programmes. This chapter will concentrate on the one feature which most have in common, that they seek to alter or determine a regional balance of power by the use or threat of force.

It is useful to compare this sort of system with two other forms of combination between nations, the power-balancing alliance and the collective security organization. Balance-of-power theorists have generally held that a country's greatest enemy would be its neighbour, but that its neighbour's neighbour was equally likely to be a useful ally. Both in Europe and amongst the Indian and Chinese princes who developed the idea of a power balance, alliance politics were seen as having a patchwork pattern. Regional arrangements, in theory as in practice, were rare. Usually only in the special case where a state threatened the whole order were geographical blocs formed. Limitations on communications, on arms technology, on economic resources and on the way in which governments defined their interests all meant that no state could transcend the existing balanced system to form the sort of global foreign policy which super Powers have pursued since 1945. Collective security, on the other hand, was originally conceived as an alternative to the balance-of-power system. It was deliberately invented to supersede that system, which was seen as not only politically unsuccessful, but also morally indefensible. This prescriptive element in the idea of collective security was an essential part of it. It assumed that Powers could band together, like men in Rousseau's model of the state, to create a General Will for peace, and furthermore for the prosecution by force of 'bandit nations' who might try to gain from war. The

[1] P. G. C. Darby, *British Defence Policy East of Suez, 1947–1968*, O.U.P., London, 1973, pp. 293 ff.

limitations of collective security were increasingly recognized with the decline of the League of Nations after 1935. By the end of the 1930s even the most optimistic supporter of the League and of collective security was forced to recognize that neither could guarantee peace in this less than best of all possible worlds.

The very limitations on the effectiveness of collective security led in part to the creation of regional arrangements. But the resulting problems were recognized rather than solved in the Charter of the United Nations. This was written in the light of the experience that great Powers will not support even a high ideal if it conflicts with their interests. Thus the Charter foresaw that states may want to act outside its provisions even to the extent of using force in certain circumstances. Article 52 was drafted as a necessarily vague admission of this: it allowed 'regional arrangements for dealing with such matters relating to the maintenance of international peace and security as are appropriate for regional action'. This article originated in a desire on the part of the United States and some of her American allies to retain an exclusive hemispheric interest through such local agreements as the Inter-American conference.[1] They wanted to keep the other Powers from interfering in the politics of the Americas. This was important since it created a structure which was a model for all subsequent formal arrangements to varying extents. It is because governments, especially the United States, took advantage of this part of the Charter that we can say that regional arrangements effectively began when it was signed. As J. S. Nye noted in the introduction to his book of readings on the subject, one can describe twenty-three 'regional groupings' (including non-military ones) which developed between 1945 and 1968.[2] Before the Charter was signed there was only the Inter-American system. Thus while the existence of the Charter obviously did not cause a sudden blossoming of regional collaboration, it did create the conditions in which many felt such association was both possible and necessary.

It is possible to disagree with Nye here. Were there not more regional arrangements before 1945? Surely the Washington Naval Agreements of 1921, which together tried to determine the balance of power in the Pacific Ocean, were 'regional arrangements'? Surely the league of Balkan States (Serbia, Montenegro, Bulgaria, Greece),

---

[1] Walter B. Sharp, 'The Inter-American System and the United Nations', *Foreign Affairs*, XXIII, 3, April 1945, p. 450.

[2] J. S. Nye (ed.), *International Regionalism*, Little, Brown & Co., Boston, 1968, p.v.

which almost totally drove Turkey out of Europe in the First Balkan War of 1912, constituted some sort of 'regional arrangement'? Perhaps even the division of Africa amongst the colonial Powers in the nineteenth century should be seen as a tacit regional arrangement? To resolve these questions is to define what is meant by 'region' and 'regional arrangement'.

There is an ambiguity in the term 'regional arrangement'. Does it refer to treaties or understandings which exist to protect its members from outside threats? Or does it refer to those created to determine the balance of power amongst the members of a region? This is not a straightforward problem since the Organization of American States, for example, a paradigm of what we mean when we talk about such agreements, exists to do both. It protects the member-states from outside attack, but it also attempts to maintain the *status quo* within the region. Yet clearly the primary importance of contemporary formal arrangements like the OAS, or like the North Atlantic Treaty Organization (NATO) and the Warsaw Pact, is defence against threats from outside their regions. If one is to be consistent, and if one is to avoid an overwhelming proliferation of arrangements, then 'informal regional arrangements' should also be a term reserved for those primarily directed against outsiders. This is a matter of convenience rather than an inflexible rule. It is also largely a matter of convenience to reserve the title of 'regional arrangement' for those which have developed since 1945, in a diplomatic, strategic and economic environment markedly different from that in which earlier alliances were formed. Thus regional arrangements are, for present purposes at least, those which are directed by a group of states in a region mainly against others outside their region. They can be distinguished analytically from balance-of-power arrangements and collective security agreements. They are different in their environment and in their tendency to look back to, or refer to, the United Nations Charter from alliances made before 1945. It is therefore useful to consider them as being distinct from those earlier alliances.

It is equally hard to define what we mean by 'region'. Ultimately this definition too – and indeed that of any universal term – rests on linguistic usage. But we can set broad limits to the idea. Consider the geographical area 'Europe', the land mass west of the Ural Mountains. Geographically that counts as a single region. But strategically it is a subsidiary area within a global military balance between the super Powers. Politically there are many regions, the Balkans, the Nordic, the Iberian, Western Europe and several others. Economically

73

there is the Europe of the Nine and the Europe of Comecon; but there are also trading regions which complicate this pattern, as for example the region of both Eastern and Western Europe which looks towards West Germany as its principle trading associate, or at least as an important source of commercial activity. On reflection there is thus no single definition which can be advanced to include all the kinds and examples of regions which one would want to allow to be such. Yet the word must be located somewhere in our intellectual landscape if we are to be able to use it. Russett saw this when he said that definitions of 'region' must be 'flexible: no single condition is either necessary or sufficient by itself'.[1] Following Russett one can, however, point out that regions *tend* to have 'geographical proximity', 'share similar political attitudes and have cultural homogeneity and/or economic interdependence'. To this one can add that those regional arrangements to which this chapter is devoted, those which use or threaten force, are bound by a conscious recognition of at least some degree of community of interest and collectivity of action amongst their decision-makers. This deliberately loose definition will become clearer as some examples and problems of regional arrangements are discussed.

NATO was the first of the major, formal regional arrangements. Its apparent success, judged by the criteria of those who set it up, led to a spread of similar alliances. They became one of the principal means of American foreign policy, and kept a special place in the hearts and minds of American decision-makers at least until the declaration of the Nixon Doctrine which marked the final end of the containment policy. Even after the President's announcement that his country's allies would in future have to play a fuller part in the maintenance of their own security, that they could no longer expect as much help from the United States through regional arrangements as they previously had, this type of *entente* still has an important place in American thinking. The motives of the founder members of NATO are interesting in themselves, but are also important as showing the thinking which underlay the spread of regional arrangements. Dean Acheson, the American Secretary of State, explained the United States's position shortly after the NATO agreement was made:

It is clear that in the world of today we can no longer rely on

---

[1] Bruce M. Russett, *International Regions and the International System*, Rand McNalley, Chicago, 1967, p. 11.

our geographical position to preserve our peace and security. Our security and peace necessarily rest in the combined security and peace of the rest of the democratic world.[1]

The emergence of the North Atlantic coalition marked the extension of American commitments to Europe, although in 1945 Americans had hoped to wind up their presence there 'within two years'. It was the perceived threat and, perhaps more, the unpredictability of the Soviet Union which led to this change of role. The policy of containment was formulated in 1947 as a response to this perception. By 1949 – how much as a result of a self-fulfilling prophecy one hesitates to guess – Russian policy seemed fully to justify the completion of a large multilateral alliance to deter and plan against the possibility of 'Soviet aggression'. There were other motives. Many Europeans wanted to get a permanent American commitment to Europe, especially the British Foreign Secretary, Ernest Bevin. While this was chiefly to balance the greatly increased power of the Soviet Union, it was also to anchor the internal security, economic and political, of Western Europe. However, there was also much truth in Bevin's remark that Molotov, the Soviet Foreign Minister, did more than anyone else to bring his (Bevin's) policy to fruition. The Russian refusal of Marshall Aid in July 1947, followed by the Czech *coup* of February 1948 and the deadlock over Germany which came to a climax with the Berlin blockade: this caravanserai of crises was quickly labelled the 'Cold War' in the press. The open hostility of Russian conduct at international conferences and in the United Nations added to Western fears and suspicions. Perhaps only this series of events could have made European decision-makers willing to join the Brussels Pact and its successor, NATO. It was only with the outbreak of the Korean War in 1950 that NATO was fully accepted in Europe. Only then did it become a fully integrated military institution.

Informal regional arrangements can be seen either as stages in the development of formal alliances or as alternatives to them. Thus before a formal treaty was signed there was co-operation between those governments which joined the NATO pact. Other states may deliberately prefer not to make a treaty which would bind them too closely or commit them to obligations too specific for their taste. They prefer the flexibility and privacy of an informal agreement, as

[1] Press statement, 8 April 1949, *Documents on International Affairs 1949–1950*, O.U.P., London, 1953, p. 265.

the white Southern African Powers seem to have done. Alternatively they may be unable to agree sufficiently on a treaty although they want to work together against a rival. This has prevented the Arab states from forming a lasting alliance against Israel. There may be a definite decision to combine regionally to use force without a formal agreement, although, as the case of the Middle East shows, the 'enemy' which the concurring states face must be easily recognizable and a major threat if the alliance is to succeed.

This introduction has examined the background to, and reasons for, the spread of regional arrangements. It is necessary to look at the purposes for which states collaborate in such arrangements, at the limitations on their usefulness and at the forms of organization which they take. From a discussion of these we should be able to reach an assessment of how important regional arrangements are when states resort to the use of force.

The purposes of regional arrangements

Regional arrangements obviously do not exist 'to use force'. They exist rather to use force or to threaten it in some agreed way for particular political ends. Although there may be exceptions, one can assume *prima facie* that they use force when it is in the interests of their members. Thus the choice of force as a means of policy represents a deliberate decision or a studied reaction to a crisis. It is hard to find a way to classify the very diverse ends to which regional arrangements are put. The approach to be adopted here will be to assume that states act in this rational manner and to look at the purposes of arrangements in terms of the different levels of force which they employ.

Before proceeding on the assumption that, in effect, Clausewitz was right, that war is but 'an extension of policy', it is important to ask if this is always the case. Do states and regional arrangements ever use what one might call 'pure force', force which has no political content or purpose at all? The very awkwardness of the phrase 'pure force' shows that this is almost inconceivable. The violence of individuals can be apolitical, but in the international environment all the actions of states have a political meaning even if the actors try to eschew a political purpose. Few Powers would wish to follow the Khan Tamburlane, who saw the destruction of Babylon and the erection on its site of a mountain of skulls as an end in itself. This is not out of moral scruple. It is because the action would serve no end and would earn its perpetrator a reputation for 'breaking the rules' (as Hitler did) and as a threat to all other members of international society. There have been cases which have come close to being examples of 'pure force', although this has been as an idea rather than as a policy. The American doctrine of massive retaliation had a marked difference from most other strategic ideas as a threat to destroy utterly and without compromise any other country which attacked the United States or her allies. But since this was designed to deter such attack it is not a clear case of 'pure force'. One can argue that in any case it was never a realistic policy. But the threat that the Strategic Air Command would obliterate the USSR if the Soviets dared to seize even the most insigificant part of the 'free world' is one in which the means of policy can hardly be said to be rationally matched to its goals. This Mr. McNamara recognized when he abandoned the policy. There is the same sort of irrationality, though in very different circumstances, about the policy of the Arab states towards Israel. In practice, they follow two lines. They hope to retake the lands seized by Israel in 1967, and to limit Israeli influence in the world and in the Middle East. But they also, though with less consistency, aim at the destruction of the state of Israel altogether. It is the first of these aims which receives support from outside the region, from the Warsaw Pact and elsewhere. But it is the second aim which is dear to the heart of Arab nationalists, and it is on their achievements towards this goal that governments are often judged at home. Most Arab governments, except in times of war, have tried to avoid the second aim in favour of the first, and even this is not a very good example of 'pure force' if one analyses the actions of Arab governments rather than the words of their nationalist leaders.

All force is thus used in a way limited by the political ends of the user in international society, with only rare exceptions. It will be valuable to look at the purposes regional arrangements have when they actually use force, and then at the purposes they have when they threaten force. This posits the existence of a threshold between uses and threats of force. This is only one of a number of thresholds which states observe, of which the most important is perhaps the decision to use nuclear arms. But there is no clear scale of importance of these thresholds, and the distinction which appears to be there may prove to be an illusion: one Power may be surprised to find that its opponent does not recognize its use of, for example, air overflights as a step less than open warfare. The crossing of the Yalu river in the Korean War was a clear threshold to the Chinese, who signalled through India that such a step would bring the People's Republic into the war. Americans ignored or misread the signal, the river was crossed and the Chinese counter-attacked in massive strength. Since the threshold between the use and the threat of force is generally recognized, it can be used here. But it is important to remember that it is not a natural division: it exists for as long and as strongly as governments choose that it should.

The limited use of force

This section will look at the role of the threshold as it is recognized by states and regional arrangements when they use force. It will look at the way in which means are adjusted to ends, and in which they are limited to the importance of those ends. It must also try to discover why groups of states decide to use force at one particular level rather than any other. Above all, both this section and the next, on threats of force, will look at the diplomacy of force, the relationship between military means and policy goals and formulation in regional alliances.

The decision to use force by an alliance must always be significant. As with individual states, the weight an alliance assigns to any matter is best indicated by the degree of risk its members are prepared to undertake. Thus when the Soviet Union enforced the Berlin blockade she was signalling not just what she wanted, which was not to seize Berlin but to gain a strong position for negotiations on the future of Germany; she also showed the risks she was prepared to take. The response of the allies was to take steps *at a level below the use of force.* They devised the airlift to relieve the city without force. The initiative, and thus the responsibility, for the use of force was thrown back to the Russians, who would have had to shoot down the transport planes to prevent the relief of Berlin. This is an example of how the refusal to use force marks a limit to the risks a state will take. If the Russians had sought the possession of Berlin, and if it had been as vital to them as one imagines the possession of Kiev is, then they would probably have shot down the transports. It incidentally shows how Powers recognize the idea of a threshold by their conduct.

Regional arrangements have used force to show their determination, to demonstrate the limit of their tolerance and for simple defence against attack. Conflict has taken the character of eighteenth-century warfare, of manoeuvre and deployment. Force is used selectively and to secure the greatest leverage.

South Africa, Rhodesia and Portugal are involved in an attempt to fend off the several groups of African liberation forces which beset them. Here the purpose of force is twofold. The guerrilla movement is strong in the Portuguese colonies, Angola and Mozambique, but weak in the other two countries. Failure to repress the successful guerrilla movements would encourage others. Therefore the first purpose is simply to destroy them. The second is to deter independent states to the north, especially Zambia, from helping the guerrillas. Massive overt collaboration would produce a strong reaction in the north, and a regional arrangement might well be formed between the independent states which was previously prevented by differences between them. The level of co-operation in Southern Africa is low compared with that in NATO, but significant, bearing in mind that the three Powers command overwhelming force in the area. There are known to be several hundred South African police in Rhodesia, and an unspecified number of Rhodesian troops in Mozambique. That the South African government was very concerned to deny press reports that several thousands of its troops were also involved in actual fighting shows its concern to underplay the confrontation.[1] In spite of political differences, the three governments have collaborated increasingly closely since 1965. They have been involved in war, but have found that they could only achieve their purpose by carefully limiting the force used: it is in their interest to present the conflict not as a war but as a mere policing operation. The minimum use of force is not simply economically efficient, it may well be more politically effective.

An important form of leverage used by groups of states involving force is that which Schelling calls 'compellence'. Whilst deterrence is the suspension over an opponent's head of the threat of force, which prevents him from acting *against* one's interests, compellence is the infliction of violence on an opponent to force him to act *in* one's favour. Thus, in a NATO scenario, if the Warsaw Pact countries seized Berlin, the NATO Powers might choose to release small-scale nuclear weapons, one at a time, at targets in the East. The first might land in uninhabited forest, to convince the Pact of NATO's will. Subsequent attacks, perhaps increasing in effect, could be used against people or military targets to compel the surrender of the

[1] Reports in *The Guardian* and *The Times*, 19 January 1973.

city. Compellence is a difficult policy to operate and is something that a small state or weak alliance would not be able to do. Only powerful combinations of states have the options to follow this sort of sophisticated 'conflict management'.

The Arab states have used force against Israel to dissuade her from certain policies. In particular, force (mainly artillery strikes) has been used to discourage the permanent settlement of the West Bank and the Golan Heights which were taken from Jordan and Syria in 1967. These actions have sometimes escalated to full-scale fighting when Israel retaliated against the destruction of a kibbutz. There is no reason why this sort of leverage using force should not be successful in other circumstances. It failed the Arab states in the late 1960s because the June war had affected the balance of power too strongly in Israel's favour: the retaliation to attempts to lever her has been deliberately savage and the cost to the Arab states has outweighed the gains.

Israel refuses, and has the power to refuse, to play the Arab 'game'. Limited uses of force where the user does not want a full-scale war depend on the recognition of these 'rules'. Either all participants will feel that the 'rules', at least for the time being, are in their interests, or one participant will be strong enough to dictate them to the others. The nature of the 'rules', and hence of the conflict, will differ qualitatively depending on who determines them. That these rules are explicit and understood is shown by the exchange of letters between Mr. Khrushchev and President Kennedy in the Cuba crisis.[1] The recognition by the two statesmen that both sought to avoid nuclear war is an example of such rules. They have since become more complex. Arguably it is pre-eminently these rules which have made possible the recent European *détente*. Talks on arms control, limitation and reduction can be seen both as rule-making and as rule-observing procedures. Two problems prevent these rules from stabilizing conflict very widely: they need a steady period of recognition of some degree of common interest; if a situation changes continually, as world politics altered between 1945 and about 1955, the 'rules' cannot emerge. Secondly, if in a dispute a state considers the issue at stake a vital one, yet follows an established tradition of behaviour, it runs the risk that its opponent will not be convinced of its resolve. The rules, in other words, wear out. They must be renewed if states are to maintain their credibility within them. The principal 'rules' are the recognition of the various

[1] See appendix to Robert Kennedy, *13 Days*, Macmillan, London, 1969.

thresholds which are important and, in a 'sophisticated' conflict, the recognition of the degree of importance to attach to these thresholds. For a regional agreement to be able to work effectively within the context of this mode of conflict it must be tightly organized and its members must share a homogeneous idea of their political interests.

One final point worth making about how regional arrangements use force is that they sometimes do so by proxy. Thus Secretary of State Dulles said in 1955 that the main business of SEATO lay outside the area covered by the Organization. As a result, SEATO countries contributed to the defence of anti-Communist governments. Laos was included in the treaty area although the Laotian government did not join. SEATO fought by proxy when mountain tribesmen such as the Montagnards fought insurgent movements in Cambodia and Vietnam. To say that the Vietnam War was war by proxy, with North Vietnam fighting on behalf of China or the Warsaw Pact, would oversimplify and underestimate the independence of decision of North Vietnam. However, the Korean War can be seen much more clearly as war by proxy on the Communist side, up to the point where American action brought China into the War in fact.

What conclusions can be drawn from this discussion of the actual use of force as a result of action by regional arrangements? Only some of the main points are made here. The idea of limited war stresses the relationship between military action and political goals. Military action must be appropriate, and it may be hard for divided allies such as the Arab states to agree on action. The importance of the goals which states have will not necessarily be shown most clearly in the quantity of force they use, but in the quantity of risk they are prepared to take. A sophisticated vocabulary of analysis has developed for armed conflict, but poor states and lesser alliances have neither the resources nor the options to afford the policy-makers and professors necessary for this style of conflict management. The purpose of the actual use of force by regional arrangements, 'defence', may be fulfilled by a range of means, stretching from pre-emptive attack and compellence to 'low-key', quasi-police operations. As states seek to bargain from strength, they also try to bargain through strength. Combination in formal or informal agreements brings together the resources of the members but requires a relatively high degree of organization and co-operation.

The threat of force

When states are not at war, military means are still useful. They are part of the range of possibilities for the implementation of foreign policy. This section looks at the uses of force at a level below that of actual shooting. It considers how military means are fitted into the context of diplomatic interaction, some different types of threats which are made, the use of the symbols of power as threats and, briefly, the idea of deterrence.

Threats as an instrument of policy are almost never used in isolation in practice. The American blockade of Cuba in 1962 to induce the USSR to withdraw missiles put into the island was accompanied by diplomatic pressure, by mobilization of resources and by increased air and naval demonstrations. This was intended to convince the Russians and Cubans that the United States really meant to bomb and invade Cuba as she threatened. As the crisis developed, American troops moved into position for the invasion. Russian submarines were forced to surface by the explosion of depth-charges close to them, whilst surface vessels were hounded. This was carefully calculated brinkmanship. President Kennedy intended to invade, but the pressure of the blockade convinced the USSR of the credibility of the threat and she withdrew. This use simultaneously of all means short of war was an impressive display of the efficacy of threats. Although the action taken against Cuba was American, it had the support, and was done in the name of, the Organization of American States. In effect a 'single state action', it concerned a clear regional arrangement, and is important as the most significant recent use of threats.

The 'rules' of conflict in international disputes have already been mentioned. Two rules are specially important with reference to threats: they must be explicit and they must be credible. The essence of a threat is that the victim of it must feel threatened. A great part of states' and alliances' defence budgets are now devoted not to using or threatening force, but to establishing that threats made will be believed.

There are several ways of analysing threats of force; it is useful to distinguish general and specific threats. A general threat to retaliate may be either the loose commitment 'not to tolerate' an action, or it may be a deliberate abstention from publicizing one's intentions, as the Americans threatened to reply to attack in the 1950s 'at a place and time of our own choosing'. The Russian threat to retaliate had

NATO sought to intervene in the suppression of the Hungarian revolt of Autumn 1956 was vague but explicit, as it was clear in the minds of the Western planners. A threat might be specific in terms of the means used, as when a country indicates that at this or that point in a conflict it will use nuclear weapons. It might be specific in terms of its target: coercion using Berlin as a target has been a specific weapon for the Warsaw Pact. As crises have developed, Pact activity has been immediately measurable by the length of time a convoy has taken to reach the city. The flexibility of this threat is almost infinite. The underlying possibility is always explicit: by making a convoy take twenty hours to get through to Berlin, the Communist states are reminding NATO of their power to seize it.

There is an effectiveness about a general threat when, like the USSR, its maker is known to have rather unpredictable responses and a devastating capability. One picks one's way on foot happily through stationary traffic but does not walk too near the edge of the pavement when drivers are racing home on New Year's Eve. Other countries do not have either the power or the reputation of the Soviet Union. Some wish in a dispute to show that their ambitions are strictly limited. They will make a specific threat. For this latter reason, American threats in the Cuba crisis were limited and made as clear as possible.

Both formal and informal alliances usually like to make a great show of force. This has a significant function as a symbol. An exercise by SEATO countries will train their navies; it will also demonstrate the solidarity and power of the alliance to neutral and hostile governments. This symbolic use of force can merge into subtle leverage: a Soviet naval demonstration was held off Singapore when the 1971 Commonwealth Prime Ministers' Conference was in progress there. The exact purpose and effect of this display were uncertain, but the Commonwealth surely has an interest in the growth of Russian naval strength which goes beyond noting the mere symbolism of a heavy cruiser. The visit of military forces to foreign countries is an interesting and important part of diplomacy. Visits may be effective in two ways: they may help to bring the visited nation into the visitor's camp, or they may counter-balance or prevent a rival state or alliance from exerting influence. Neither goal will be achieved without diplomatic preparation and, if ill conceived, such a use of force will be counter-productive: the sight of Western ships making unchallenged use of Chinese waters in the first thirty years of this century contributed to the emergence of Chinese nationalism.

The spread of Soviet naval power since about 1965 has presented NATO with major problems which illustrate both the small, detailed business of 'visit diplomacy' and some general difficulties of tactical adjustment by regional arrangements in the face of changes in the power balance. NATO has always been mainly concerned with the position on the 'iron curtain' frontier. This involved land and air forces. Naval organization took second place and was managed by a simple division of the sea area into British- and American-controlled zones. They formerly enjoyed a considerable superiority. Since the recognition that Russian strength at sea was growing, NATO's command structure has evolved to counter it. An important Russian 'threat' has been perceived outside the NATO area, in the Southern Atlantic. The Organization cannot work there as a result of the terms of the Treaty. Consequently, since it has been agreed that it is in the interests of NATO to do something, the Chiefs of Naval Staffs of the Organization have suggested the deployment of a naval force off the coast of West Africa.[1] This is intended to counter-balance Russian visits to the area. It is also designed to encourage states like Nigeria to lean to the Western side.

The effectiveness of symbolic and diplomatic uses of force is hard to assess. They are part of a process of activity and bargaining in which states seek to gain influence and not, like the issuing of an ultimatum or the escalation to nuclear war, easily recognizable as major events. At some time Soviet influence in the Mediterranean became a crucial factor in the politics of the area. It was not when the first ship passed through the Bosphorus, but only after a series of diplomatic forays of which naval visits were an essential part. Crude gunboat diplomacy might seem out of place in a world of 'controlled response' and Mutual Balanced Force Reductions. Nevertheless, nations feel that it is important in some cases, and the effectiveness of a threat is determined largely by the attitudes to it of the participants in it. The visit of ships and the parade of aircraft may seem quite innocuous uses of force. In a remote way they do nonetheless contain threats. The best example of this kind of 'concealed threat' was the first Sputnik of October 1957: this great scientific achievement would have been nothing more if the implication that for the first time the USSR could destroy American

---

[1] Alvin Paul Drischler, 'Standing Naval Forces for NATO', *Survival*, XIV, September/October 1972, p. 227.

cities had not been evident. It should be noted that there is an important difference between this type of threat of force, which is used for leverage and manoeuvre, and that used for defence or deterrence, which is examined below. In this type of action, regional arrangements strike postures: they show the extension of their interests and the intention of their policy.

The basic idea of deterrence is simple. As a diplomatic pursuit and an academic game it has endless complications. Regional arrangements use force to deter very much as states do, which is to say that they threaten reprisal against attack thereby hoping to prevent it. It follows from this that they deploy their forces in order to threaten and deter most credibly rather than to defend most effectively. This can lead to conflict within an arrangement: there was a complicated debate on whether Britain could fulfil her obligations in the Far East best by an actual presence, which could defend, or by a token force together with a promise to send more troops in an emergency, thus deterring attack. The discussion came to centre not on whether or not the United Kingdom should stay 'East of Suez', so much as on the question of how to deter most effectively. Few policy-makers wanted a commitment to defend which would have been unconditional. The Malaysian government, and many in the Conservative Party, wanted a defence commitment, but this has not existed since the end of the Malaysian–Indonesian Confrontation in 1966.

Of course deterrence is not a new idea. Rome sought to stabilize her frontier in the East in the first century A.D. by creating a barrier of client states in each of which a few Roman soldiers were stationed. They had no hope of fending off a Parthian attack. Their intention was to deter such an attack by making it clear that the loss of Roman life would bring 'massive retaliation' from the Empire. For long periods this was not credible owing to the weakness of Rome. As a result, Parthia ignored the threats and deposed princes appointed by her rival, only to be chased out when Roman strength recovered. Conventional deterrence is still very similar: the certainty of South African intervention deters any likelihood of overt warfare by independent African countries against Rhodesia. A serious economic or political crisis in the Republic would endanger the credibility of her support for the illegal régime.

Nuclear deterrence, on the other hand, is new. The threat of atomic violence is not simply one of a greater level of damage. It is also a more certain threat since there is far less defence against nuclear weapons, especially if they are delivered by missiles. However, as the American intervention in Asia shows, reliance on these weapons alone would leave the policy of an alliance incredible. The nuclear threshold is so great that it would only be crossed in defence of a narrowly defined vital interest. An opponent could thus threaten one's lesser concerns with impunity knowing that one would not risk total war in their defence. The Warsaw Pact countries have always had a considerable superiority over NATO in conventional forces and have, as a result, always been able to respond very flexibly to a NATO threat. NATO countries have therefore had to pay special attention to the problem of when, where and how they would consider using nuclear weapons of different sizes. This is a partial explanation of why the study of strategic questions and the barbaric language often associated with it has been so highly developed in the West. But one must remember that nuclear arms are remarkably unimportant in the day-to-day business of states. Perhaps this is even more true of regional arrangements since governments are especially loath to surrender to them the national control of the weapons. Thus SEATO, although officially able to draw on American atomic weapons, has always in practice relied on conventional threats and force.

The different forms and qualities of threats of force which regional arrangements make are thus a function of their purposes. There are several different ways of analysing threats and there is some controversy about the best way of doing this. One can, however, divide each of the types of uses of force according to the methods used: nuclear and conventional deterrence and defence on the one hand, a whole spectrum of diplomatic uses of force on the other. General and specific threats are both means of securing leverage; the choice of which to use facing the decision-maker may well be resolved by a decision whether an ambiguous or unambiguous threat is thought likely to be more effective. But as the practice of this sort of policy has become more familiar, states have increasingly sought to create and obey rules which have come to shape the approach to the use of threats by regional alliances.

Other functions of force used by regional arrangements

It has been said that regional arrangements use force primarily against those outside the region. But they also use it within the region quite often, and in some particular cases this has been very important.

Regional arrangements can provide states with a means of disciplining others. They may also be used to legitimize a use of force. Finally, membership of such an arrangement may offer some states particular opportunities for exerting leverage within the alliance by the manipulation of forceful means.

Small Powers are often more willing to use force than large ones and, for various reasons, they may care less about the scale of force they employ. It is possible for some small states, especially those controlled by dictators, to use force in a completely irrational way (at least in the very limited sense of there being no relationship between ends and means). The Chaco War of June 1932–June 1935 was fought between Paraguay and Bolivia. It was a conflict of supreme political insignificance, yet by the end of it the male population of Paraguay was halved. The disputed land for which the war was fought was an area of the most infertile, inhospitable semi-desert to be found on this earth; the Chaco can have been coveted only by the dictators who directed the war. This was a major cause of the establishment of the Inter-American Conference. The United States set about bringing together the governments of the continent and influencing their policies. Since it was formed, the Organization of American States, which was the successor to this growing co-operation, has been a device for political debate where the United States can exercise a degree of control over her neighbours without having to follow an obvious 'big stick' policy. Alliances can allow big Powers to control small Powers. The Warsaw Pact offers other examples of this.[1]

The regional arrangements which states form may serve to legitimize the use of force. 'Legitimize' is a flexible word. It is ambiguous in the sense that it can either mean 'provide a justification for', or it can mean 'sanction, give authority to'. The Russian action in Hungary in 1956 was justified publicly in terms of the Warsaw Pact treaty, but the authority for it is not to be found in any international agreement. The blockade of Guatemala in 1954, instituted by the United States to stop arms supplies from Communist sources, was similarly legitimized in terms of the agreement of the Organization of American States. When one says that an arrangement is used to 'legitimize' an action, it is worth asking, 'In who's eyes?' It may be that a state seeks the approval of some vague 'world opinion'. Or

[1] Examples of this are looked at in further detail in Chapters 2 and 4 in this book by Kenneth Kinney and Adrian Guelke.

alternatively, the state may try to fit its actions to the terms of a treaty to which it is a party in order to obtain the sanction of international law. A use of force may be couched in terms of a regional arrangement so that the force-using state may get the support, or try to get the support, of other states or of public opinion in the force-using state itself. Thus agreements may be used to provide a sort of camouflage for the pursuit of interests that have little to do with the 'defence aspects' of the arrangements.

Force may be used within an alliance or agreement for leverage purposes within that same alliance. Obviously this would not normally involve the firing of shots in anger. The British and French possession of nuclear weapons is designed to secure them advantages in dealing with their allies as much as with their foes. Force may also be used to reassure an ally of one's intentions. The presence of Rhodesian troops in Mozambique, or of American troops in Taiwan, shows that their commitments to their allies are real. As a corollary of this, states have to be wary of how they change their commitments: Britain and the United States are deterred from reducing their forces in Europe by the belief of their allies, especially the West Germans, that this would imply a reduction in their will to defend Europe. These examples show that the disposition of force within an alliance may well be a function of politics amongst supposedly friendly nations. Thus it has often been said that Britain keeps her nuclear capability in order to 'win a seat at the top tables', to gain influence with the United States and to maintain a status above that of her non-nuclear allies.

The organizations of regional arrangements

Although institutions are important and must be mentioned, this chapter need not say much about them. There are two reasons for this. Firstly, details of the institutional aspects of regional arrangements are covered very well in several standard works. Secondly, the institutions which an alliance may set up and the formal treaty agreements Powers may agree on are not necessarily a good indication of the political realities underlying them. Thus this section will concern itself only with these questions: What different ways of organizing are there? How do they effect the decision to use force? What purposes do they serve in relation to the use of force? These organizations not only reflect force-using purposes: most regional arrangements have at least a few other roles, and in some, the other roles are vital. The Organization of American States, for instance, is a channel for aid as well as a defence pact.

The most basic form of organization between allies is that used by the British and French in the Crimean War. The two sides fought the same enemy, at least most of the time. Co-operation at staff level was non-existent, there was no common planning and no common equipment or supply system. This was a disaster which every subsequent agreement to use force between states has taken care to avoid. Nevertheless, states sometimes organize only at the staff level, whilst even in a major alliance, such as NATO, co-operation below brigade level is limited. But NATO's organization is not purely military. There is technological and logistic co-operation and a considerable standardization of weapons. NATO is controlled by a Council and a bureaucracy which rivals that of the European Economic Community in complexity. Economic and scientific resources were allotted to the Organization, whose duties were enhanced by its control of German rearmament. A Military Committee, composed of Chiefs of Staff, was established for planning. To recognize the 'special interests' of Britain, France and the United States the so-called 'Standing Group' was set up, where the three Powers sat and where they could resolve differences. NATO is designed to satisfy its participants of American involvement in Europe, to provide a framework for German rearmament, and to reflect simultaneously the local interests of states like Italy and Norway and the regional interests of Britain and the United States. To some extent its organization, in the separation of military and civil business, the creation of a Cabinet-style Council and the holding of parliamentary-style debates, reflects the political organization of the member countries. At the same time, the *de facto* control of the military organs by the United States mirrors the fact that that nation has provided and continues to provide by far the greatest part of NATO's strength.

The Warsaw Pact is organized in a superficially similar way to NATO. In fact, whereas NATO has to balance the diverse goals and interests of its members, the Warsaw Pact is arranged in a much more single-minded way. This is not simply because the Soviet Union exerts a monolithic control of the Pact: in the period 1968–72 the USSR found her former satellites, notably Romania, willing to use the Pact to gain independent positions. The political purpose of the alliance is a very particular piece of leverage. NATO was formed in April 1949, the West German state later that year. The Warsaw

Pact was formed in response to neither of these events. Rather, it was created on 14 May 1955 as a direct result of the admission of West Germany to NATO a week earlier. Provisions for a joint command structure to be set up were made (Article 5).[1] However, the real purpose of the Pact was contained in Article 11, which provides that the alliance would lapse 'on the day a general European treaty of collective security' came into force. This was a direct invitation to the West to dissolve NATO and join in a general European treaty. The Pact has a command structure, holds exercises and has become a vital part of Soviet policy. Yet all this co-operation could have been accomplished without the Pact itself: there already was close collaboration between the USSR and the forces which she nurtured in her satellites. The Pact is thus as it is for the special purpose of putting pressure on the Western Powers in favour of a European Security Conference. This is not to say that the Pact would in fact be dissolved if European agreement was reached, or that co-operation between its members would cease even if Article 11 ever were to be invoked.

The terms of agreements and the working of organizations within a regional arrangement may be designed to limit the obligations of states: all governments will, if at all possible, avoid entangling alliances where their commitment to use force may become unlimited. The formal organizations illustrate this, as they reflect power differences between members. Large Powers which are producers of security control both policy and planning, both bureaucracy and field commands. A country like Belgium is at a double disadvantage: it is small and has little influence in NATO, yet it is, by virtue of its geographical position, completely dependent on the Organization for its defence. The small country may be wholly dependent whilst the larger can change its commitment, and hence the credibility of the agreement of which both are members, as exigency dictates. The fate of Czechoslovakia between the two World Wars demonstrates one possible outcome of unequal alliances. This may also apply to informal agreements. Saudi Arabia has often voiced her support for the Arab cause. She gave substantial aid to Jordan after her defeat in the June War of 1967. Yet Saudi Arabia has kept carefully away from anything which might bring her into armed confrontation with Israel. Her oil, commercial interests and internal development are quite reasonably of more importance to her than the success of a Pan–Arabic movement led

---

[1] *Documents on International Affairs, 1955*, O.U.P., London, 1958, p. 183.

by states with which she has long-standing rivalries, Egypt and Syria in particular.

The immediate purposes of organizations developed by regional arrangements are to co-ordinate the methods, contingency planning and goals of the participants in the agreements. Different organizations reflect differences both in the goals of an alliance and in the methods available to it: co-operation between Arab governments is unsophisticated compared to the structure of NATO, but their resources are more limited and their concerns (arguably) more straightforward. Power differentials and the degree of commitment of members clearly inform the structures of both types of arrangement for the use of force. The extent of organization will also depend on past attitudes. The OAS took some time to adjust to the fact that its isolation had been permanently ended by the Cuban revolution and the Soviet development of ICBMs at the end of the 1950s. Long-standing organizations may develop an inertia of their own: changes in either NATO or the Warsaw Pact are hard to effect. In contrast, the Southern African *entente* has great flexibility both because it lacks organization and because it is still comparatively new.

Limits on the use of force by regional arrangements

If regional arrangements have so many purposes and can often organize so effectively, one should perhaps be surprised only that there are so few of them. But there are also important reasons why they have not spread further. These limitations on the usefulness to states of regional arrangements may derive from disagreements between members of them, lack of common purpose, outside pressures or changes in political attitudes. There may also be cultural or technological factors such as language barriers which prevent an alliance from developing. Much of this analysis will look at the South-East Asia Treaty Organization (SEATO) since that Organization has displayed many of these limitations.

States may prefer to act outside an alliance. They may not be able to reach that degree of common understanding necessary for effective co-operation. They choose to ignore machinery which they believe cannot be adapted to their purposes. The principal limit on how far SEATO can use force is quite simply that some uses of force will not be supported by some of the members. Alliances and understandings often pledge their signatories to defensive action and rarely to attack. An agreement for offensive action would probably encourage each

91

state to believe that every other was climbing to dominance through its aid. The defence of the *status quo*, on the other hand, by definition maintains the existing power balance. One of the most famous examples of offensive agreements, the secret protocol made by Stalin and Hitler to divide Poland, certainly affords an excellent example of the suspicions aroused by them. Thus arrangements are more likely to work if they have clearly defined, defensive purposes.

The United States has had difficulties with its policy towards SEATO which are particularly instructive bearing in mind that country's desire to use multilateral organizations in her external relations since 1945. The SEATO treaty, which was signed at Manila on 8 September 1954,[1] is a carefully worded attempt to balance the interests of the US and of the other signatories. Thus in spite of US disagreement, the treaty area was carefully defined to exclude Taiwan (Article 8). The other Powers had no wish to be tied to the American chariot in any confrontation between the United States and the Chinese People's Republic over the Nationalist Chinese régime. They were prepared to join in the defence of Cambodia, Laos and the 'free territory under the jurisdiction of the State of Vietnam', that is, South Vietnam. This meant that, among others, Australia and New Zealand linked their interests to those of the United States in South-East Asia. Until changes of government occurred in those two countries, they sent small expeditionary forces to the Vietnam conflict. Many New Zealanders and Australians came to have doubts as to whether their national interests should be stretched to justify this action. The resulting desire for a redefinition of the national interest, which is to say for a change in foreign policy, was an important factor in the success of the opposition Labour Parties in the elections held in both countries in the autumn of 1972. The success of co-operation between states will be conditioned by changes in domestic politics in the member states; furthermore, if a member of an alliance comes to perceive that his interests have changed, he may affect the capacity of the alliance, or even withdraw from it altogether.

Other SEATO members avoided commitments in Vietnam. The SEATO Council had met in May 1965 to discuss how the Organization could help the Americans with their operation there. Pakistan refused to sign the resulting communiqué; France did not even attend the session. The conflicting interests here are evident. Paki-

---

[1] For full text see *Documents on International Affairs, 1954*, O.U.P., London, 1957, p. 157.

stan's foreign policy is dominated by her geographical position. She faced India in suspicious hostility which took much of her available foreign policy resources and which led to war later that year. Russia is too close to Pakistan for her government to have slighted her by anti-Communist activity abroad. And in any case Pakistan hardly has the means to launch ambitious projects far from her borders. The French position was influenced by public opinion, which would not lightly have tolerated a return to the area where the Republic had met a disastrous defeat in 1954, but perhaps more by her new interests and by ideology. For by 1965 General de Gaulle was anxious to cultivate influence in the Third World, whilst the nationalist ideology of his policy could not bring itself to sacrifice independence for the prosecution of American interests.

When the SEATO agreement was made, the United States also wished to restrict her obligations under the terms of the Treaty. An 'understanding' was included to the effect that the US duty to intervene by force in the event of an attack on a member was limited to the case of 'Communist aggression'. With any other sort of aggression, the United States undertook only to 'consult' with the other members. This allowed the President considerable latitude in any decision as to how America would react to any fighting in the SEATO area, since he reserved the right to define what constituted 'Communist aggression'. When war broke out between India (not a SEATO member) and Pakistan in 1965 and again in 1971, the official American policy was to leave the settlement of the dispute to the United Nations.

SEATO is a loose alliance for several reasons. Its membership is diverse. Members' political interests vary considerably. Britain is concerned with the defence of her remaining trading interests. The United States has traditionally looked to the alliance as a glacis forming the southern flank of her frontier against the Communist Powers. The success of SEATO used to be seen as essential to the security of Thailand as a result of that country's salient position. Australia and New Zealand spent the first fifteen years of their membership seeking defence against 'Asia' to maintain their security. Since then they have increasingly come to think of themselves as Asian states. Asian Powers had mixed feelings about the alliance: Burma would perhaps have joined, but she would not co-operate with Thailand, with whom she had a frontier dispute; India had a major dispute with Pakistan over the hegemony of Kashmir, and wished to maintain her independent, neutralist position. It would be

93

true to say that the greatest difficulty faced in the organization of SEATO came not so much from its opponents, China and the USSR, as from its rivals, the Third World organizations which loosely but perhaps more effectively represented the interests of their members. The principal of these were the Colombo (1950) and Bandung (1955) Conferences. Although these did not set up permanent institutions, and they certainly cannot be described as regional arrangements, they began a co-operation and created a solidarity amongst underdeveloped nations which enabled them to win greater political independence of the blocs dominated by the major Powers. The development of a sense of identity separate from that of the Great Powers by African and Asian states has limited the spread of regional arrangements in so far as they are seen as instruments of traditional super-Power diplomacy. Thus the Organization of African Unity and even to some extent the United Nations have been developed as alternatives to regional arrangements.[1]

The history of SEATO illustrates the analogy that regional arrangements both formal and informal have the character of Galsworthy's bourgeois families: their members are always ready to fend off an attack from outside when it is a distinct threat, but are often more ready to quarrel jealously within the family.

Limits on the value of regional arrangements are also shown by the failure of two schemes put forward for closer intra-alliance co-operation. Pressures from members within an alliance or from Powers outside may kill the prospect of collaboration, if those opponents of it are strong enough. For this reason, the proposed Multilateral Naval Force (MLF) failed in the 1960s. Some members of NATO were keen to join a scheme which would give them some share in responsibility for handling nuclear weapons. But Britain and France received the American idea (which was not always taken very seriously in the Pentagon either) so coldly that it failed. Soviet opposition from outside the region has limited the development of co-operation in Scandinavia. The USSR regards Finnish neutrality as a vital interest for which she has fought twice, in 1939–40 and in 1941. It has long been known that the establishment of a Nordic Security Community would be seen in Moscow as a threat even if it were to be officially neutral. Nordic co-operation has a long history which has brought mutual action on law, on trade, economic and

---

[1] Arnold Wolfers observed this in 1959 in 'Collective Defence Versus Collective Security', in *Discord and Collaboration*, Johns Hopkins Press, Baltimore, Maryland, 1965 edn., pp. 181 ff.

social policy, and in the cultural field. The powerful but discreetly expressed displeasure of the Soviet Union has been the greatest constraint on political and defence collaboration.

Difficulties amongst prospective allies can prevent the formation of regional arrangements. Even if states can work together in one set of problems, they may be rivals in another. Attempts were made to create an alliance system in the Middle East, which was called at various times the Northern Tier, the Baghdad Pact and the Central Treaty Organization (CENTO). The membership and purpose of these systems differed. British and American interests clashed and, as Coral Bell has shown,[1] the conflict exposes the Special Relationship at its worst. Suffice it to say here that it was only after the loss of many of their interests and the collapse of British influence between 1948 and 1956 that the two came together in 1958, when they sent troops into Lebanon and Jordan to prevent the revolution in Iraq from spreading to those two countries. However, by 1958 the original purpose which the alliance might have served had disappeared: the Iraqi revolution had broken the defensive 'line' against Russia, whilst the after-effects of the Suez crisis gave the Soviet Union much regional influence. America had taken over many British oil interests, except in the Persian Gulf.

British and American policy was torn by oil competition and was sometimes downright incompetent. The division of policy and purpose in both countries prevented a rational assessment of the problems that each faced, especially where they had to deal with Arab nationalism: they did not believe that it could be a genuinely popular movement, or that anti-colonialist movements might wish not to move too close to the Soviet bloc if they were not driven in that direction. It is true that misperception is hard to avoid in a period of rapid political change. That is not the point here. For it remains the case that alliances can fail because of difficulties caused by the prospective allies.

The United Nations and regional arrangements

An analytical distinction was drawn earlier in this chapter between the idea of regional arrangements and that of collective security organizations. In practice this division is not nearly so rigid. The United Nations has occasionally acted as a regional arrangement.

---

[1] Coral Bell, *The Debatable Alliance*, O.U.P., London, 1964, pp. 40–55.

The politics of regional arrangements appear in the United Nations. And it has already been seen that the United Nations can offer an alternative to regional arrangements as a mode of combination or as a means of diplomatic intercourse.

The United Nations can be said to have acted as a regional organization when it undertook the Korean operation. This was a result of the deliberate policy of the Soviet Union, which boycotted the UN. As a result of this withdrawal, which ended in August 1950, the United States was able to take the opportunity to use the institution as a prop for its own policy. When the Russian boycott ended and her representative returned to veto proposed actions in the Security Council, the UN ceased to have effective control of the war, which passed to the United States. That country's forces bore the brunt of the fighting and, as a result of the initial decision to intervene, what was in fact an intervention by a group of states was represented as a collective security operation. There is an obvious limit on the degree to which the United Nations can act as a regional arrangement: the USSR is unlikely to be so foolish as to allow the United States to exploit the UN for its own national interests again if they conflict with her own. The UN is, precisely because it has acted as a universal body, an unsuitable instrument for any particular state's national policy.

It is more usual for the UN to become a forum for conflict between regional arrangements which, because neither can predominate, does not lead to any positive action. The Middle East disputes have been resolved in a series of resolutions calling for Israeli restraint or withdrawal, but schemes for more active responses to the fighting have always met with either American or Russian vetoes. In terms of the use or threat of force, the UN is largely a restraint on states' resort to arms, although it is very debatable how effective it is in that role. The most important exception to this might seem to be the Suez crisis, when the USSR and America joined in condemning the Anglo–French–Israeli invasion. But this dispute was settled first by great-Power action, leaving the UN a role only in the mopping-up operations. The uses of force by the UN since the Korean War, in Cyprus, the Congo and in the Middle East, have been conducted with the acquiescence of the Security Council Powers, if not always with the approval of them all.

As a centre of diplomatic activity where many states have their chief representatives, the UN has helped to bring some governments together: contacts made there have perhaps contributed to the evolution of regional arrangements. This is most clearly the case of the Southern African *entente*: all three members have been the victims of a series of UN resolutions against their racist policies. This condemnation has helped to bring the three white Powers to a recognition of their common interests. Diplomatic contacts at the United Nations have also brought together African and Asian states which are too distant and of too limited resources to have ordinary bilateral contacts. But this has not in itself led to co-operation. For it is very likely that states which have a common interest would come together with or without the UN; those which do not have a common interest will not form it there.

Conclusion

The first paragraphs of this chapter raised the question of how important regional arrangements are when force is used. They have certainly been of great importance in the past in specific instances. But one should not mistake the unique environment of the Cold War in which they were prominent for an immutable condition of international society. Regional arrangements were an important part of the reaction of states to the post-war changes in the nature of power and of military force. However, they were informed by the peculiar role of ideology in states' foreign policy-making. One can certainly argue that the past decade has seen a decrease in ideological attitudes amongst the great Powers. If the United States and the Soviet Union see each other less and less as embattled agents of evil, then the alliances which grew partly out of that attitude are likely to change. But they need not disappear. There are several influences on the states which direct them to join regional arrangements. They include the wish to organize their commitments, the desire for security, the common recognition of threats and the hope that an alliance can secure more effective leverage than individual states could. This chapter has examined how these motives have worked in the past; some changes are already noticeable. SEATO, for example, is now almost defunct; but it has been seen that SEATO was never a very cohesive arrangement. European developments have been significant too: some NATO and Warsaw Pact countries are perhaps coming to feel that they have much in common as Europeans and that they are not inevitably antagonists. Both America and Russia, as well as the People's Republic of China have tried to limit their commitments abroad and to manage their conflicts by the recognition of each other's vital interests and of rules which aid conflict resolution.

It is thus impossible to make a general statement of how important regional arrangements are. One can still claim that they have a role, that even the most powerful state will probably find that these combinations extend the boundaries of possibility in foreign policy-making, in spite of their costs. This chapter has also raised a number of questions which it has no space to answer. It has simply tried to introduce a subject which is open to deep examination and, as the state system changes, to wide speculation.

4 Force, Intervention and Internal Conflict

The changing role of force

Force has long been regarded as the last resort of a state whose territory or interests are threatened by a hostile neighbour. Unlike the individual in domestic society, it is argued that in international society a state must usually rely on its own resources to defend itself. Indeed, armed conflict between states has been looked on as inherent in the very nature of the international political system; inherent because of the absence among the multiplicity of sovereign states that make up international society of an overarching authority analogous to that within domestic society. In these circumstances, the development of nuclear weapons has encouraged the belief that the anarchic character of international relations threatens the very future of mankind. Some have taken the argument to its logical conclusion. For example, Bertrand Russell has predicted that within a few decades mankind will be faced with a choice between a world-state and annihilation.

Yet ironically, few of the more than fifty local wars[1] since the end of the Second World War have been conventional interstate wars. The vast majority have been civil wars or have started as internal conflicts or insurrections that have led to the intervention of other states. Examples of 'aggression' in the accepted sense of an un-provoked attack by conventional armed forces across an inter-nationally recognized frontier have been rare. More remarkably, it is difficult to single out a clear-cut example of territorial aggrandize-ment in the post-war period. Thus it is arguable whether even India's conquest in 1960 of the Portuguese territory of Goa, superficially the most blatant case of 'aggression', fits into this category, given the colonial background to the dispute. In any event, India's action against Goa pales into insignificance when compared to the

---

[1] Figure given in Lincoln P. Bloomfield and Amelia C. Lewis, *Controlling Small Wars*, Allen Lane The Penguin Press, London, 1970, p. 18.

territorial changes in the subcontinent that have resulted from internal conflict and upheaval.

In general, though border disputes between neighbours are still not uncommon and have occasionally led to war, coveting someone else's territory has since 1945 ceased to be a major cause of war. Throughout the world there has been a gradual acceptance by states that existing boundaries are permanent. Exceptions, though improtant, are rare. Even in Africa, where new states have inherited the artificial frontiers created by the colonial Powers without regard to ethnic divisions, acceptance of the territorial *status quo* has been firmly established and written into the constitution of the Organization of African Unity. Indeed, most African states opposed the secession of Katanga from the Congo and of Biafra from Nigeria precisely because they believed that to allow a single exception would create a precedent that threatened their own existence. In Europe, West Germany's acceptance of the Oder-Neisse frontier between East Germany and Poland has finalized the territorial consequences of the Second World War, and today it is almost inconceivable that any European state would resort to the use of force over a territorial question.

Though important and novel, the greater firmness of frontiers is not the only reason for the decline in the number of wars between states. The sheer destructiveness of nuclear weapons has encouraged the super Powers to avoid confrontation and they in turn have restrained smaller Powers out of the fear that a local conflict might intensify to the point where they themselves would become involved with unpredictable consequences. Finally, states can no longer as readily rely on force or the threat of force as an instrument for compelling obedience to their demands. People in modern societies are more conscious of their identity and more aware of their power. They are therefore less inclined to accept dictation from above, especially when its source lies outside their own society. In particular, states recognize that it is no longer sufficient to occupy a country's capital to secure the capitulation of an enemy state, still less its population. The days too, are long past when the native populations of Africa or Asia could be awed into submission by the appearance of a gunboat on the horizon.

Indeed, it is tempting to conclude that in relations between states, conventional military forces have largely lost their usefulness as an instrument of foreign policy, except as deterrents. However, that would be carrying the argument too far. What is true is that the effective use of force has become contingent upon political circumstances. These in general have operated to limit the power of states to use force in the international arena. At the same time the reverse has happened within states: political circumstances have tended to extend the role of force. Paradoxically, in an age when states possess the military capacity to destroy the world, the vulnerability of states to the violent acts of individuals or groups within society bent on securing radical political change has increased. In many societies government is continually threatened by revolution and the state exists on the brink of civil war or disintegration. But because of the interdependence of the world today and the existence of a global conflict of ideologies, it is in practice impossible to prevent the internal weaknesses of states from impinging upon relations between states. As a result force has acquired a role in international relations that is distinct from its traditional role in interstate conflicts: the military intervention of foreign states in internal conflicts and civil wars.

Intervention is an imprecise term that is difficult to define because virtually every transaction between two states constitutes some degree of interference in each other's domestic affairs. Hence Talleyrand's famous aphorism: 'Non-intervention is a metaphysical term, which means about the same as intervention.' Nonetheless, it is possible to single out a few salient features that provide the core of its meaning. Generally, it is an act limited in time and scope, that is directed at changing or preserving the political structure of the target state and which lies outside the ambit of normal relations among states.[1] It can take non-military as well as military forms, for example, the application of economic sanctions. However, it is when intervention has taken the form of the use or threat of force that it has presented the most serious challenge to international peace.

Intervention is not a new feature of international relations, but historically its role has generally been limited, involving the threat rather than the actual use of force. In the nineteenth century it was typically used by powerful states to enforce the payment of a debt, to secure the punishment of a wrongdoer, or to protect the rights of its nationals or of an ill-treated Christian minority. But more ambitious forms of intervention were envisaged. As early as 1815 the Holy Alliance, the coalition of European Powers against revolutionary France, declared its readiness to intervene against revolutionary

[1] See Urs Schwarz, *Confrontation and Intervention in the Modern World*, Oceana Publications, New York, 1970, p. 83.

movements. In the second half of the century the United States expanded the scope of the Monroe Doctrine to justify regular intervention in the domestic affairs of Latin American states. In the main, however, states were reluctant to intervene militarily in internal conflicts or civil wars. Their reluctance in part stemmed from the fact that such intervention was likely to prove taxing if not ineffective. More important, since states largely followed historic objectives in their conduct of foreign policy which did not change with successive governments, there was little incentive for states to intervene in domestic conflicts that were unlikely to impinge on international relations. By contrast, today internal conflicts appear to have become the main source of change in the international political system and consequently intervention has become a more pressing international question.

The habitual use of force in interventions rather than in wars between states has wider implications. It has meant a shift away from the purely military to the political or coercive use of force. The distinction is a difficult one to specify exactly for force is rarely used without some political end in mind. The purely military use of force here means the direct application of force to seize or occupy territory and to repel, disable or even exterminate enemy forces. More subtle is the coercive use of force, when it is employed to inflict suffering or hardship upon an adversary so as to influence his behaviour and secure his compliance. To take an analogy from domestic society, it is the difference between forcibly taking, say, a wallet from someone and twisting his arm until he voluntarily hands over the wallet because he can no longer stand the pain. In the first case, the most important factor in determining the outcome is whether the person applying the force is physically stronger than his victim. In the second case, assuming that the first strategy is not feasible, the readiness of the victim to endure pain may totally frustrate the superior physical strength of his adversary.

Of course, suffering almost invariably results from any use of force but in the case of, for example, the capture of a fort, it is strictly speaking incidental to the military purpose of the action. By contrast, to take a contemporary example, the placing of bombs in pubs and shops in Northern Ireland by the IRA is not in any sense part of a conventional military campaign. The bombings' principal, arguably, sole purpose is to coerce the population of the province and the British government by inflicting politically unacceptable losses upon both civilians and the British Army. A contemporary example from international relations was the extensive bombing of North Vietnam by the United States in December 1972. Explaining on television why the bombing raids had been made, President Nixon's Special Advisor on National Security, Dr. Henry Kissinger, said that the United States had reached the conclusion that the North Vietnamese were protracting the negotiations.

> The more difficult Hanoi was, the more rigid Saigon grew. . . . And therefore it was decided to try to bring home really to both Vietnamese parties that the continuation of the war had its price.[1]

In effect, his statement was an admission that the purpose of American bombing had been coercive and not military. In general, however, governments prefer to justify actions of this kind in military terms because they are less emotive. Indeed, one of the reasons why civil wars have a reputation in the public mind for cruelty and wanton destruction is precisely because of the dominant role of the coercive use of force.

In fact, at least an element of coercion is implicit in virtually any use of force in international relations. At the end of the day when the battle has been won and the enemy forces routed, military victory has to be translated into political terms. As one of Napoleon's commanders remarked after the conquest of Spain: 'You cannot sit on bayonets.' If the population of a conquered country is indifferent or easily awed into submission, the country's new rulers may have little difficulty in establishing their authority and the mere presence of their troops may be sufficient to deter any opposition. Indeed, coercion almost by definition is most effective when it takes the form of the threat of force rather than its actual use. Today, in part because people are generally more knowledgeable about how to offer resistance and less afraid of the military force at the disposal of the state, the mere threat of force frequently fails to compel obedience in a disaffected society. The implications of the decline in many societies of the authority of the state are principally internal, but in the context of international relations they serve to make a strategy of intervention by other states generally more demanding and more costly. To understand why, nevertheless, intervention remains a prominent feature of the international political system we must first examine the pattern of internal conflict in the modern world.

[1] Quoted in *Newsweek*, 12 February 1973, p. 13.

The pattern of internal conflict

Internal conflict of varying degrees of seriousness afflicts the majority of states in the world today. Something of the scale of the problem may be gauged from remarks made in 1966 by the United States's Secretary of Defence, Robert McNamara. He estimated then that there had been '149 serious internal insurgencies' within the previous decade. In particular, much of the Third World presents an almost continuous picture of pervasive disorder and violence. Professor Zolberg's description of post-independent Africa is scarcely an exaggeration.

> The most salient characteristic of political life in Africa is that it constitutes an almost institutionless arena with conflict and disorder as its most prominent features. . . . Almost every new African state has experienced more or less successful military or civilian *coups*, insurrections, mutinies, severe riots, and significant political assassinations. Some of them appear to be permanently on the brink of disintegration.[1]

However, although the problem of disorder is most acute in the Third World, it would be a mistake to regard internal conflict as principally a disease of underdevelopment or as simply the product of the frustrations of extreme poverty. The disturbances in France in 1968 and the continuing violence in Northern Ireland are reminders of the vulnerability of even the wealthiest, most well-ordered and open societies. In fact, it makes more sense to look on internal conflict in its modern forms as specifically a disease of industrialization and modernization, a product of the social strains resulting from the imposition of change from above which the majority of the population has generally not welcomed or sought.[2] We should therefore look first at Europe where historically the process of industrialization and modernization began.

A hundred years ago when Europe's newly created industrial might encouraged her statesmen to think in terms of the conquest of continents, there seemed to be almost no limit to the power of a

[1] A. Zolberg, 'The Structure of Political Conflict in the New States of Tropical Africa', *American Political Science Review*, LXII, March 1968, p. 70.
[2] See Barrington Moore, *Social Origins of Dictatorship and Democracy*, Penguin, Harmondsworth, 1969, p. 506.

modern state. The megalomania of Cecil John Rhodes was not untypical.

> Expansion is everything ... these stars ... these vast worlds which we can never reach. I would annex the planets if I could.[1]

No one represented better than he the assertive self-confidence of the new era of imperialism that gripped Europe after 1870. Few doubted Europe's superiority in any field, but what clinched the argument was her possession of a monopoly of modern weapons. As Hilaire Belloc put it:

> Whatever happens we have got
> The maxim gun and they have not.

At the same time, the very industrial processes that formed the basis of Europe's superiority over the rest of the world at the end of the nineteenth century were ushering in social changes that were fundamentally altering the political structure of every state in Europe. The most important of these was that 'the overruling intervention in public life of the masses ... passed from the casual and infrequent to being the normal'.[2] Everywhere in Europe the rise of the masses was reflected in the creation of mass political movements and the transformation of existing political parties. Indeed, in its most radical manifestations the new political power of the masses challenged the power of the state itself. 'Freedom', wrote Engels, 'consists in converting the state from an organ standing above society into one completely subordinated to it.'[3] Extreme hostility towards the state as an institution similarly characterized the ideology of both Pan-German and Pan-Slav nationalism. In every society the spread of modern communications encouraged the emergence of political groups that sought to subordinate the interests of the state to political ideology, thereby laying the basis for the internationalization of every domestic conflict.

The traditional structure of society was further shattered by the First World War, which brought about the internal collapse of the continental empires of Russia, Austria-Hungary and Germany and led to the creation of new, politically volatile states in the vacuum

---

[1] Quoted in H. Arendt, *The Origins of Totalitarianism*, Allen & Unwin, London, 1958, p. 124.
[2] Ortega y Gasset, *The Revolt of the Masses*, Allen & Unwin, London, 1961 edn., p. 57.
[3] Quoted in B. Crick, *In Defence of Politics*, Penguin, Harmondsworth, 1962, p. 41.

left by their fall. In the inter-war years the territorial revisionism of Germany and the bombastic imperialism of Fascist Italy threatened a renewed outbreak of general war among the states of Europe. But more important was the fact that during this period resort to the use of force became an increasingly common feature of domestic, as opposed to international, society and force in the hands of mass political movements emerged as a potent instrument of domestic political change. It is doubtful whether Hitler or Mussolini would have succeeded in subverting the normal political process in Germany and Italy had they not enjoyed the support of para-military party organizations.

Further, the universal appeal of the doctrines of Communism and Fascism ensured that other states not directly affected had a considerable stake in the outcome of civil conflict. The prominent role of intervention in the two largest civil wars of the period, in Russia after the Bolshevik revolution and in Spain between 1936 and 1939, is consequently not surprising. During the Second World War itself the exploitation of internal tensions in other states was a significant factor in Hitler's early successes and, initially at least, greatly facilitated the task of German forces in, for example, France, the Ukraine and Yugoslavia.

Outside Europe the spread of industrialization and modernization through imperialism unleashed social forces not altogether different from those which disrupted Europe in the first half of this century. Indeed, the pattern of change in Asia and Africa in the post-war period has some obvious similarities to that in the Balkans and Eastern Europe at the turn of the century. Both involved the mobilization of the masses by an educated élite under the banner of nationalism. However, there are important differences. In most Asian and African states the tensions between town and countryside and between forces of modernization and tradition have been very much greater than in Europe though they have yet to cope with the full impact of industrialization. Further, as many of the new states are 'highly artificial umbrella structures tying together a clump of divergent societies with fragile and alien institutions',[1] problems of integrating different ethnic communities loom larger than class warfare.

In tropical Africa, the problems of integration or nation-building as it is often called are particularly acute. The characteristic features

[1] R. Higham (ed.), *Civil War in the 20th Century*, University Press of Kentucky, Lexington, 1972, p. 218.

of these states are extremely weak national centres and a periphery made up of more or less self-contained traditional societies.[1] In the smaller less-developed states especially, the process of modernization has not extended very far into the countryside, despite the spread of communications and the growth of political awareness during the independence struggle. In many, a similar pattern of internal conflict has emerged since independence. All too often the failure of nationalist leaders to meet the expectations that they aroused in the struggle against the colonial Power has quickly exhausted their legitimacy in the eyes of the population, especially among those involved in the modern sector of the economy. Government by consent has progressively given way to rule by coercion, at least within the nation's capital. In these circumstances, civilian leaders have been increasingly forced to rely on the support of the police and army. Inevitably some military leaders have become disenchanted with their role as instruments of political terror and have taken over themselves.

In most cases, their intervention has been initially welcomed and they have quickly gained the support of opposition groups that bore the brunt of oppression under the old government. However, disillusion has usually followed because of the military's failure to restore rule by the ballot box. In fact, successive *coups* in Africa with a few exceptions have done little to restore public confidence or participation in government. The frequency of *coups* cannot therefore be ascribed to their popularity. A more salient factor has been the indifference of those living outside the national centre, in the periphery, to the political process within the modern sector. Another factor is the ease with which *coups* can be staged in countries with a single political centre, as is typical of most small African countries. In 1963 the Togolese government was overthrown by an army numbering 600, while in the same year in Ghana the deployment of some 500 men out of an army of 10,000 toppled Nkrumah. Hardly a shot was fired. By contrast, the loyalty of a single battalion of airborne troops frustrated a *coup* to oust President Senghor of Senegal in 1962.

On occasions, foreign intervention has effectively prevented a *coup*. Unlike other forms of military intervention, but like the most spectacular *coup*, it may be relatively bloodless. In general, it provides rare examples of relatively painless intervention. France's intervention in Gabon in 1964 is perhaps the best-known case. On

[1] A. Zolberg, op. cit., p. 70.

18 February, a group of young officers staged a *coup* in the country's capital in Libreville. Government offices were occupied and President Leon Mba arrested. The same day French troops were flown in from Brazzaville in the former Congo. They quickly routed the forces of the young officers, numbering only 150 men, and successfully restored President Mba to power. France justified her action under a 1961 treaty which provided for French assistance at the request of the Gabonese government. No such request was made, in fact, but the French government argued that the arrest of the President justified unilateral action because it prevented the government from seeking help in the normal way. French action brought an angry reaction in West Africa where it was widely believed that the reasons for France's swift response was her economic stake in Gabon's deposits of manganese and uranium ore. France's failure to restore President Fulbert Youlou of the Congo (Brazzaville) in 1963 or President Hubert Maga of Dahomy in 1965 was pointedly noted by the states in the area. In practice, the difficulty of appraising the likely domestic political reaction of the target country, the requirement of exact timing, and the resentment likely to be engendered by the interference by a former colonial Power set limits to this form of intervention.

The almost comic-opera pattern of conflict in many small tropical states in Africa is by no means typical of the Third World as a whole. In larger and more developed states, where the spread of modernization and industrialization has been more extensive, conflict is less likely to be confined to the bloodless *coup d'état*. Largeness by itself is an important factor as the existence of regional centres of power diminishes the prospects of overturning a government at a single stroke. At the same time, a regional centre may provide the nucleus for secession, a direct threat to the existence of the state itself, as happened in Nigeria and the former Belgian Congo. When regions broadly coincide with ethnic divisions or when the distribution of natural resources among the regions is unequal, the dangers of secession and of civil war become especially great.

In the case of the Biafran secession, Ibo fears for their security within new regional arrangements after massacres of their countrymen in the north was probably the primary consideration and monopolizing the region's oil revenues only secondary. By contrast, ethnic divisions played a minor role in the Katangese secession. From the outset, the distribution among other areas of the revenues from the region's large copper deposits was the nub of the question.

In both cases, partly because of the economic importance of the conflicts to foreign companies and states, external intervention played a significant, though limited role. In particular, states which supported secession took considerable pains to disguise their involvement. For example, while France indicated her general support for Biafra's secession by recognizing Colonel Ojukwu's government in July 1968, the French government's role in the raising of loans for military equipment for Biafra in return for mineral rights still remains largely a matter of speculation.[1] In the case of Katanga the role of white mercenaries in the conflict raises interesting questions about South African and Rhodesian involvement. Public knowledge is largely confined to the fact that office space was made available to the Katangese authorities in Salisbury and Johannesburg.

Insurgency and revolution

One of the cruel ironies that Third World states face is that internal conflict may arise not out of economic failure or stagnation but out of their very success in stimulating economic development. There is a superficial sense in which this may be true. Thus Edward Luttwak argues:

> Nkrumah in spite of his eccentricities, was largely defeated by his own success: the by-product of the considerable economic development achieved by Ghana was to stimulate and educate the masses and the new élite, their attitude to Nkrumah's régime becoming more and more critical in the light of the education which the régime itself provided.[2]

More fundamentally, the impact of modernization on the countryside through, for example, the commercialization of agriculture may have the effect of intensifying potentially explosive ethnic rivalries by extending the area of competition between the different communities. Because development tends to be uneven, it usually has the result of increasing inequalities within society at least in the short term. This is especially true of private enterprise economies in the early stages of development. In Third World countries the problem tends to be exacerbated by their need to attract foreign capital for development. As 'beggars cannot be choosers', governments are reluctant to reject any proposal for investment, whatever its social

[1] See R. Higham (ed.), op. cit., p. 208.
[2] Edward Luttwak, *Coup d'état*, Allen Lane The Penguin Press, London, 1968, p. 172.

costs. But probably the most important factor inhibiting government action against the growth of inequalities is the political strength of sectional interests in the modern sector of the economy. A report by the International Labour Organization to the Kenyan government in 1972 highlighted many of these problems and warned that, notwithstanding the high rate of growth of the Kenyan economy since independence,

> unless strong measures are taken to reduce the impact of these inequalities the frustrations and resentments they engender could be a real threat to the nation's stability, particularly if allowed to interact with tribalism.[1]

The particular form internal conflict takes in countries in this category will vary considerably according to their particular domestic political circumstances. But whatever form it takes, conflict is likely to be more deeply rooted than in less developed countries, in which the struggle for power tends to remain confined to the élite. Change is likely to be more violent. Further, in these states, because of the spread of disaffection into the countryside, insurgency may emerge as a major challenge to the government's authority. Typically, though not invariably, insurgency depends on some measure of external support, especially for arms. At the same time, without roots in the countryside, insurgency is unlikely to become a serious menace. In particular, there is little evidence to support the belief that insurgents can manufacture disaffection and gain support for their cause by provoking government counter-measures against the local population. Government action punishing a local community for the presence of insurgents does not usually take place unless the government's authority has already broken down or there is some evidence of local support for the insurgents.

Normally, villagers will hand over guerrillas to the authorities unless they closely identify with the cause of the insurgents. Usually with good reason, the peasants' fear of government authority is considerably greater than any fear of guerrillas without local roots, who, to coin a phrase, are like fish out of water. In general, both the crassness of governments and the amenability of peasants to intimidation or to persuasion have been much exaggerated by revolutionaries and counter-insurgency experts alike.

For example, the British counter-insurgency expert, Sir Robert Thompson, has graphically compared the impact of insurgents to the

---

[1] Quoted in *Africa*, 18 February, 1973, p. 32.

terror created among a peasant population by a man-eating leopard or tiger.[1] Equally dubious is the contention of the French revolutionary and companion of Ché Guevara that the failure of revolutionary movements in Latin America is due in part to their concentration on political as opposed to military action.[2]

The record of attempts to bring about political change from the outside through insurgency is not impressive. None of the subversive movements promoted by Nkrumah in West Africa met with any success or proved to be more than minor irritants to his neighbours. At the same time, successive bloodless *coups* in these countries hardly suggested that the governments Nkrumah was trying to overthrow enjoyed any widespread political support themselves. The Bay of Pigs intervention by the United States in Cuba in 1961 was a disastrous failure, while Ché Guevara's attempts to export revolution to Bolivia similarly bore little fruit. Nevertheless, because even with local roots, insurgents regularly depend on external support in some measure, insurgency is rarely a purely domestic matter and continually impinges on relations between states. Indeed, precisely because the domestic and external elements often cannot easily be disentangled, insurgency creates the most vexing problems for international relations. From the vantage point of the state fighting insurgents it appears to be externally aided subversion: from that of unsympathetic or hostile neighbours, civil war. In practice, it may well contain elements of both.

Further, insurgency and government efforts to suppress it not uncommonly have a considerable impact on the domestic affairs of neighbouring states. Where ethnic loyalties cross national boundaries, insurgency itself may spread into a neighbouring state, or more typically, the influx of refugees escaping from government repression aimed at quelling the insurgency may excite opinion in a neighbouring state in favour of the insurgents. In this event, the increasing involvement of a neighbour in the conflict may lead to war between the two states. For example, when India intervened in East Pakistan at the end of 1971, her action was probably dictated less by a desire to establish her hegemony in the subcontinent by weakening a rival, than by domestic pressures arising out of the impact of the massive influx of refugees from East Pakistan on the

[1] See Sir Robert Thompson, *Defeating Communist Insurgency*, Chatto & Windus, London, 1966, pp. 10–11.
[2] See Régis Debray, *Revolution in the Revolution?*, Monthly Review Press, New York, 1967; Penguin, Harmondsworth, 1968, pp. 119–20.

politically sensitive state of West Bengal. Nonetheless, it is worth noting that insurgency is a form of internal conflict that regularly provides pretexts for wars between hostile neighbours. The fact that it has not led to more such wars is in part due to the restraints on interstate war in the modern world. But as important a reason is the nature of insurgency itself.

Although sometimes associated with infiltration and urban guerrilla warfare or terrorism, insurgency is essentially different from both. At the heart of the matter is the fact that insurgency occurs when the authority of the government in a particular region, or more extensively, breaks down or is open to challenge due to the spread of disaffection. Characteristically, insurgents represent a new source of authority and control; in short, an alternative government, even if only contingent upon changes in the central government. Like most governments they may employ a limited measure of intimidation or even terror to enforce their rule. But their rule is as unlikely to depend upon terror alone as that of any established government. They may also only rule by night in certain areas as has, for example, been said of the Vietcong control of some villages in South Vietnam. Nonetheless, extension of their authority and control is usually the purpose, not simply the basis of their military activities. Indeed, once insurgents have finally established their control in a particular area, military operations may become secondary to their political and administrative functions.[1]

In this respect, insurgency differs from infiltration, which usually has defined military rather than political objectives. For instance, infiltration typically results in an attack on enemy installations or bases, but no more than that. Generally, it may more reasonably be regarded as a disguised form of aggression or as part of a limited unconventional war between states. An example is the infiltration of Arab guerrillas into Israel across the borders of Syria and Lebanon. Although it creates a measure of insecurity in border areas it does not represent a threat to Israel's political authority within her own borders. Similarly, terrorist attacks by Arab guerrillas on civilians represent attempts to coerce the Israeli government, not to replace it, notwithstanding their ultimate objectives.

Similarly, urban guerrillas, while they may rely on the support of a disaffected section of the population to provide a base for their operations, do not represent an alternative city government. Typic-

[1] See for example, E. Mondlane, *The Struggle for Mozambique*, Penguin, Harmondsworth, 1969, pp. 167–83.

ally, they aim to bring about changes in the behaviour or even composition of the government through the coercive use of force. Taking hostages and bombing police stations are their characteristic modes of action. The violence they create may be considerable. Nevertheless, their aims are more limited than those of rural insurgents, for in general the city is too complex a social organization for guerrillas to take over except in the context of a full-scale revolution or the total collapse of government authority. Partly for this reason insurgency is a phenomenon of the Third World rather than industrial society. Significantly, although guerrilla forces in Vietnam, Angola and Mozambique have established their control over vast tracts of territory, they have not succeeded in subverting, or holding for more than a short interlude, a single city.

Because insurgency attacks the very roots of authority in society, unless confined to a very small area it generally presents a greater threat to the state than either infiltration or urban guerrilla warfare. It is rarely amenable to a military solution. Once insurgents have established their authority within a particular village, it is likely to persist and even survive temporary occupation by military forces of the government. Just as a country occupied by foreign troops usually adjusts to the re-establishment of the old authorities once the troops leave, so on a smaller scale a village will tend to revert to the control of the insurgents once the government forces withdraw. Only if the government succeeds in discrediting the insurgents in the eyes of the local population can it expect any lasting change in the allegiance of the villagers. Circumstances usually favour the insurgents and militate against such a change as the government cannot hope to influence villagers without first establishing its physical control over the village.

As it can only do this by the use of force, it risks initially intensifying peasant opposition to its cause. In particular, government violence in areas where its authority does not run is blind. Rarely can government forces distinguish between the enemy and potential allies or waverers. Their lack of political intelligence, in practice, raises the level of force they will need to use to capture any position. Further, the possession by insurgents of increasingly sophisticated weapons has meant that it has become more and more difficult for government forces to wrest control of a village from insurgents without destroying it. In these circumstances massacres on an unprecedented scale, as, for example, in East Pakistan in 1971, and refugees have become common by-products of civil war involving

113

insurgency. At the same time, attempts by insurgents to extend their control into cities, which are less amenable to political subversion, often bears somewhat similar features to that of government action in the countryside. The largely indiscriminate massacre of civilians in Hué by the Vietcong during the Tet offensive in 1968 is an example.

The battle between the state and insurgency has often been described as a struggle for the hearts and minds of the people. It is an accurate enough description, for what is involved is nothing less than the allegiance of the masses to the existing state. For that reason a state is bound to treat the problem of insurgency as principally an internal one whatever play it makes of external involvement. Consequently, unless the involvement of other states extends to widespread infiltration of their military forces in support of the insurgents, a state fighting insurgents is likely to concentrate its military resources on combating the enemy within and employ other pressures to secure the compliance of neighbours to demands that they desist from aiding guerrillas. Indeed, insurgency has acquired its international significance not just because of its association with revolutionary doctrines, but because some states grappling with insurgency have been unable to meet the challenge to their authority by themselves and have involved other states in their defence. The political advantages of insurgents have not infrequently outweighed the state's possession of very much larger military resources.

The most serious form of insurgency is that linked with a revolutionary movement, not just because of its international ramifications, but because it generally rules out the possibility of political compromise, of a change in the central government directed at meeting the parochial grievances of a region or ethnic community in rebellion against the state. Of course, it will only become serious if the revolutionary movement is able to establish itself as a credible alternative to the existing government. Nonetheless, even when its control is confined to a limited area, it is more difficult to isolate its impact from the rest of society than in the case of a secessionist movement.

The generally close association in our time between revolution and insurgency is not accidental. Both are intimately connected with the decline of the authority of the state due to the loss of traditional and religious sanctions and to the rise of the masses. Many other factors, economic and social, have contributed to the waning of the state's authority. Of particular importance in the twentieth century has been the disruption brought about by two World Wars. In South-

East Asia Japanese occupation during the Second World War struck a blow against colonial authority from which it never recovered. Elsewhere in Africa and Asia the example of the grant of independence to neighbouring states and the expectation of success springing from colonial withdrawal on a global basis provided a powerful stimulant to anti-colonial revolt. Indeed, since 1945 anti-colonial movements have been the main source of large scale insurgencies. Peasant revolutions in independent countries are more difficult to characterize, but the particular system of land tenure has nearly always been a critical factor. In Barrington Moore's view:

> the most important causes of peasant revolutions have been the absence of a commercial revolution in agriculture led by the landed upper classes and the concomitant survival of peasant social institutions into the modern era when they are subject to new stresses and strains.[1]

In developing countries where the process of modernization does not have roots within indigenous society, the survival of feudal social institutions is more likely and the social impact of, for example, the introduction of a cash crop is likely to be more disruptive. Nonetheless, only where traditional social institutions are hierarchically structured and these inequalities acutely aggravated, is it probable that the tensions arising out of modernization will take the specific form of an extensive clash between town and countryside.

Finally, less specifically material factors generally play an important role in the development of internal conflict. Culture, religion, or traditions that stress resignation or fatalism as a response to social upheaval and that confer legitimacy on the role of traditional leaders may be as significant as the more obvious interaction between social groups and economic forces in determining the character of internal conflict. The relation of these factors to material circumstances is itself problematic. They underline, too, the importance of specific national factors in the development of conflict that cannot be encompassed in broad generalizations.

The role of intervention

When insurgency is linked to a revolutionary movement it is likely to have wide international repercussions, often not just regionally but

---

[1] B. Moore, op. cit., p. 477.

on a global basis due to the world-wide conflict of ideologies between the super Powers. Both Russia's commitment to support wars of 'national liberation' and that of the United States to 'contain Communism' have internationalized revolutionary war. Nonetheless, few of the local conflicts that have arisen since the end of the Second World War can reasonably be regarded as proxy wars fought on behalf of the super Powers by local representatives. Only North Korea's attack on South Korea in 1950, which was in part prompted by Russian encouragement, would appear to fit into this category. Nor does it make much sense to regard local conflicts as a form of war between the super Powers themselves, though from an international perspective the involvement of the super Powers in any conflict tends to obscure its indigenous roots.

For more concrete reasons than ideology, internal conflict is rarely a matter of purely domestic concern or even limited in its impact to one region. The reasons are not hard to find. The cliché of our time is that we live in a shrinking world in which the interdependence of states in both political and economic terms has grown to a point where it is difficult for even the smallest state to be indifferent to important internal conflicts in other parts of the globe. The tendency in recent years for local or domestic conflicts to spill over into the international arena has highlighted the importance of local conflicts to the ordinary citizen. In particular, it has become increasingly difficult to contain political violence within the societies in which it originates. The frequent hijacking of planes by revolutionary groups ranging from Croat nationalists to Palestinian guerrillas currently provides the most obvious illustration. The helplessness of the international community in the face of these attacks on civilian bystanders in a sense merely matches that of states afflicted by internal conflict. But the most important link between conflict in domestic society and the international political system is the regular intervention of states in internal conflicts.

Intervention is a persistent feature of international society arising out of the fact that states possess tangible as well as intangible assets outside their national boundaries, which ensure their continuing interest in the domestic affairs of other states. These assets may be economic in character or may relate to a state's particular perception of its security needs. They form the bread and butter of any state's foreign relations and are the main basis of negotiation and bargaining between states. However, in the last analysis, if a state's interests in another society are threatened, and if it has the power to do so, it will intervene, though its intervention may be disguised or limited to the application of political, economic, or diplomatic pressures. Indeed, direct military intervention in internal conflicts is only the tip of the iceberg. Visible intervention of this kind is a serious step for any state to take especially as it may prove both costly and ineffective, if not actually counter-productive. For this reason, it is a step that is usually only undertaken by a powerful state, or by a state whose essential security is threatened by an internal conflict in a neighbouring country. The larger the Power, the more extensive its view of its security is likely to be. Indeed, within the ambit of its security, a government of a super Power may include its national prestige, its international standing, the credibility of its will to use force and even the vindication of its own political values. At the same time, technological change, especially the development of inter-continental ballistic missiles, has widened the super Powers' conception of their security even in its narrow sense.

Because internal conflict may bring about a change in the international political system that alters the overall balance among the major Powers, a super Power may feel that its failure to act in these situations would encourage its rivals to ferment trouble within its sphere of influence and seriously weaken the resolve of its allies to resist aggression. This has typically characterized the attitude of the United States in the post-war period. For example, President Johnson's Secretary of State, Dean Rusk, argued that the defence of the United States began at the seventeenth parallel – in Vietnam. Indeed, since the enunciation of the Truman Doctrine of containment in 1947, successive United States's governments have adopted the position that a failure to intervene against Communist-led insurgency would constitute appeasement of its rivals. The reasons for the United States's determination to play an active and direct role in combating revolutionary movements are partly historical, stemming from a belief that during the 1930s isolationism, encompassed in the concept of 'Fortress America', failed to safeguard American interests. In particular, the shock of Pearl Harbor in 1941 had produced a reaction in the United States which led her policy-makers to conclude that the costs of acting as the world's policeman were less than that of allowing aggression even in regions outside her sphere of influence. Both these extremes of policy have proved very expensive to the United States.

However, an account of United States's policy in terms of her perception of her self-interest alone would be inadequate. In the post-war period, the belief that as a super Power the United States has a special responsibility to be, in President Kennedy's words, 'the watchman on the walls of world freedom', has played an important part in American thinking. Successive United States's governments have viewed this responsibility in terms that go beyond the United States's recurrent fear that any sign of weakness would encourage her rivals to step up their support for wars of 'national liberation'. The United States's conception of her role as the guardian of international standards was forcibly expressed by Vice-President Hubert Humphrey in April 1966 at the height of the Vietnam War:

> The day that this country does not honour its commitments, it is on that day that the whole fabric of international law and order is torn apart and breaks down.[1]

In recent years, largely as a result of Vietnam, a somewhat more modest conception of America's world role has emerged out of President Nixon's pronouncements on foreign policy, which have emphasized the responsibility of America's allies, where possible, 'to stand on their two feet' and to provide for their own defence. As early as 1967, Hans Morgenthau expressed a fundamentally sceptical view of America's capacity to 'bear any burden':

> We have come to overrate enormously what a nation can do for another nation by intervening in its affairs – even with the latter's consent.[2]

Any discussion of intervention in the post-war world tends naturally to focus on the role of the United States because her intervention has been both more extensive and more visible than that of any other country. Direct military intervention by the other super Power, Russia, has been confined to her sphere of influence in Eastern Europe. Russian action, like that of the United States, has been justified in broad ideological terms. Since Stalin's conquests during the Second World War, Soviet leaders have spoken of a sacred duty to prevent counter-revolution in Communist-ruled countries. After the invasion of Czechoslovakia in 1968 by Warsaw Pact troops, this duty was elevated to the status of a doctrine by the Soviet Party leader, Leonid Brezhnev. In a series of speeches he argued that as the Socialist countries of Eastern Europe owed their

---

[1] Quoted in R. Higham (ed.), op. cit. p. 127.
[2] H. Morgenthau, 'To Intervene or not to Intervene', *Foreign Affairs*, XLV, 3 April 1967, p. 436.

independence to the strength of a wider Socialist community, any opposition to the interests of the world revolutionary movement, of which Russia by reason of her power was the head, was an abuse of their sovereignty. In practice, the guardianship which Russia has assumed over Eastern Europe and supported by the use of force reflects Russia's perception since the Second World War of her security needs and her economic interests, as much as her ideological preoccupations.

Direct military intervention in internal conflicts by states less powerful than the United States and Russia is not as common – at least since the ending of colonial rule in all but a few territories. French intervention in the civil war in Chad, Egyptian in the Yemeni civil war, and Indian in the conflict in East Pakistan are recent examples of action taken by states in regions in which for historical and geographical reason they have special interests and the capacity to intervene. Traditionally, intervention has been regarded as the prerogative of great Powers or of the wider international community. Today, however, there is a growing revolt against the pretensions of the super Powers to police the world. At the same time, the almost frozen state of international relations due to the limitations on inter-state war has increased the interest of states in influencing political decision-making at its source within domestic society. In the nineteenth century intervention by great Powers to enforce international standards of behaviour was widely accepted by small states largely because there was a considerable measure of consensus among the Powers themselves as to what these standards were. Consequently, small states which were not themselves the victims of great-Power interference were not inclined to view intervention as a threat to international peace. Indeed, many felt the opposite to be the case; that intervention contributed to the maintenance of international law.

But since the end of the Second World War there has been a growing recognition that the conflicting conceptions that the two super Powers have of intervention present a threat to international peace, especially in local conflicts involving insurgency. For example, in the 1960s many non-aligned states expressed fears that the war in Vietnam might intensify into a confrontation between the super Powers. In particular, the belief that great-Power involvement exacerbates internal conflict and aggravates rather than diminishes its impact on the international political system has gained wide currency. Indeed, even humanitarian intervention by large Powers

119

to enforce international standards of behaviour has been sharply criticized. For example, the joint United States–Belgian airlift to rescue Europeans trapped in Stanleyville during an uprising in the Congo in 1964 was greeted by a torrent of abuse from African states. As protection of foreign nationals has frequently been used as a pretext for politically motivated intervention, the reaction of militant African states to the renewed involvement of these two Western states in the affairs of the Congo cannot be considered surprising. In fact, a year later, in 1965, the protection of foreign nationals was used by the United States as a pretext for extensive interference in the political affairs of the Dominican Republic. The same argument had been put forward by the British government as a justification for the Suez operation in 1956.

Because of widespread criticism of unilateral intervention, both the United States and Russia have sought to legitimize their actions by securing a measure of collective backing for military intervention. When Russia intervened in Czechoslovakia in August 1968 to reverse the trend towards liberalization, she secured in advance the support of some other members of the Warsaw Pact, and forces from East Germany, Hungary and Poland participated in the invasion itself. Similarly, largely token forces from Australia, New Zealand and South Korea provided a collective basis for American involvement in Vietnam. Invitations from the government of the target country have also been regarded as important in conferring a degree of legitimacy upon the actions of an intervening Power; indeed, so important that they have, on occasion, been manufactured. Thus, when Russia intervened in Czechoslovakia, she coerced the country's leaders to sign a document after the invasion that formally sanctioned her actions.

The unpopularity of intervention among the new states of Africa and Asia does not simply stem from the behaviour of the two super Powers. Their hostility is directed towards the concept of intervention itself as it implies the existence of a hierarchy of states in fundamental conflict with the principle that all independent states are legally sovereign and equal. Ex-colonial states, in particular, resent an institution which appears to confer special rights on major Powers in the interests of international order. To many non-aligned states intervention smacks of neo-colonialism and imperialism. In view of the ideological conflict between the two super Powers, it seems unlikely that a genuinely multilateral basis for intervention to enforce accepted international standards of behaviour will be established. Even more deep-seated is the conflict between states broadly satisfied with the *status quo* and those which regard the present structure of the international political system as fundamentally unjust. This conflict has come to the fore in the United Nations in which many new states have sought to limit the policing role of the major Powers in support of the *status quo*, while pressing for international action over apartheid and related issues.

The United Nations itself is specifically excluded by its Charter from intervening in matters which are 'essentially within the domestic jurisdiction of any state'. While the UN has not kept to the letter of this article, its interventionary role has, in practice, been very limited; confined basically to its peace-keeping function in Cyprus and its controversial involvement in the Congo after independence. In the Congolese case, the role of the United Nations's forces turned out to be much more extensive than was originally envisaged. Indeed, the Security Council resolution under which the troops were sent specifically barred their use to influence the outcome of any internal conflict. Their sole purpose was to assist in the restoration of law and order. Yet by the end of 1961 the United Nations's forces, with the support of the United States in the Security Council, had become involved in operations to end Katanga's secession. Though the result was, perhaps, a happy one for the Congo, the international repercussions came close to wrecking the United Nations. France and Russia refused to make any contribution to the costs of the United Nations's Congolese operations on the grounds that they breached the Charter and sparked off a financial and constitutional crisis within the United Nations that further damaged the organization's sagging credibility.

In the present climate of world opinion, a repetition of the Congolese experience seems unlikely and it is difficult to envisage any circumstance in which the major Powers would again sanction the use of United Nations's forces in an extensive interventionary role. Ironically, at a time when the importance of internal conflict as a source of changing alignments within the international political system has enlarged the potential of intervention, international hostility towards the idea of a world police force has never been greater. There is little prospect that the international community will arrive at a consensus on an acceptable form of intervention.

Conclusion

Despite the general unpopularity of intervention in a world community of new states, jealous of their independence, intervention by the super Powers within their own spheres of influence has come to be accepted as almost inherent in the nature of the international society. In fact, the super Powers themselves have generally recognized each other's special interests within these areas and it is very unlikely that either would intervene in a domestic conflict in the other's backyard. But, outside these areas, insurgency presents special dangers of increasing tension; special because insurgency typically challenges the political viability of a state. When an outside Power intervenes in a conflict of this kind, whether in support of or against the insurgents, it is in a sense putting its political as much as its military credibility to the test. Partly for this reason, when a state becomes involved in a guerrilla war, the original reasons for its intervention may become secondary to the preservation of its prestige and credibility among its allies.

In these circumstances, the intervention of one super Power is likely to lead to that of the other, if only in a supportive role. Because insurgency often involves a measure of external support even in its initial stages, it often provides a pretext for intervention of a directly military character, leading inevitably to widely different perceptions of the conflict's origins. Because of the wider ideological implications of a revolutionary insurgency, if both super Powers become involved, the danger of a confrontation between them is always present as either might prefer the risks of brinkmanship to humiliating defeat. In any event, the costs of the conflict may bear little relation to the military strength of the insurgents. Indeed, the persistent character of insurgency rests on the fact that insurgents are often able to combat force with their political authority. This is of particular importance in the event of external intervention as political authority is one resource that a foreign Power can rarely bring to a domestic conflict. It is principally this factor rather than external restraints on the use of force by an intervening Power that may enable insurgents to challenge the international standing of a major Power.

The nature of these internationalized domestic conflicts, of which the war in Vietnam is the outstanding example, accounts too for the shift from the purely military to the coercive use of force. Broadly political, rather than conventional military considerations place limits on the use of force in domestic society that differ from those operating in the international arena. In particular, force can rarely be used effectively in a domestic conflict without political intelligence, which commonly an intervening Power does not possess. Indeed, a foreign army in an internal conflict in certain respects resembles a police force that has lost its files. As a conventional military campaign is unlikely by itself to restore the authority of a state that has been subverted from within, the use of force as an instrument of coercion will usually become the outstanding feature of the conflict, not least because insurgents themselves will resort to terror in areas they cannot subvert politically. Nonetheless, a powerful state may choose to flounder in an internal conflict of this kind rather than see an ally succumb to insurgency supported by a rival.

Indeed, the limits imposed on the use of force in an international context by the suicidal potential of nuclear weapons paradoxically provide an incentive for military intervention in internal conflicts, notwithstanding the risks involved. The reason is that in absence of interstate war, internal conflict provides an opportunity for a major Power to extend its influence or, more commonly, a last chance to prevent revolutionary or radical change that is perceived as threatening its interests. In view of the continuing importance of force within domestic society as an instrument of social control and as an outlet for disaffection, it would be foolish to predict the demise of force in international relations. In fact, it is possible that it will become more, not less, difficult for states to isolate violence in domestic society from the international arena and the interplay of political interests on a global level.

5 Substitutes for Force: the Example of Subversion

The spectrum of forms of force available for use in the international system has been greatly expanded since the Second World War. At one end of the spectrum the capacity to destroy has been vastly extended by the invention of nuclear weapons and the vehicles for transporting them from one country to another. At the other end the power to influence and undermine institutions for political control within another state through the use of subversive activity has given new significance to low levels of force. The present chapter will concentrate on subversive activity in international relations as an example of the low-level use of force and will consider it as an alternative to or substitute for the national military use of force and at times in opposition to it.

Subversive activity is defined for the purposes of this discussion as the covert intervention by force in the internal affairs of one state by another state in order to extend the political control of the latter over the former. This activity is as old as the history of international relations. However, since all the actors in any political system, including the international system, are at all times involved in one another's affairs, the concept of subversive intervention must be broadly based. For example, the expression may be used to characterize activities – such as the exchange of newspapers, teachers or diplomatic agents – which in most instances would not normally be regarded as intervention at all. In fact, it is hardly possible to draw any hard and fast line between the point at which 'normal' intercourse between two states ends and the point at which covert intervention for the purpose of enlarging political control begins.

A common denominator of subversive methods is their purpose – political control; they are used to extend the influence of one state either directly or indirectly over another by means short of a general or even a limited war. But limited military operations, such as border raids and street demonstrations, guerrilla activities, and armed internal resistance or insurgency, may also be an integral part of

124

covert political activity. This common denominator of purpose underlying the aggressive use of political, economic and social instruments of foreign policy has in the past been the ultimate extension of influence through direct military force and conquest. Such aggression has been recognized as an instrument of policy, and an elaborate super-structure of international law dealing with the rules of war has been generally accepted. However, with the rise to power of Hitler in the 1930s and the rapid expansion of Nazi Germany, the Soviet Union drew official attention to the need for a definition of 'indirect aggression'. Hitler was adept at using diplomatic pressure on a country in conjunction with the internal pressures generated by a dissident minority or Nazi-supported movement. The demands of the Sudeten German Party against the Czechoslovak government, for example, were carefully co-ordinated with the official activities of the German government.

If subversive activity is a central feature of cold warfare today, it was also the distinctive feature of cold warfare yesterday, for cold warfare antedates the Cold War.

Cold warfare during the interwar period was normally referred to by such terms as 'Trojan horse tactics' or 'fifth column activities', but the substance was the same. Yesterday's 'fifth column' activity is today's 'cold warfare', 'protracted struggle', or 'guerrilla insurgency'. Subversive activity, however, as a contemporary use of force is a twentieth-century phenomenon or, more precisely, a post-First World War phenomenon. This is not to say, however, that isolated examples of subversion did not extend back through history. Examples can be readily identified during times of revolutionary change, such as the American, French or Russian revolutions and the Wars of Religion, the development of empires, and the diplomatic history of European nations. For a contemporary study, Andrew M. Scott in his book *The Revolution in Statecraft*[1] lists twelve factors which distinguish twentieth-century subversive activity from what has gone before. However, for our purpose only those characteristics are listed in the following paragraphs which have a direct bearing on the use of force within the contemporary international system.

(1) 'Informal access' may characterize the relations of countries working together as well as of those in conflict.

[1] Andrew M. Scott, *The Revolution in Statecraft: Informal Penetration*, Random House, New York, 1965, pp. 9–11.

(2) It is used to achieve a variety of objectives ranging from attack at one end of the spectrum to support at the other.

(3) 'Informal attack' may be used as a prelude to military operations or as an adjunct to them.

(4) The variety of techniques employed have expanded. They may be violent or non-violent, covert or overt, from technical assistance and military training missions to militant party formations and the organization of *coups d'état.*

(5) These techniques are used against a variety of targets – nations, minorities, groups, parties.

(6) Participants in 'informal relations' have become more extensive – labour organizers and economic aid advisers; guerrilla or counter-insurgency instructors; Central Intelligence Agency (CIA) agents and foreign service officers. This accounts for the fact that since both the techniques of 'informal penetration' and the target against which they are used are diverse, personnel must also be varied.

The relationship between subversive activity as a covert operation and informal penetration needs further development. There has been a marked increase in subversive activities in recent decades, but subversive activity and informal penetration are not one and the same thing since informal access may involve either covert or overt operations. It may, for example, make a difference whether the United States operates an information programme through the United States Information Agency (USIA) in a country (overt) or whether it engages in covert propaganda activities, but both programmes are types of informal penetration. It may also make a difference whether tactically the United States Army trains guerrillas in South Vietnam (overt) or whether it hires 'volunteers' to do it (covert), but, here again, both programmes would involve informal access.

The other question is one of identification, for when is the use of force identified with subversive activities? There is still no commonly held definition of what constitutes subversive activity and its relation to force, although there is a general recognition of its operational techniques. The late United States Secretary of State, John Foster Dulles, at the time of the Lebanon crisis, denounced the political warfare activities of Nasser's régime as 'indirect aggression', which he characterized as one of the most dangerous features of contemporary international life and one that required particular attention in the Middle East.[1] Dulles stated:

> We do not think that the words 'armed attack' (in Article 51 of the United Nations Charter) preclude treating as such an armed revolution which is fomented from abroad.

In a speech to the American Society of Newspaper Editors on 21 April 1961 on 'recent events in Cuba' President Kennedy described and evaluated Soviet political warfare:[2]

> We face a relentless struggle in every corner of the globe that goes far beyond the clash of armies or even nuclear armaments. The armies are there and in large numbers. The nuclear armaments are there. But they serve primarily as a shield behind which subversion, infiltration, and a host of other tactics steadily advance, picking off vulnerable areas, one by one, in situations which do not permit our own armed intervention ...

Although the overt/covert question may be of considerable operating importance in a discussion of subversive activities, we will deliberately restrict our discussion here to the question of covert operations and its relation to the use of force and how it affects the international system.

With regard to the theoretical aspect of covert operations, it is the common element of purpose which becomes distinctive. It marks the watershed between reciprocal involvement and deliberate covert intervention. The aggressive motive behind such intervention is implicit in the terms military force or political warfare.

Let us assume an over-simplified situation in which an aggressor state deliberately sets out to extend its control politically or militarily over another by intervening within its internal affairs. With this model in mind, covert intervention by the aggressor state may take several forms and each a type of force in itself. These categories may be classed as either operational techniques or stages within the forceful extension of control or influence by the aggressor. Three such stages or processes may be distinguished and described as infiltration, disintegration, and subversion.[3] The application of these three techniques usually results in a period of covert control.

[1] Richard P. Stebbins, *The United States in World Affairs, 1958,* New York, 1959, p. 212, as cited in Paul W. Blackstock, *The Strategy of Subversion*, Quadrangle, Chicago, 1964, p. 25.

[2] *New York Times*, 21 April 1961, as cited in ibid. p., 26.

[3] These three processes are enumerated in P. W. Blackstock, op. cit.,

Infiltration

Infiltration is the deliberate or planned penetration of political and social groups within a given state by agents of an intervening power for manipulative purposes; that is, for the aggressor state forcefully to extend its influence and control over the target-state. This technique is usually covert to the extent that such penetration is deliberately manipulative. Here, as in all forms of political control, the motive or purpose is again the distinctive criterion, and the term penetration is much more accurate in conveying this essential motive than infiltration, which has been widely used in popular literature dealing with Communist subversive activities. Agencies such as the Intelligence Unit of the United States Agency for International Development (AID mission in Saigon) directed by a former CIA agent, Rufus Phillips, operated under the cover name of 'Rural Affairs Section'.[1] The secret United States military training mission which operated in Laos under the cover name of 'Programs Evaluation Office' carried on covert political activities aimed at penetrating select political and social groups in order to gather classified information which could not be obtained through open sources. Because of such circumstances these agencies were given an innocuous cover to conceal both their existence and their extent. Thus, if disclosed, such offices would be regarded as 'unfriendly' or 'aggressive' by the host country.

In planning the covert use of force for political control, one of the first steps is the establishment of an operational base from which selected political and social groups may be penetrated. The approach adopted will vary widely according to the historical situation and the immediate context of the relationships between the aggressor state and its target. The existence in Malaysia of political parties which for communal or Communist reasons sought either Indonesian domination or assistance in pursuit of their partisan ambitions as against the national interest, gave Indonesian officials the opportunity they sought for exploiting internal differences in Malaysia to their own advantage.[2] In Cambodia, Prince Sihanouk complained of subversive activity practised by 'Sino-Khmer Communist elements'

---

p. 43. For an example of this theory applied in practice, see the case study of Malaysia and Indonesia which appears later in this chapter.

[1] *New York Times*, 8 October 1963, as cited in P. W. Blackstock, op. cit., p. 44.

[2] Malaysia Information Office, *Indonesian Intentions Towards Malaysia*, Kuala Lumpur, 1964, p. 17.

in the Khmer-Chinese Friendship Association as well as in several schools and that organizations directing subversion were the Thailand Patriotic Front and the Pathet Lao, acting as proxies for Peking and Hanoi.[1]

Disintegration

This particular stage employs the use of force in order to split the political and social structure of a target-state until the fabric of its national morale disintegrates and the state is unable to resist further covert intervention. Tensions created by competing political and social élites for power and status may be exploited by setting such groups against each other in hostile, uncompromising opposition. Through the use of force, the social fabric can be destroyed and the political structure so weakened that the target-state is unable to resist further intervention. However, it should be added that this 'softening up', or disintegration of political and social institutions, may serve other ends than mere covert intervention by one state in the internal affairs of another. For example, it may facilitate the seizure of power by a revolutionary conspiracy (overt intervention) or by an aggressive political faction within the state such as the Secret Army Organization (OAS) in Algeria.

The idea of exploiting the political, psychological and sociological vulnerability of another state is by no means new, but only since the Nazi era of the Second World War has this ideology become an explicit part of the use of force within political and military planning. The 'Crush Malaysia' campaign initiated by Indonesia in 1964 evidenced the use of subversive force within the movement. For Malaysia there was the rising pressure of guerrilla warfare not only in Borneo, but also in Singapore and on the Malayan mainland itself. Particularly significant were the racial clashes in Singapore for they struck at the roots of Malaysia's national solidarity. A good argument may be made for saying that Indonesian pressure may in fact have provided the furnace for national unification in Malaysia. External difficulties may conceivably have helped to mould diverse communal elements into a homogeneous people. Experience shows, however, that unity is not the invariable result of such processes. External pressure may just as often lay bare the weak points of a society, widen the lines of fission and shake up the whole political

[1] Michael Leifer, 'Rebellion or Subversion in Cambodia?', *Current History*, February 1969, pp. 91 and 93.

system. Indonesia was doing its best to open up the wounds and aggravate the tensions that would in any case beset a newly born state.

Subversion

This final stage is the undermining or detachment of the loyalties of significant political and social groups within the target-state, and their transference, under ideal conditions, to the symbols and institutions of the aggressor. The assumption behind this manipulative use of force is that public morale and the will to resist covert intervention are the product of combined political and social or class loyalties which are usually attached to national symbols. Following infiltration and parallel with the disintegration of political and social institutions of the state, the loyalties may then be detached and transferred to the political or ideological cause of the aggressor.

The ultimate goal of the intervening state may be maximal, that is, the seizure of power by a controlled internal faction within the target-state, or liberation by invading forces trained and equipped outside the target-state. In both cases the use of force would be the optimal criterion and could prove the transition and characteristic from covert to overt operations.

Within our general theoretical framework, it becomes necessary to distinguish at what point covert acts become overt realities. As was mentioned earlier, penetration, disintegration, and subversion within the target-state usually results in a period of covert control. Such control may be divided into three broad areas: (1) those which affect the relative power position of the target-state *vis-à-vis* the aggressor, (2) the vital foreign-policy interests of the latter, and (3) actions which affect the relative power position within the target-state of the political party, military group, or faction through which the intervening power seeks by force to extend its influence and control. The term overt control best describes the relationship between an intervening power and its victim when an advanced stage of infiltration, disintegration, and subversion has been achieved. Along with propaganda and violence, preliminary operations have created the proper degree of public apathy and defeatism; when a society is already badly disintegrated, and when public corruption is widespread, it is then possible for covert techniques to be converted into open intervention.[1]

[1] P. W. Blackstock, op. cit., p. 69.

The open military attack on Germany by the Allies at the end of the Second World War was accompanied by clandestine resistance operations on a scale without precedent in terms of size, organization, depth and intensity. The United States organized an independent covert operational agency, the Organization of Strategic Services (OSS) which co-operated with the British and French clandestine intelligence services. In Poland an underground state was organized, and, until destroyed by advancing troops of the Soviet Union, carried on effective resistance to the Nazi occupation. Smaller, more divided resistance groups engaged Nazi occupation forces in Italy, Yugoslavia and Greece. In the German-occupied territory of the Soviet Union partisan bands also developed. This pattern of guerrilla warfare and resistance operations likewise spread to the Asian and South-East Asian theatres of the war. In the Philippines, guerrillas were notorious for their harassment of Japanese occupation troops during the war. In the post-war period, with the exception of the Korean police action conducted along traditional military lines, guerrilla and counter-guerrilla warfare has become a dominant pattern in the underdeveloped areas of the world.

An evaluation of the use of force in subversive activity

Like most revolutionary movements, subversive warfare thrives on conditions of political repression and economic and social injustice. Even the most refined security police technique of surveillance penetration, betrayal and repression will not remove the underlying causes of revolution. As suggested by Allen Dulles, former CIA director, many states in underdeveloped areas need professional guidance or assistance in the use of intelligence and counter-intelligence techniques,[1] just as they used military force and economic aid. But short-term or one-shot operations to thwart a Communist seizure of power are not enough.

In 1954, for example, when the Communist-dominated government of Arbenz was in power in Guatemala, an advantage was to be gained for the so-called 'free world' by its military overthrow. A covert operation was therefore planned, insurgent members armed, and subsequently the government was overthrown. However, was the long-term interest of the United States served by this covert operation of force? The CIA helped a group of Guatemalans based in Honduras and Nicaragua to overthrow Arbenz's régime. The

---

[1] P. W. Blackstock, op. cit., p. 288.

man whom the CIA assisted to power, Castillo Armas, was assassinated in 1957. An election to find a successor was cancelled as corrupt, but in a subsequent vote, General Miguel Ydigoras, who was openly opposed by Washington, came to power. General Ydigoras in turn was ousted by a military *coup* aimed 'to quash Red inroads' led by Defence Minister Enrique Peralta Azurida, who took over as Chief Executive in March 1963, re-establishing again United States ascendancy.

Reflecting on the United States's motives in Guatamala, C.L. Sulzberger commented:

> We were able to train anti-Castro forces in obscure jungles and to de-nationalize vast properties of the United Fruit Company (United States owned company) seized by Arbenz. . . . Nevertheless, we still looked like champions of the rich and the *status quo*. One hundred million dollars in aid had a dismally insufficient impact. . . . Seventy per cent of Guatemalans were still illiterate and a large number were hungry. . . . We had failed to find guaranteed market outlets for basic agricultural products, to assure honest government or requisite sweeping reforms. We had shown decency, sympathy and good intentions. But one knows where mere good intentions lead.[1]

The ill-planned Bay of Pigs Cuban invasion in 1961 further illustrates the difficulty of discerning where one's national interest lie in the covert use of force for military purposes. At the time the Kennedy administration had concluded that Castro's continuance in office was contrary to America's interests. It then had to decide whether to try to overthrow that government by subversive force or to confine its actions to the political and economic sphere. This latter action involved economic embargo and boycott coupled with political and psychological warfare.

The decision was made to proceed with the invasion, and a disaster soon followed. The allies of the United States were stunned, leaders in neutral nations were denunciatory, criticisms in Latin America were savage. Anti-American rioting and demonstrations broke out in Bogota, Caracas, Montevideo, Mexico City, the Canal

---

[1] *New York Times*, 15 November 1961, as cited in P. W. Blackstock, op. cit., p. 288 (the parenthesis my own). A more detailed study of the Guatemala case appears in David Wise and Thomas Ross, *The Invisible Government*, Cape, London, 1965, pp. 158–75.

Zone, Buenos Aires, Guatemala City, Rio de Janiero and La Paz.[1] Since the invasion failed, it was easy to conclude that the entire operation was a mistake. If it had led to the overthrow of Castro, however, would that automatically have made it a wise undertaking?

The perennial struggle against Communist or other revolutionary movements will not be won merely by the use of force in covert operations which seek, however, successfully, to do no more than thwart threatened seizures of power, or merely to overthrow a Communist régime which has seized power. The argument here is not that intervention by the United States in the internal affairs of Guatemala may not have been a necessary expedient at the time. CIA intervention in the Congo in support of Colonel Joseph Mobutu contributed materially to the stabilization of his native régime, especially during its first year (1960–1). Andrew Tully, in *CIA, the Inside Story*, summarizes his account of this covert operation with the statement:

> CIA had played an important role in the patient's sometimes irritating but continuing recuperation from over-indulgence in the excesses of freedom.[2]

This kind of clandestine operation is exemplary. But the CIA record of supporting repressive factions or régimes (such as the former Diem régime in South Vietnam) simply because they were anti-Communist and therefore 'our friends' indicates an approach to the Cold War which is already obsolete. The United States's military establishment has developed an alternative approach in a 'counter-insurgency' doctrine which calls for combined military and 'civic action' at the village level, where it could be more useful.

Covert political operations rather than covert military operations may be useful in helping to meet this need, but the idiom that such technical assistance is not a subversive technique employing force is somewhat short sighted.

An example of this technique in covert operations is the military civic action programme. The interest in civic action grew out of efforts to cope with guerrilla activities.[3] If the support of the people

---

[1] A. M. Scott, op. cit., p. 94, The Cuban invasion also appears in detail in O. Wise and T. Ross, op. cit., pp. 9–90.

[2] Raymond Roubins, 'The United States in Relation to the European Situation', *Annals of the American Academy*, 126 (July 1926), reprinted in R. A. Goldwin, et al., *Readings in Russian Foreign Policy*, O.U.P., New York, 1959, p. 229, as cited in P. W. Blackstock, op. cit., p. 290.

[3] A discussion of civic action programmes appears in Robert W. Komer,

in a given area is indeed essential to the success of a guerrilla movement, then denying this support to the guerrilla forces is quite as important as winning combat actions against them.[1] Military civic action has been defined as:

> The use of preponderantly indigenous military forces or projects useful to the local population at all levels in fields such as education, training, public works, agriculture, transport, communication, health, sanitation and other contributions to economic and social development, which would also serve to improve the standing of the military forces with the population.[2]

Civic action programmes have been developed in a number of countries including those faced with guerrilla activity, those threatened with insurgency, and those that were simply facing the problems of development. Thus, for example, in Guatemala a United States Army unit aided the Guatemalan Army in building irrigation facilities, purifying water and in improving roads. In Ethiopia American military advisers worked with the Ethiopian armed forces in building schools, drilling wells, and clearing roads. In Korea, during the ten years from 1953 to 1963, Armed Forces Assistance to Korea completed 4,537 projects, including the construction of schools, churches, orphanages, civic buildings and bridges.[3] Whether the United States Army developed its own capabilities in this field, as it did in South Vietnam, or acted in an advisory capacity, it was still using a technique separate from the direct use of force in the strict military sense of the term with regard to covert operations.

In the realm of economic aid, the use of force in subversive activities is usually based on the criterion that the success or failure of a given aid programme is likely to hinge on the political conditions that exist in the host country. It is an easy step from this realization to the conclusion that aid officials ought to take steps to bring about political conditions that would be compatible with the programmes they favour. Covert American efforts in support of former Philippine

---

'Impact of Pacification on Insurgency in South Vietnam', *International Affairs*, XXV, 1, 1961, p. 53.

[1] Samuel B. Griffith, Brig. Gen. USMC (ret.), translater, *Mao Tse-tung on Guerrilla Warfare*, Praeger, New York, 1961, p. 44.

[2] Major General William B. Rosson, 'Understanding Civic Action', *Army*, July 1963, p. 47, as cited in A. M. Scott, op. cit., p. 85.

[3] Jack Ramond, *Power at the Pentagon*, Harper, New York, 1964, as cited in A. M. Scott, op. cit., p. 85.

President Magsaysay prior to the 1955 elections illustrates the point:

> Gradually, moreover, the increased involvement of America aroused by a sense of urgency in the frustrating quest for solutions to these problems led them to the consciousness of a need for, and finally to a sense of responsibility for, a creative solution of a third set of problems: those of political leadership in the Philippine Republic. Americans found themselves involved in influencing the Philippine election as a means of securing a leadership that would make their other proposed reforms effective.[1]

American aid officials did not want their efforts wasted and hence wanted to be sure that the right economic decisions were made. The only way to make certain of this was to see to it that the right decision-makers were in office, which implied covert intervention in the political process. However, the political realm is much more sensitive than the economic and covert intervention in this quarter more easily provokes charges of subversion. When foreign advisers become concerned with campaigns, elections, and the press, it is easy for nationals of the penetrated country to conclude that they are being forcefully influenced and that their sovereignty is being infringed. This is why many of the political activities of the United States are handled covertly by the CIA or other such organizations. Often, however, the political activities that are needed, or the scale that they require, are not well adapted to covert execution. For this reason, officials have begun to reach out for new ways of wielding influence. Military civic action, as already noted, is one such way.

For centuries the Great European Powers have used subversion, that is, covert operations, as an instrument of their statecraft, as an ally of diplomacy in peacetime, and as a valuable auxiliary to military force in time of war. However, the effectiveness of subversive activity as a means of control or conquest through its use of force has been at times overrated and its employment oversold.

During the eighteenth and nineteenth centuries, the major Powers spent large sums of money on covert operations, such as bribery of political party leaders and even legislators abroad, with little lasting effect on major foreign-policy decisions or concessions. Allied experiments in covert operations during the First World War period

---

[1] H. Bradford Westerfield, *The Instruments of America's Foreign Policy*, Crowell, New York, 1963, pp. 409–10.

of Allied intervention in the Soviet Union likewise proved counter-productive. Early Soviet attempts to export permanent revolution to Germany, Austria and Hungary through the Comintern were also abortive. Furthermore, the Soviet take-over of Central Europe after the Second World War was more the result of the military situation at the war's end than the effect of Communist subversive force, although, especially in the case of Czechoslovakia in 1948, these were very skilfully conducted.

The Cold War era was a period during which the CIA leadership regarded the extensive use of covert operations as a means of raising the 'iron curtain' in Europe and the 'bamboo curtain' in Asia. In spite of an uprising in East Germany in 1953, revolts in Poland and Hungary in 1956, the Czechoslovak crisis in 1968, and continued widespread dissidence in the area, the Eastern European states, with the exception of Yugoslavia and Albania, have remained within the Soviet sphere of influence. Moreover, the defections of Yugoslavia and Albania were self-initiated; they were not brought about by Western-controlled covert operations by a force of arms. In addition to the following examples, the CIA has had notable short-term successes in blocking Communist take-overs in Iran, Guatemala, in the Congo and Cuba during the decade from 1954 to 1964.

Under this dichotomy between the United States and the Soviet Union, a successful covert operation by one side, in the clandestine use of force, automatically implied a coercive failure of the other. now However, with the advent of China, another major Power has become actively engaged in the use of subversive force and is furthermore presenting a formidable challenge to Soviet control and a bitter ideological rival within the Socialist camp.

Suspicion regarding Chinese sponsorship of subversive activity can be traced back to 1954 and especially in relation to the Overseas Chinese problem within South-East Asia. It was at the Bandung conference (April 1955) that Chinese leaders were confronted directly with the suspicion of China's relations with the Overseas Chinese which existed in the minds of many Asian leaders. Writing in the *Jen-min jih-pao*, Chang Hsi-jo referred to the 'nonsensical talk' about an Overseas Chinese 'fifth column' which had arisen at the Bandung conference. He asserted that it was a well-known fact that 'revolutions could not be exported', and that although the Overseas Chinese were patriotic it was 'absolutely unthinkable' that the Chinese government would use them to interfere in the internal affairs of other countries.[1] However, more illustrative of Chinese activities were those in Sarawak, where a large majority of the 230,000 Overseas Chinese (out of a total population of about 745,000) fell into line with the policies of the Sarawak United People's Party (SUPP), an organization which the Sarawak government described as the principal tool of the Communist underground in the territory. This Communist apparatus had made its strength felt not only through the SUPP, but through the predominantly Chinese trade unions and through student organizations of the private Chinese schools, where a mixture of Communism and Chinese cultural chauvinism had strongly influenced instruction.

Convinced of China's eventual hegemony in the Nanyang region, desirous of establishing closer ties with the mainland for business reasons, fearful of their position and of a possible 'desinicization' campaign in a new Malaysian federation, the Sarawak Chinese community offered an ideal recruiting ground for the Communist-inspired anti-Malaysia campaign. In January 1963, only a few weeks after Arahari's unsuccessful *coup* in Brunei and Sarawak, the Chinese Premier Chou En-lai, referring to Arahari's venture, expressed 'the resolute support of the Chinese people for the just struggle of the people of Brunei'. He declared that the latter had undertaken 'a heroic armed uprising to win national independence and overthrow colonialist rule'.[2] Later the same year, Marshal Chou Teh, Chairman of China's National People's Congress, reiterated that the Chinese people 'firmly supported' Indonesia's struggle against 'neo-colonialism propagated by the imperialists in the name of Malaysia'.[3] By this time Chinese Communists and Chinese youths wearing SUPP emblems were training with Indonesian 'volunteers' and with the remnants of Arahari's National Army of the Government of North Kalimantan at various bases in Indonesian Borneo, and Indonesian military personnel were leading bands of Chinese and Indonesian guerrillas. Shortly afterwards the Sarawak government announced that armed Indonesian terrorists had landed along the coast of Sarawak, and that Sarawak 'Communists were giving the Indonesians their full and willing co-operation'.[4]

In investigations of and deportation proceedings against Sarawak Chinese, the Sarawak government captured documents which left

---

[1] *Kuang-ming jih-pao*, 17 December 1956.
[2] *North Borneo News* and *Sabah Times*, 4 January 1963.
[3] New China News Agency, 28 September 1963.
[4] *Strait Times*, 19 October and 29 November 1963.

little doubt of Peking's hand in the anti-Malaysia campaign and the guerrilla war in Sarawak. As a government spokesman put it:

> It is Sarawak's misfortune to have a well-organized Communist group at work inside the country. This group is entirely Chinese in set-up and its numbers owe their loyalty not to Sarawak but to the cause of international Communism and particularly to the forces of Communist China. Their aim was to establish a Communist Chinese state right here in Sarawak.[1]

The same spokesman noted that in these same documents captured from arrested subversives, 'considerable attention was being paid to imparting knowledge of guerrilla war tactics, with special reference to the work of Mao Tse-tung'.[2]

The advent of subversive activity on a large scale adds an important new dimension to international politics. Subversive force alters the way in which the nations of the world compete with one another. This is true of both the lesser and greater Powers. For one thing, a nation may be powerful in the traditional terms of power, resources, or military capabilities and also have a substantial capacity for subversive force. The Soviet Union, in the classic Cold War context, provides a case in point. Under the pretence of 'peaceful coexistence', the Soviet Union mounted a threat to Western security through the exploitation of unrest and instability in the underdeveloped regions of the world. Frustrated generally in Europe after 1948, the Soviet Union, especially after the death of Stalin in 1953, increasingly turned its attention to the Third World. Offering the new countries trade and aid and friendly relations with one hand, Soviet leaders used the other to assist national liberation movements. When Mr. Khrushchev announced that national liberation wars were not only justified but inevitable, he notified the West that this form of competition under the aegis of peaceful coexistence would become perhaps the major weapon in the Communist arsenal.

A second possibility is a nation that is strong in traditional terms and yet weak in its capacity for subversive aggression. United States foreign policy is beset by no problem more exasperating and urgent than the development of an adequate counter-insurgent doctrine to cope with wars of national liberation. With Cuba and Zanzibar turning into schoolhouses of subversion and Moscow and Peking continuing to espouse their wars of national liberation, this doctrine

[1] *Sunday Times* (Singapore and Kuala Lumpur), 21 April 1963.
[2] Ibid.

is having an increasing critical affect within Latin America, Africa and Asia. The following quotation illustrates the fundamental irrelevance of United States doctrine to Communist operational methodology. In his April 1963 message to Congress the late President Kennedy, pleading for more foreign aid, said:

> Had the needs of the people of Cuba been met in the pre-Castro period – their need for food, housing, education, jobs, above all for a democratic response in the fulfilment of their own hopes – there would have been no Castro, no missiles in Cuba, and no need for Cuba's neighbours to incur the immense risks of resistence to threatened aggression from that island.

This situation was not changed in the least by former President Johnson's announcement that the United States Army had 344 guerrilla 'teams' working in forty-nine countries to train the local military in the 'most advanced techniques of internal defence against subversive war'.[1]

More interesting is a third case where a nation might be weak in traditional terms and yet strong in the area of subversive force. One that is relatively poor with regard to resources, population, and military power may yet possess notable capabilities for subversive force. Schools for subversive activities may be inside such a nation as in the case of the National Cadres School launched by the Cuban Communists under the Batista régime in 1954 or the Aurora School run by the Argentine Communists in Buenos Aires in 1958. Or it may be outside the target-state's territory, such as the training in Hanoi and Communist-held areas of Laos given to cadres infiltrating into Thailand, the training in Cuba of cadres from all over Latin America and Africa for action in Panama and Zanzibar, or the Communist Chinese training of Congolese guerrillas in hotel rooms in Bujumbura, Burundi.

Nasser's Egypt is another case in point. It was weak according to the traditional indices of power and was even weaker during the early years of Nasser's régime. Nevertheless, by means of agitating political threats, terrorism, the propaganda of Radio Cairo, the appeal of pan-Arabism, and the conception of a United Arab Republic (UAR), this weak country had a marked effect on the political climate within the Middle East. In a period of six months in 1963 Iraq, Syria and Yemen all experienced *coups* by groups favourably disposed toward Nasser and the UAR.

[1] *New York Herald Tribune*, 4 June 1964.

Castro's Cuba in a period immediately after coming to power and with few of the traditional resources at his command, managed to throw a sizeable portion of Latin America into turmoil with his efforts to foment revolution in neighbouring countries. In February 1964 a special investigative commission of the Organization of American States found Cuba guilty on four counts of aggression against Venezuela. A five-nation group (Argentina, Colombia, Costa Rica, Paraguay and the United States) spent several weeks examining evidence and drafting a report which included several hundred pages of annexes and documents. The evidence submitted by Venezuela against Cuba and on which the Organization investigators based their findings[1] consisted of:

(1) Subversive propaganda – one hundred hours of magnetic tape of Castro and other anti-Venezuelan Communist broadcasts from Cuba.

(2) Cuban training of Venezuelan terrorists. Documents showing more than sixty key members of the Venezuelan Communist Party and its affiliate, the Revolutionary Movement of the Left, as having received subversive training in Cuba since 1960. The training in Cuba in guerrilla warfare in the past year of more than 400 Venezuelans.

(3) Cuban financing of insurrectionary acts in Venezuela.

(4) Cuban dispatch of arms and instructions for subversion and terrorism.

There is no inherent reason, therefore, why subversive force and aggression, including attempts at *coups d'état*, cannot be designed and promoted in Cairo, Havana, or in the capitals of other small countries as well as in Moscow, Peking or Washington.

There are a number of reasons for concern about the use of subversive force on the stability of the international system. For one thing, the techniques of subversive activity can be highly effective under favourable conditions. The covert subsidy of one or two newspapers in a country could make a substantial difference in the expression of public thought. Organizing a guerrilla movement can create greater difficulties for a government or can even lead to its overthrow. In Malaya a guerrilla movement supported by Indonesia achieved its minimum objective of harassing the British and Malayans; in Indochina a guerrilla movement (converted later into

[1] *Washington Post*, 14 February 1964, as cited in P. W. Blackstock, op. cit., p. 25.

a regular army) achieved its maximum objective of driving the French out of the area. The organization of a successful *coup d'état* can change the entire political orientation of a nation.

For the United States and the Soviet Union, their traditional attitudes towards the use of force within subversive activities can be summarized in the formula of public disavowal and covert practice. In 1950 the TASS overseas news service repeated this theme:

> It is universally well known that the USSR . . . never interferes in the internal affairs of other countries . . .[1]

And the Soviet handbook, *The USSR as it is*, published in 1959 reaffirmed the same general line:

> In its relations with other countries the USSR is guided by the Leninist principle of the peaceful coexistence of states with different social systems and stands for peaceful economic competition between Socialism and Capitalism. . . . The USSR has never taken up arms in order to impose its system, its ideology, on any country and never will.[2] *Humor!*

Further illustrative is an exchange of notes between the two nations at the time of the Cuban invasion in April 1961. In reply to a Soviet note which charged that 'the armed bands which invaded that country had been trained, equipped and armed in the United States', President Kennedy stated:

> The United States intends no military intervention. . . . While refraining from military intervention in Cuba, the people of the United States do not conceal their admiration for Cuban patriots who wish to see a democratic system in an independent Cuba.[3]

President Kennedy's reasoning was following that of former CIA chief Allen Dulles who, in 1954 in response to the question 'Is that part of your function – to stir up revolution in these countries?', replied that the USSR was

> using all the techniques that Communist inventiveness could supply . . . in order to bring about Communist revolution, that

[1] TASS Overseas Service, 18 June 1947, as cited in P. W. Blackstock, op. cit., p. 28.
[2] Ibid.
[3] Sanche de Gramont, *The Secret War*, Putnam, New York, 1962, p. 24, as cited in P. W. Blackstock, op.cit., p. 28.

whole movement constituted a threat to the stability of the free world. . . . We would be foolish if we did not co-operate with our friends abroad to help them do everything they can to explore and counter the Communist subversive movement.[1]

Aggressive states inclined to use force within the international system that would normally be prevented from playing a major role in international affairs by the cost of modern weaponry would find that subversive activity has much to recommend it. Traditionally, a state's imperial ambitions have been sharply limited by its resources and general power position. In the realm of subversive force, however, resources go a long way. If a small nation chooses to concentrate its efforts (or if it has access to outside support), it can become quite influential in a restricted area. Speaking along these lines, President Soekarno at an Independence Day address on 17 August 1963 stated:

> Still fresh in our minds are the subversions from outside at the time of PRRI and PERMESTA rebellions. They operated from bases abroad, around us! Some operated from Malaya, some operated from Singapore, some operated from Taiwan, and some operated from South Korea, and some from foreign bases in the Philippines! In brief, all the foreign bases around Indonesia were used as bases of subversion against Indonesia.[2]

The strategists in Indonesia's 'Confrontation' with Malaysia thought of Malaysia in two parts. The campaign in Sabah and Sarawak came under army control, while the campaign against Singapore and the Peninsula Malaya came under navy control. The tactics were as follows:

> (1) To use the returned West Irian volunteers and the fringe of members of Malay extremist anti-Malaysia elements in PMIP (Pan-Malaya Islamic Party), PMU (Peninsula Malay Union), and Party Ra'ayat as recruits for an Indonesian 'fifth column'.
> (2) To organize training for them in sabotage and subversion, and to build up a number of encircling front-line bases in the Rhio Islands and Sumatra overlooking Singapore and Malaya on which stores of explosives could accumulate and from which the attacks could be launched.
> (3) To organize bogus commercial shipping companies as his

[1] Ibid.
[2] 'The Forceful Echo of the Indonesian Revolution', *Warta Berita*, issued by Butara News Agency, 17 August 1963.

(Ibrahim bin Haji Yaacob) links with Singapore and as employment agencies for his agents.

(4) To place agents in Singapore and Malaya to penetrate defence secrets, to attack public utilities with explosives and to create alarm by sporadic explosions.

(5) To prepare for a naval landing in Singapore and Malaya. The agents were urged to join army units stationed near the west coast, to find suitable landing places, and to think in terms of the capture by political activity of a state which could be built up as an Indonesian 'Yenan' in Malaya.

(6) To prepare a plan of subversion in Singapore and Malaya both to create present terror and to weaken Singapore and Malaya's power of resistance to a future attack.

(7) To encourage Malay political parties in deliberate subversive and repressive anti-Chinese policies and in activity which would lead to the overthrow of the freely elected Government of Malaysia under the Prime Minister Tunku Abdul Rahman.[1]

(8) In the long-term aim to split Sabah and Sarawak from Malaysia, to bring Singapore and the Federation of Malaya under a common government subservient to the Soekarno-guided Java-based 'Democratic Centralism' of Djakarta. Behind this in support of this sustained political warfare would be the army attacks on Sarawak and Sabah, the naval attacks on fishing boats, the stream of scurrilities from Radio Kemam, and the reported variations by President Soekarno on the theme of 'crushing' Malaysia.

A final argument for the use of force in subversive techniques is that an aggressively inclined state can probe for weak spots without being forced to take overtly aggressive action. It need not deliver an ultimatum to its neighbour or declare war or invade. Instead it can attack that neighbour covertly while maintaining correct relations formally. Under a screen of diplomatic privileges Indonesian officials assisted political parties which were working for the incorporation of Malaysia into Greater Indonesia. These officials openly and secretly worked for the overthrow of the

elected Government of the Malaysia territories which had been established constitutionally and democratically. They encouraged the organization of extremist groups, sworn to the violent

[1] Malaysia Information Office, *Indonesian Intentions Towards Malaysia*, Kuala Lumpur, 1964, pp. 28–9.

overthrow of the legitimate government of Malaysia and trained saboteurs, supplying them with arms and explosives. They also harboured and gave aid and encouragement to those in Indonesia who wished to see the destruction of independent Malaysia. This has been the action of official Indonesian diplomatic representatives, acting in fulfilment of their government's policy and on direct instructions from their departments in Indonesia.[1]

Conclusion

The general argument underlying this chapter is that the cost of using force has increased while that of subversive activity has lessened. Military force is comparatively cheap, especially for a *status-quo* Power, considering that its very existence works against its use. It is important to think of the argument of deterrence in cataclysmic terms, to live in dread of all-out war and to base military calculations on the forces needed for the ultimate but unlikely crisis. Nuclear weapons deter nuclear war; they also serve as a means of dampening rising tension. The temptation of one state to employ larger and larger amounts of force is lessened if its opponent has the ability to raise the ante. Conventional force may be used more hesitantly than it would be in the absence of nuclear weapons because it cannot be assumed that increased tension will be perfectly regulated. But subversive force can be used with less hesitation by states able to parry, to thrust and to threaten at varied levels of military endeavour.

Where military force is seen to be balanced, whether or not the balance is nuclear, it appears that the resultant of opposing forces is zero. The vectors of national force, however, do not meet at a point, if only because the force employed by a state does not resolve into a single vector. Military force is divisible, especially for the state that can afford a lot of it.

In a nuclear world, contrary to some assertions, the dialectic of inequality does not produce a strict hierarchy of strong and weak states. Lesser states that decide to employ the techniques of subversive force can at least compete with states which possess nuclear arsenals.

[1] Dato (Dr.) Ismail Bin DATO Haji Abdul Rahman, Minister of Internal Security, Malaysia, *Indonesian Intentions Toward Malaysia*, Malaysia Information Office, Kuala Lumpur, 1964, p. vi.

In short, instability in the international system may be increased by the emergence of new states that make excellent targets for subversive attack and by the existence of three major power centres willing and able to encourage and finance the subversive activities of a variety of nations. In addition, states not aggressively disposed to use force may, when they find themselves the victim of covert attack, be compelled to reply in kind, thus adding to the general instability within the system and in turn increasing the complexities which in the last forty or fifty years have enlarged the spectrum of force in international relations.

The contemporary international arena is conditioned today by many factors which do not rely on military force alone. The constant tensions and pressures which we have referred to in this chapter owe their existence to many causes and developments not the least of which include political, ideological, psychological, economic and social factors in addition to the ever-present military force of arms. These additional factors must be carefully taken into account when we consider the contemporary international system as an arena for the play of force. It is only through this combination of affecting elements that we can arrive at a clearer picture of what constitutes conflict between the states of the world and what conclusions from this must be drawn for the study of contemporary international relations.

6 Force in the Relations between Great Powers and the Third World

This chapter is concerned with the great Powers' use of force in the Third World. The United States, the Soviet Union, Britain and France are generally associated together as the great Powers of the present day, with China's status still undetermined since, at the time of writing, that country shows little intention or capability of military intervention far beyond its own borders. Moreover, China has no history of such intervention during the nineteenth and twentieth centuries (apart, of course, from the invasion of Tibet in 1950); indeed until the last few years it may be regarded as having been an object rather than a subject of international relations. Japan, on the other hand, though having a considerable history of the use of force against other states, has been quiescent since the Second World War. The Third World is defined as constituting the relatively new states of Africa and Asia but also as including the countries of Central and South America. The use of force is defined broadly as the employment of the military instrumentalities of foreign policy.

During the twentieth century, and especially since 1945, the world has undergone extremely rapid technological, social and economic change, one effect of which has been to render increasingly hazardous the use of large-scale military power by the strongest states of the world against each other. Given the destructive force of present-day weapons and the second-strike capabilities of the United States and the Soviet Union, in any major nuclear exchange between the super Powers there could be no victor in any meaningful sense. However, change has also had a notable impact on the use of force in the so-called 'Third World' and it is to this question that what follows is addressed.

The obsolescence of traditional techniques

In general, prior to 1945 the great Powers found that to protect their political, economic and strategic interests in their colonies and to

146

control these areas, it was enough to station there small numbers of troops, reinforced by native levies and police forces. Special dangers were met by the despatch of additional forces, as happened when the Boers in southern Africa rebelled at the end of the nineteenth century; but usually the colonies were easy, and therefore inexpensive, to control. The colonized peoples were poorly armed and anyway were largely indifferent to their rulers.

After 1945, however, much of this changed. Nationalist sentiments and expectations spread from Europe, partly as a result of the Second World War, and reached not only the intellectual élites of colonies but also the large mass of the population. These became increasingly hostile to their alien rulers and, with large dissenting masses, the enforcement of the colonizing state's law became increasingly difficult. The small military units stationed in colonies could no longer fulfil their tasks, especially where they were harassed by attacks from local irregular forces.

The cost of keeping colonies began to exceed the gain. Britain was persuaded to leave India, mainly by passive resistance techniques, and fought costly actions in Palestine, Kenya, Cyprus and Aden, for example. The final outcome was that Britain granted independence to all parts of its empire which desired it. France suffered extremely heavy casualties in Indochina and Algeria in the process of abandoning its empire, and of the imperial states of nineteenth-century Europe, only Portugal persists in retaining its possessions overseas. However, it is paying a heavy economic price in terms of the effort it has to make to try to suppress guerrilla movements in Angola, Mozambique and Guinea-Bissau.

It is perhaps basic to any study of warfare in the Third World to realize that military forces cannot force. They can exercise vigorous pressure on the population and may impose severe punishments if their orders are disregarded but they cannot compel individuals to act in a specified fashion. The psychological condition of the people is of vital importance for they will be able to resist severe pressure if their determination is great. As far as the post-1945 world is concerned, there was sufficient determination to achieve independence in many developing areas that the European states acquiesced. Further, resistance to alien rule cannot be destroyed by simply increasing the amount of military pressure applied and the severity of punishments. In many cases such action may serve to stiffen resistance, as the French found in Algeria. Hostility towards the colonizing state can be increased by reprisals against the innocent, even if this occurs by accident. As Tom Schelling wrote, war becomes 'not so much a contest of strength as one of endurance, nerve, obstinacy and pain'.

Although during the fifties and sixties Britain and France realized that their armed forces were incapable of controlling their colonies, the states of Europe and North America nevertheless have continued to use their armed forces on an *ad hoc* basis to intervene in independent developing countries. The US has been the most active, sending its forces to lead the United Nations action in Korea in 1950, to restore order in Lebanon in 1958, to prevent the establishment of an anti-American régime in the Dominican Republic in 1965 and to prevent a Communist take-over in Indochina after 1960. The main occasions when Britain has acted were in 1956, when an invasion force was sent to Egypt in an attempt to regain control of the Suez Canal and to overthrow President Nasser's régime; in 1958, when troops were sent to Jordan to protect King Hussein; and in 1961, when a force was airlifted to Kuwait to deter a threatened invasion from Iraq. Troops were also sent briefly to Tanzania, Uganda and Kenya in the mid-sixties to restore stability in a difficult period soon after independence. France also joined in the Suez operation and sent troops to Chad between 1968 and 1972 to protect the régime of President Tombalbaye. The Soviet Union has been very restrained in the Third World and has sent a large number of troops only to Egypt in the 1967–72 period. The major Soviet military interventions have taken place within Europe: in Hungary in 1956 and in Czechoslovakia in 1968.

Each of these military activities led the Power involved to learn specific lessons but some generalization is possible also. First, they were almost all expensive in financial terms, with the most extreme instance being the Vietnam War, the cost of which to the US reached millions of dollars a day. The total cost will perhaps never be known. An official US estimate made in 1956 of the Korean War assessed its total cost to the US at $83,000 million. Even such brief and minor actions as the US intervention in Lebanon involve millions of dollars, and costs are dramatically increased when the despatch of forces has to be followed by substantial aid programmes. Thus the expense of the Dominican Republic expedition was made up not only of the cost of the despatch of the troops but also of the $100 million emergency aid programme which the US introduced to shore up the government of President Hector Garzia-Godoy which it had placed in power.

Military actions abroad can have a direct effect on the domestic economy. The Vietnam conflict was a persistent drain on the American balance of payments and the Suez crisis caused important oil shortages in Britain and damaged the position of sterling as a world reserve currency. Despite theories which have been put forward about the US economy depending on defence spending for its health, it still appears that low defence spending is more likely to stimulate economic growth, as the post-war experience of Japan and Germany illustrates. A high level of expenditure on defence inevitably involves the diversion of resources, including trained manpower, into non-productive activities.

Furthermore, it is the experience of the great Powers since 1945 that their expeditions abroad have proved costly also in political terms. Again, the clearest case is the Vietnam War which resulted in damage to US relations with much of the Third World and even with its European allies. The Suez invasion proved similarly traumatic for Britain. Even a comparatively popular action, such as Britain's in 1961 when it went to the aid of Kuwait, was met with some suspicion and the Arab states insisted on replacing the British force with one from the Arab League. Basically the states of the Third World are jealous of their independence and resent actions by developed states which threaten their sovereignty. Thus it may be that the act of military intervention itself is less opposed than its implications. The US action in the Dominican Republic in 1965 caused outrage throughout Latin America because the US was asserting the principle of its right to exclude certain kinds of régime from the hemisphere. In the Kuwait case, the Arab states did not disapprove of Britain's action to any extent, but they did not wish to see the principle asserted that Arab affairs were a British military concern.

Adding to the costs incurred by a great Power sending its troops abroad in the post-1945 world is the dislocation that it may cause at home and the unpopularity which the government may suffer. In the democratic societies of Western Europe and North America the values of the people must be taken into account and increasingly these values reject the use of military force in foreign policy unless it is absolutely necessary. As a result the Vietnam War dislocated American society and politics as the Algerian conflict did to French society. Increasingly it seems that the only circumstances under which an intervention in the developing world may not be costly in financial and political terms are if the intervention itself can be given minimum publicity, as was the case with the French action in Chad, and if the tasks involved can be completed speedily before many lives are lost, as when Britain acted in East Africa in 1964. It is most important also that there should be widespread sympathy in the world for the aims of the intervention, as was definitely not the case with the US action in the Dominican Republic in 1965.

A further serious criticism of the use of military force by the great Powers is that it has proved often to be an inefficient and ineffective tool of policy. Despite an enormous effort, the US failed to defeat the Vietnamese Communists. The Suez invasion failed to restore control of the Canal to the maritime states and actually strengthened Nasser's position. The departure of French combat troops from Chad in 1972 left the rebels there undefeated. In Lebanon in 1958, the US did succeed in restoring order but only by allowing a President to take over who was more anti-American than Chamoun, his predecessor. Even in the Dominican Republic case, where the US appeared to have succeeded in its basic aims of protecting US citizens, halting the violence, preventing a Communist take-over and restoring constitutional processes, there are doubts about the long-term efficacy of the US action. Did it not, for instance, cause a polarization in Dominican politics which weakened the political structure of the country? Did it not also reassure conservative forces elsewhere in Latin America that they could rely on US aid if they failed to introduce needed changes called for by popular demand? One study of the Dominican intervention concludes that 'review of the 1965 Dominican crisis, therefore, does not provide the United States with a manual for successful intervention. What it shows, on the contrary, is the very high price of military intervention and the uncertainty of its consequences, even under conditions relatively favourable to the exercise of American power'.[1]

Often success for intervention forces depends on their obtaining the support of the indigenous population, especially if operations against guerrilla forces are involved. The guerrilla's main asset is usually the support received from the population and this must be wrested from him. However, troops intervening in developing states (indeed in developed states also) find it easier to arouse hostility than friendship from the populace; the presence of alien troops with different customs and little respect for local ways rarely provokes a favourable response. Hence the unpopularity of Soviet troops in

[1] A. A. Lowenthal, in S. L. Spiegel and K. N. Waltz (eds.), *Conflict in World Politics*, Winthrop, Cambridge, Mass., 1971, p. 114.

Egypt up to 1972. In Vietnam a major American error was to concentrate excessively on killing suspected Communists at the expense of trying to win popular support in rural areas.

One final disadvantage of the despatch of troops to Third World conflicts should be mentioned: it is a dangerous activity. In the bipolar environment there has been a constant danger that intervention in a conflict on one side by the West could coincide with intervention by the USSR on the other. A process of escalation could occur ending in global war. This danger helped to restrain the USSR from sending its troops to fight in Korea and Vietnam and it is the reason why the Arab–Israeli situation has often been seen as the potential source of a third world war. Awareness of this danger has made the US and the Soviet Union extremely cautious. At the beginning of the June 1967 war, both Powers agreed not to intervene and later, when the USSR did provide pilots and other air defence personnel for Egypt, it was made clear that they would not help any offensive operation involving the crossing of the Suez Canal. This, in the last analysis, was the reason why the Egyptians asked the Soviets to leave in 1972.

So far it has been argued that, since 1945, one form of the use of force, namely the sending of troops from developed states to Third World conflicts, has often proved an expensive and risky business for the great Powers involved. Such operations have frequently failed to achieve even their immediate objectives and their side-effects are long lasting and difficult to foresee. For instance, it has been argued that the Dominican Republic intervention in 1965 and the US statements justifying it were later used by the USSR to rationalize its invasion of Czechoslovakia. The US, by acting in a certain manner in Latin America, its traditional sphere of influence, virtually endorsed similar Soviet action in Eastern Europe.[1]

However, while the great Powers have found that one traditional method of using force, the despatch of their troops abroad, may often prove inefficient in Third World situations, they still have a great many interests in developing states which require protection. States bordering on either the USSR or the US, such as Cuba and Iran, remain of strategic significance as do states which can provide access to major oceans. Despite advances in synthetics, North America and Europe remain dependent on the Third World for many vital raw materials with obvious examples being oil, chrome

[1] T. M. Franck and E. Weisband, *World Politics: Verbal Strategy among the Superpowers*, O.U.P., London, 1971, pp. 96–109.

and copper. Furthermore, although the Cold War has given way to a degree of cordiality between the US and the USSR, the two still compete strongly for political support from neutralist countries. This competition provides added significance to the political attitudes of Afro-Asian governments.

In considering the protection of their interests in the Third World, the great Powers cannot ignore the use of force just because the intervention of their own troops is not likely to be effective. Force is frequently used in developing states by indigenous elements for the settlement of disputes. The usual method of changing governments in many states is the organization of a *coup d'état* using key units of the armed forces. *Coups* are essentially technical operations which usually depend for their success on the sudden seizure of important buildings such as communications centres.[1] Many governments in developing countries face movements which use guerrilla warfare to achieve their aims. These movements, which aim slowly to weaken the central régime, often have revolutionary social goals and they are especially common in Latin America. Some of them, in particular in Africa and Asia, also have separatist goals involving the break-up of established states. For instance, force has been used by and against separatist movements in Sudan, Nigeria and Ethiopia.

Also, military power remains an important factor in many inter-state disputes in the Third World, despite the efforts of regional organizations such as the Organization of African Unity, the Organization of American States and the League of Arab States. India and Pakistan, the Arab states and Israel, Uganda and Tanzania have all used force against each other as a result of their disputes and there are many other cases in which military power is important, for instance the relationship between Iraq and Iran.

To sum up: the spread of national sentiments in the developing world coupled with changes in military techniques has meant that the great Powers can rarely use their own troops in the Third World. Yet they still have substantial interests in these areas which require protection and which are often threatened by various military activities from within the countries of the developing world. The *coup d'état*, guerrilla warfare and interstate conflict are common features of Third World politics. In this situation, the problem of the great Powers is to strengthen those indigenous military elements in

[1] Edward Luttwak, *Coup d'État: A Practical Handbook*, Penguin, Harmondsworth, 1968.

the Third World which are favourable to them and which have qualities of effectiveness and efficiency.

New approaches to the use of force in the Third World

Local armed forces and insurgents can most obviously be strengthened by the provision of training and equipment. Training aid encompasses a wide range of activities and may include anything from help with the establishment of basic procedures and discipline in a new army to instruction in the operation and maintenance of sophisticated electronic equipment. It has been provided in varying amounts since 1945 by all the great Powers with Britain and France helping in the main their former colonies; the US those states in Africa and Asia which were perceived to be threatened by Communism, as well as most Latin American countries, and the USSR those Third World governments and movements which were expected in the long term to favour the Soviet side in the Cold War. France's entire military aid programme is dominated by training aid with most help going to its former colonies south of the Sahara.

Military training help is vital when local forces are being built up for actual combat purposes. However, this latter condition is not always present since some states improve their armed forces merely for prestige purposes. When inadequate attention is paid to training in the expectation that combat will not occur, the results may be disastrous, as the USSR and Egypt found to their cost in 1956 and 1967. If a state's armed forces are insufficiently disciplined, they can become a major source of disorder, as in Amin's Uganda.

The provision of training aid has been seen by all the great Powers as a means of maintaining and strengthening their influence in Third World states, in many of which the military sector is of primary political importance. Through training aid, armies in developing states, and especially their officers, can be indoctrinated with the aiding state's ideas about the role of the army in politics, the proper ordering of society, the nature of world politics and other major issues. Two statements by US training aid administrators summarize their views as to its value in terms of US relations with developing states:

> We feel that if we can get an officer of the field grade into one of our courses at the Command and General Staff College, the

153

mere association with Western people there would rub off on him during the course of his ten-month period and we feel that expenditure of such funds might have some effect in making this man a little bit more pro-Western.[1]

The training programs requested provide ... the best investment available, dollar for dollar, in maintaining or promoting a considerable measure of constructive influence and pro-US orientation within these foreign military establishments.[2]

While the arguments for political influence accruing from training aid remain far from proven and there are several cases of Western-trained officers overthrowing pro-Western governments, there remain two points in their favour. The first is that training aid supplies the first requirement for influence in a state in that it provides regular contact and communication with important segments of society in developing states. Its provision means that there is regular formal and informal contact with soldiers who have or will hold important government posts. Without this contact, there would be less opportunity for influence. Second, a state which is providing training aid can do so in the knowledge that, even if it is perhaps gaining little influence of its own, it is at least keeping out other states which otherwise would supply the required training help and might have more success in gaining sway over the recipient régime.

A specific danger with training aid is that, if carried out on a large scale, it acquires some of the characteristics of military intervention of the type discussed at first where a great Power simply sends its own troops abroad to fight in a conflict. Hence, too large a training mission can become unpopular; for instance, the very size of the Soviet military training mission in Egypt and the way in which it behaved served to turn Egyptians against the USSR.

The dividing line between a great Power sending training aid and actually intervening with its own troops in a conflict is often hard to discern if fighting is going on. In the early 1960s the US activities in Vietnam were officially limited to advisory roles but in fact US advisers went out on patrol with South Vietnamese forces. These forces frequently were attacked and US soldiers were killed. Until

[1] General Fuqua, US House Committee on Foreign Affairs, Hearings on the Foreign Assistance Act of 1963, p. 727.
[2] General Strickland, US House Committee on Foreign Affairs, Hearings on the Foreign Assistance Act of 1965, pp. 732–3.

1972 it was thought that the British role in Oman was restricted to training the Omani armed forces but then it emerged that British officers were leading patrols against rebels.

There is substantial evidence both historical and logical to suggest that the provision of military training can lead directly to the despatch of troops for combat duties. When military training aid is provided either to allow one side to triumph in a conflict or at least to hold its own, and then is proved inadequate, the great Power in question is obviously tempted to increase its involvement and to send troops. This was the case with the Americans in Vietnam, the British in Oman, the Soviets in Egypt and the French in Chad.

Military training aid can also lead to increased great-Power involvement in another situation. If a state sends troops abroad to train others, there is a danger that these troops may become accidentally involved in combat. For instance, their camp may be attacked by the enemies of the aid-receiving state. Awareness of these factors has led to the development of two fairly common practices. First, a great deal of training aid is provided in the territory of the donating state. Israelis go to the US to learn how to fly American aircraft, thus minimizing the number of Americans who need to risk involvement in Arab–Israeli clashes by being in Israel. Similarly, China and the USSR, which provide help to many revolutionary movements, implement their training programmes within their own boundaries whenever possible.

Second, the aid-providing states may organize mercenaries of one sort or another to undertake the training programme. Such men are usually former professional soldiers who sell their services where required. They are recruited usually on an *ad hoc* basis by private companies, which are hired by foreign governments and movements, usually with the support of their home governments.[1] Other training help is sometimes provided by employees of companies which manufacture arms, whose use and maintenance require substantial instruction. Here the 1965 Saudi air defence deal with British and American companies makes an interesting study. The arrangement made was that Raytheon and English Electric along with other British and US firms would provide the several hundred personnel needed for a five-year period to train Saudis. It is likely also that these men helped to operate the weapons. Certainly the Lightning

---

[1] See *Observer*, 13 May 1973, p. 29, for extracts from a book by Patrick Seale and Maureen McConville, *The Hilton Assignment*, Maurice Temple Smith, London, 1973.

aircraft involved were flown by British mercenary pilots and later by Pakistanis.

The use of mercenaries makes training-aid contracts more commercial and less political in appearance. Officially, Britain and the US were simply providing services which the Saudis paid for. Had the individuals concerned with training got involved in fighting with, for example, Egyptian forces, it would have been much less difficult and embarrassing for the US and Britain than if active members of their armed forces had been involved. The use of mercenaries, then, is most appropriate when the aid-supplying state does not wish formally to commit itself to a certain cause.

Military training aid, however, is usually accompanied by the supply of weaponry and military equipment and it is the flow of weaponry from the developed world which largely determines how force is and can be used in developing areas. All developing states depend on external suppliers for their military equipment. Indeed, only two states, the US and the USSR, are virtually self-sufficient in arms production and outside Europe and North America very few states produce any substantial range of armaments. Australia, India, Israel and South Africa are the most important of them but even for these imported arms are very important.[1] China is a special case and can be interpreted either as being in the process of achieving self-sufficiency in weapons manufacture or as being simply deprived of suppliers since its split with the USSR.

The threats or use of force which governments and revolutionary movements can make depend on the resources, especially the military resources, available. It is true that other factors besides arms can determine the outcome of conflicts fought with conventional arms, factors such as the courage and morale of soldiers, the effective organization of the forces concerned and the strategy and tactics devised by commanders. However, the initial determinant is the resources available. Strategies are formulated on the basis of weapons possessed. Decisions to launch massive bombing raids require the availability of aircraft or missiles. Two neighbouring islands, perhaps each with large armies, need not perceive each other as dangerous until a capability to transport the armies across water is acquired. Generals who are faced with dramatic shortages of weapons, ammunition and spare parts have to adjust their tactics accordingly.

[1] These states are all trying to achieve a greater degree of self-sufficiency in weapons production so as to reduce dependence on foreign suppliers.

Arms help determine the structure and duration of battle. In the European wars of the twentieth century, technological developments in weaponry meant ever-increasing civilian involvement and casualties. In post-1945 Asia, the availability of very mobile, high-firepower equipment contributed greatly to the brevity of the Arab–Israeli Wars of 1956 and 1967 and the India–Pakistan conflicts of 1965 and 1971. On the other hand, if only light arms are available in large quantities, wars may be more protracted, especially if there is suitable terrain for the application of guerrilla war doctrines.

The examination of the use of force in developing states by looking at arms transfers has obvious limitations. It does not seek to explain, for instance, why developing states go to war. Arms, after all, are usually acquired as a result of political disputes and do not in themselves cause such quarrels, although in some circumstances the acquisition of arms by one state may stimulate perceptions of danger by another.

Furthermore, the governments of developing states could still resort to the use of force even if arms supplies from friendly governments in the developed world were unavailable. There is a large stock of surplus light weaponry in existence, and, therefore, rifles and machine guns may be acquired through private dealers. In an extreme case, governments could fight wars with primitive explosives, cudgels and spears and it is far from certain that such conflicts would be less bloody than a modern war of great intensity but brief duration.

The abolition of the arms traffic between the states of Europe and North America and the Third World would not, then, eliminate the use of force in the Third World, especially as some developing states such as South Vietnam, and Egypt have surplus stocks of weaponry which they can re-export. But the arms traffic is important in determining how force is used and which side emerges as victor. The great Powers therefore provide arms in an attempt to ensure that the side which they support in a dispute is the stronger.

The reasons why the great Powers export arms and why developing states acquire them can be examined in more detail. An initial point is that arms may be exported for reasons which have little to do with the threat or use of force but which have much to do with politics. Arms may be acquired to bolster the prestige of the recipient government and in these instances the main occasions on which arms are 'used' in any meaningful sense are independence day parades and the like, when they are displayed to the watching world.

There are several groups which arms obtained for prestige reasons are designed to impress. The general public in a developing country may be expected to see the arms as symbols or even as proof of its country's independence and strength. Also, in almost all the states of Latin America, Asia and Africa the military élite represents an extremely important political force and it is necessary to please it if its support for the government of the day is to be maintained. One obvious way of doing it is to provide it with modern equipment. In Latin America, different branches of armed forces frequently compete for the most expensive items. Arms may finally be seen as a way of impressing neighbouring governments and peoples, as a means of demonstrating to neighbours the power and modernity of a state's armed forces and society.

As status symbols, heavy, modern weapons such as tanks, missiles and jet aircraft are more appropriate than light arms although what constitutes a prestigious weapon varies from area to area. Supersonic aircraft in the Middle East are commonplace and therefore of little prestige value unless they are of the most modern vintage. In Latin America, however, they are still comparatively rare as for many years the US opposed their introduction to the region. The first sale was by France in 1968 when the Mirage V was sold to Peru.

Indeed, almost all tanks, aircraft and capital naval vessels in Latin America can be said to have been acquired for prestige reasons. It is difficult to envisage their use in combat as, while war is always a theoretical possibility, in Latin America it is in practice at least remote. There has not been a major interstate war in the region for decades. Perhaps the outstanding examples of prestige sales were the aircraft carriers sold by Britain to Argentina and Brazil in 1958.

There are obvious disadvantages in the acquisition of arms to bolster a government's standing. Prestigious arms by their nature are expensive and they require the services of skilled manpower, which is frequently scarce in developing states, for their operation and maintenance. It is, therefore, all too easy for a state to damage its prospects for economic growth by diverting too many resources to obtaining prestigious weapons. Also, although arms may be acquired for prestige purposes, neighbouring states may nevertheless feel threatened and seek to obtain arms for themselves. Even if no threat is perceived, states may well feel that they must keep their place in the political order of an area and so, if a weapon is acquired by one country, others will also try to obtain it. This was one reason for the increase in demand for naval vessels in Latin America in the

158

late sixties and early seventies. There is always a danger that obtaining arms for prestige reasons can lead to arms races.

Presige is a factor which affects largely the demand for arms. Economics, on the other hand, is a factor which influences the supply side of the equation. Both factors have it in common that they are determinants of the arms trade which are not directly related to the actual use or threat of force.

The economic aspects of the arms trade has traditionally received a good deal of attention ever since one of the subsidiary causes of the First World War was perceived to have been the activities of private arms salesmen who fostered conflict for financial gain. Since the Second World War the arms trade has been a government-dominated activity but it remains of considerable commercial importance.

There are two basic, economic reasons why arms are sold. The first is that, sold on a large scale, they can considerably improve a state's balance of payments position. Related to this, like all manufactured goods, arms provide employment at home and help to keep the economy running and employment at a high level. Second, it is increasingly the case that sophisticated arms cannot be produced except at an enormous loss unless they are exported. With the enormous research and development costs involved with the production of a new aircraft or missile, large-scale production is essential if a weapon is to be marketed at a reasonable price.[1]

Of the great Powers, Britain and France are under much greater economic pressure to export than either the USSR or the US. The system of government in the USSR enables the régime to override economic considerations without fear of public complaint while both the US and the USSR have large domestic markets for arms which enable them to produce a substantial number before they need to export.

Nonetheless, the key factor behind any arms transfer for the great Powers is rarely its domestic economic effect but its political and military impact on the recipient state and its neighbours. When a great Power feels it is vital that arms go to a certain state, it may be willing to provide them free. Hence an American policy of providing large amounts of military aid to states threatened by Communism was applied after 1947. The important issues for the supplier are

[1] See John H. Hoagland, *World Combat Aircraft Inventories and Production: 1970–75*, Arms Control Project, Center for International Studies, M.I.T. Press, Cambridge, Mass., February 1970.

whose capabilities are being increased, whether they are being increased in an appropriate manner and why the recipient should be strengthened. The supply of arms to strengthen a régime's political position by providing it with prestige has already been discussed but arms also have other impacts in the political and military spheres.

When military training aid was discussed, it was seen to be a method of acquiring influence with the recipient state and this applies also to many arms supply arrangements. In the nineteenth and early twentieth centuries, the great Powers could easily dominate the political attitudes of régimes in areas of the Third World which were of importance. Many of these areas were under direct military and political control as colonies while other areas, such as China, could be controlled through the despatch of a special military expedition. Since 1945, however, these techniques have been neither successful nor even practicable. Instead the great Powers have had to use other means, including the supply of arms, to deal with governments in the developing world. There are basically three kinds of activity in which the great Powers become involved; the protection of existing governments, the overthrow of governments, and the modification of their attitudes. Arms supplies can and do play a role with each.

They can first of all serve to modify the behaviour and attitudes of governments. After 1967, France agreed to sell Mirages to Libya and Iraq partly to persuade Arab governments to adopt a more friendly stance towards France. France provided military aid for its former colonies south of the Sahara so that it would maintain contact and influence with their régimes. The US policy to Latin America and the Soviet policy towards the Middle East are also determined partly by the belief that they will derive influence in these areas from arms supply activities. Soviet–American competition for the favours of India is carried out partly in the field of arms supplies.

As with military training aid, there is no proof that arms supplies inevitably bring political influence. Despite being the major source of weaponry, the USSR was unable to prevent the governments of Egypt, Iraq and Indonesia from repressing and, in the latter case, slaughtering members of local Communist parties. The US does not exercise control over the actions of Israel despite the Jewish state's dependence on US military supplies. In Indochina, President Diem could not be induced to reform his country by his American patrons and there is little evidence that China and the USSR possess exceptional control over the government in Hanoi.

In theory at least, arms supplies would seem to bring most

influence when they are needed desperately with the receipient having no other source available. However, such conditions are rare. The USSR has pursued a policy of aiding those states which have been refused military help by the West, especially in the Middle East. China is willing to help revolutionary movements rejected by the USSR. Thus, an alternative supplier is usually available. Also, if only light arms are required, they can be obtained privately, while heavier items are expensive and therefore attractive sales propositions for Britain and France.

In some cases, even if no other sources are available, a régime may strengthen its position by standing up to a great Power. President Sadat could be said to have done this by the prestige he gained by expelling Soviet military advisers, but it should be added that this decision was taken in the hope that Britain would emerge as an arms supplier to Egypt. China has suffered the greatest isolation from foreign suppliers since its split with the Soviet Union but even this may be ending, as at the time of writing (mid 1973) Britain is reported to be considering selling the Harrier aircraft to Peking.

So it can be concluded that arms are a dubious source of influence and a suspect means of winning favour from existing governments. It may well be, in fact, that arms deals reflect existing political preferences rather than change them. Arms are traded mainly between régimes which already look favourably on each other. Arms deals, however, like military training aid, increase the potential for influence in that they result in high-level contact with a régime and therefore deny that contact to others.

Another aspect of the supply of arms is that they may be despatched to strengthen friendly governments. Third World régimes face threats of three sorts; from external enemies threatening invasion, from revolutionary forces waging protracted campaigns within a state and from the sudden *coup* organized by dissatisfied elements in the armed forces. To deal with revolutionary groups, the internal security forces of a government require mainly light arms, transport items including helicopters and perhaps ground-strike aircraft. Tanks and heavy bombers are usually ineffective and may alienate the population by the indiscriminate damage which they can cause. Only when revolutionary units decide to fight main force battles, as the North Vietnamese and Vietcong did in Vietnam in the mid 1960s, will heavy-firepower items be of any use to a régime.

The definition of weapons suitable to stave off a possible *coup* is

161

not easy. There is no real way to defend against it in any military sense except to ensure that the troops which protect key installations are loyal and well armed. A good internal intelligence service provides the best defence against *coups*. To keep the armed forces loyal, it may be sensible to ensure that they are well paid, have a respected role in society and have some modern, sophisticated weapons to show off. This, however, is no defence against officers who are dissatisfied with their government's social, economic and foreign policies. In the Middle East and Africa it is usually such officers who revolt.

When a government faces an external enemy, the type of weapons suitable for its defence will depend on the terrain, the human resources of the recipient state and the configuration of enemy forces. With developing countries which lack skilled personnel, the supply of equipment which is too sophisticated and difficult to operate may prove counter-productive, as the Soviets found with Egypt in June 1967 and after. Advanced technology in a weapons system is not the same as utility. In the early 1950s, for instance, the US supplied several hundred donkeys to Turkey because it was felt that they represented the best method of transport in the mountains. A study at the Massachusetts Institute of Technology has shown some surprising results about the usefulness of older weapons for the situations in which many Third World states find themselves.[1]

Arms sent to affect interstate conflicts are rarely despatched when fighting is in progress. In fact, when fighting does occur, the great Powers often impose total, or at least partial, embargoes. These may cover arms, spare parts and ammunition. Most arms are sent when both sides in a dispute perceive a danger from each other and therefore feel in need of extra protection. In the early 1970s Zambia and South Africa began to build up their defences in anticipation of clashes.

The great Powers despatch arms to states involved in serious disputes with others usually either to maintain the peace by establishing a condition of deterrence or to ensure that, if deterrence fails, their side will survive or win. For example, this is the rationale behind US supplies to Israel. The supplier may choose to aid both sides in certain circumstances; for instance the US has provided both India and Pakistan with weapons with the hope of reassuring

---

[1] Geoffrey Kemp, *Classification of Weapons Systems and Force Designs in Less Developed Country Environments*, Arms Control Project, Center for International Studies, M.I.T. Press, Cambridge, Mass., February 1970.

each about its ability to deal with, and therefore deter, an attack by the other. However, to establish a state of mutual deterrence in disputes involving conventional weapons is by no means easy in theory or in practice, even if the great Powers co-operate. Mutual second strike capability, which is relatively easy to apply in nuclear terms and which forms the basis of deterrence theory, is difficult to establish using conventional weapons. As a result, what happens is that one side becomes appreciably more powerful than the other. Thus Israel gained the capability to defeat all its Arab neighbours and deter an attack by them. The Arabs, however, were unable to deter Israeli attacks. Similarly India became more powerful than Pakistan and the latter was unable to deter the use of force by India to resolve the problem of Bangladesh. In brief, although a great Power may send arms to a state involved in a dispute in the hope that peace will be preserved through deterrence, it is often forced, not to try to establish a situation of mutual deterrence, but instead to ensure that the side being supported is superior and can deter an attack by its opponent.

It has been argued throughout that arms supplies and military training aid are essentially substitutes for the use of great-Power forces in the Third World at a time when the use of such forces is frequently inefficient. In one type of situation, however, this hypothesis does not apply. This is when a great Power provides arms to a Third-World state which is threatened by another great Power which, by definition, has much greater military strength and potential. In this situation, arms supplies tend to be an indicator of great-Power support for the recipient and a sign that the supplier will send its forces if the recipient is attacked. To reinforce this message, a treaty of alliance may be signed between the arms supplier and recipient. Thus, after 1947 the US sent arms to a great range of states on the Sino–Soviet periphery and concluded alliances with them. The US aim was to deter Soviet expansionism. This strategy has been enunciated in the Nixon Doctrine first outlined at Guam in July 1969 which emphasizes that Asian states, using US arms, must deal with local conflicts but envisages the use of US troops if another great Power uses its forces aggressively.

Finally, just as arms may be provided to secure influence with existing governments and to strengthen them against the dangers of external attack, they may also be used as part of an effort to overthrow a régime. In the past, a great Power could remove an unfriendly régime by using its own forces but since 1945 this has become a politically and financially expensive exercise unsure of success. Instead, the great Powers have adopted different tactics. The US has frequently used the subversive capabilities and finances of its Central Intelligence Agency to finance *coups* in Latin America and occasionally in the Middle East, with its greatest failure undoubtedly being the Bay of Pigs incident. In arranging *coups*, however, the supply of arms is rarely important as the armed force units which carry them out already have weapons at their disposal.[1] On the other hand, arms are important to groups practising guerrilla warfare. The USSR and, to a lesser extent China, have given considerable support in the form of arms to revolutionary movements throughout the Third World which use guerrilla strategies. Such movements, however, can also acquire weaponry in the early stages of their activities by seizing them from the forces which they oppose.

For the USSR and China, the supply of weapons to revolutionary movements is a cheap and risk-free way of furthering their ideological ends. The weapons needed are light and therefore inexpensive, except in special cases such as that of the Vietnam War, and there is minimal danger of a confrontation arising with the US. However, the export of arms must be seen as a means of weakening pro-Western régimes rather than as a method of overthrowing them. Of Soviet-backed revolutionary movements in the Third World, only those in Vietnam, China and Cuba can be said to have been at all successful in seizing power in an independent state. The others have proved simply difficult to defeat and so have been a constant distraction for governments in power.

These are the ways in which military training aid and arms supply have been used by the great Powers to build up effective military forces in the Third World after the use of their own forces became costly and inefficient. This analysis has sought to differentiate between the different causes of and drives behind arms transfers and training aid, with distinctions being drawn between suppliers' searches for influence and profit, recipients' wishes for prestige, as well as the different military capabilities required. Although examples were provided to illustrate most points, it should be emphasized that most decisions about the provision of military strength to the Third World are determined by a mixture of factors. Hence France agreed to sell 110 Mirage V aircraft to Libya in 1970 because there were financial rewards (the sale was worth $145 million), prospects of

---

[1] The US-sponsored *coup* in Guatemala was exceptional in that armed Guatemalan rebels invaded and overthrew the Arbenz régime.

164

better relations with the Arab states as a whole, and little apparent chance that the balance of power between Israel and the Arabs, which strongly favoured Israel, would be disturbed. Libya bought the arms because it was hoped they would prove of military significance, because they would bring prestige to the Qaddafi government and because France was politically more acceptable than other potential suppliers. The USSR had an atheistic, anti-Muslim government, the US supported Israel and Britain was in dispute with Libya over arms contracts signed with the Idris régime which preceded Qaddafi's.

The determinants of arms transfers, then, are extremely complex. But complexity should not disguise the basic points introduced earlier; that the great Powers have interests in the Third World which face military threats and therefore require the threat or use of force for their protection. For the great Powers to use their own forces to provide this protection is no longer practicable and therefore they have turned increasingly to building up forces in the Third World which can and do have interests and goals compatible with those of their military patrons.

7 Internal Restraints on the Use of Force

Internal restraints on the state's use of force form a topic that requires far more space for a full analysis than the present chapter allows. An offspring of 'domestic sources of foreign policy', it nonetheless encompasses almost as large a number of variables as its parent. In this context, the word 'restraints' implies a set of factors which work in orderly ways to inhibit a state's use of force. But in reality, they are a varied collection of factors which may or may not act as restraints depending on the circumstances of the particular situation. What follows, therefore, is a general discussion of these factors in the light of four questions: What kinds of factors are there which might act as restraints? How do these factors work? How effective are they? Is their operation predictable? The discussion will particularly emphasize the contemporary role of the public as a restraint on the state's use of force.

How restraints work

The state's use of force varies over two dimensions: the frequency of use, and the intensity of application. This duality complicates the concept of a restraint because a factor which restrains use in one dimension may encourage it in the other. For example, the nuclear balance of terror is sometimes credited with ending the intermittent use of force among the major Powers, but only at the risk of enormously increased intensity of use should such a conflict occur. So long as no such conflict occurs, the nuclear balance is a restraint, but if nuclear war broke out, the nuclear balance, and the careful preparations behind it, would appear as the diametric opposite of a restraint. Ideally, a restraint should work to diminish both frequency and intensity, or at least to diminish one without increasing the other. Since it is exceptionally difficult to balance frequency with intensity, factors which inhibit one and encourage the other are questionable as restraints.

Restraints can be classified according to the way in which they are produced as either *direct* or *indirect*. Direct restraints influence decision-makers against using force either by restricting their legal right to do so, or by reducing or setting limits on the military capability at their disposal for use abroad. A technical inability to produce nuclear weapons or a legal undertaking not to do so would both be direct restraints. Indirect restraints influence decision-makers against using force by more subtle methods than an immediate restriction of legal rights or military capabilities. A personal moral conviction on the part of the decision-maker that force was a bad method, or a similar conviction widely held among the population, would be typical examples. Both types are important, but direct restraints are by their nature visible in operation, whereas indirect restraints tend to be complicated, long-term and obscure in operation.

In addition, restraints can be categorized according to the way they take effect as either *long-term* or *short-term*. Long-term restraints are those that work over time to reduce a state's use of force. They may not operate visibly in terms of a particular use of force, but would show up in an analysis of the state's use of force over a period of many years. An example of this might be a slowly developing change in political structure which worked to make the use of force more difficult by requiring a broader base of political support for it. Short-term restraints are those that have a relatively immediate impact and can usually be traced as a factor influencing a particular use of force. A great outcry of public opinion accompanied by strikes and demonstrations against a specific use of force would be an example. Short-term restraints are invariably more visible in action than long-term ones.

Restraints can be further categorized according to the way in which they inhibit the use of force as *anticipatory* or *reactive*. Anticipatory restraints are those which operate before a use of force occurs. They influence decision-makers to reduce their capability for using force, or not to initiate a use of force, or to use less rather than greater intensity of force. Reactive restraints come into operation only after a use of force is underway. They influence decision-makers to stop a use of force, or to reduce its intensity or duration, or not to implement a planned increase in intensity or duration. Unfortunately, the important concept of anticipatory restraint is exceptionally difficult to test. Decision-makers constantly have many options which they do not use simply because they are not relevant to the situations in hand. For example, one could say that Tanzania is restrained from launching a nuclear attack on China. The restraints would include lack of capability, adverse public opinion, fear of retaliation, moral qualms and so forth. Yet even if Tanzania were free from all these restraints it is still highly unlikely that she would want to attack China. Some anticipatory restraints can be uncovered by careful historical research into decision-making, and others are made clear by the declarations of movements working to achieve a restraint, but other than these sources the full extent of anticipatory restraints on the state's use of force remains unclear.

Restraints can also, of course, be classified according to source as *internal* or *external* to the state. In this chapter we shall be dealing only with internal restraints, but it is impossible to ignore completely the many links and interactions between internal and external factors. Any restraint on a state's use of force that actually occurs is invariably the result of both internal and external factors. In addition, external factors frequently disrupt the work of internal ones. For example, if a wealthy empire unilaterally disarmed itself in response to internal economic, political and moral factors, and renounced the use of aggressive force in its international relations, it might find itself under attack from armed Powers desirous of its wealth or anxious to supersede its influence. If it then fought to defend itself, it would be using force directly for external reasons, but indirectly because of the initial effect of its internal restraints. Its moral position might be strong, but nonetheless it would still be using force, and in part because of what were initially seen as restraints on its use of force. In this sense, it is important to look at any operative restraint from a broad and long-term viewpoint in order to avoid accepting a distorted analysis of a factor's true value in minimizing a state's use of force.

Britain's mobilization during the Second World War bears witness that in complex and highly integrated modern states, almost every thread in the social, economic and political fabric is relevant to the use of force. The next sections will briefly survey the major characteristics of the state in relation to the use of force, and look at some of the theories, many highly partisan, about these relationships.

Governmental factors

One of the most fruitful sources of theories is the idea that a state's form of government will influence its propensity to use force. Quincy Wright, for example, argues that:

Absolutistic states with geographically and functionally central-ized governments under autocratic leadership are likely to be most belligerent, whereas constitutional states with geographi-cally and functionally federalized governments under demo-cratic leadership are likely to be most peaceful.[1]

During the 1920s and 1930s, the argument was frequently voiced that liberal democracy was the most non-violent form of govern-ment, and Socialists and Communists sometimes make the same claim for their form of government. Such claims are usually qualified by the statement: 'If all governments were (democratic/Socialist/Communist) there would be no more war.' Conversely, democratic, Socialist and Communist proponents often assert that Fascist, military and autocratic governments are inherently warlike, while also accusing each other's form of government of being the major cause of the world's violence.

For the most part these arguments involve factors other than strictly the form of government. Communists and Socialists blame the social inequalities and rapacious economic competitiveness of capitalist systems for the prevalence of force, and look to their own systems as the cure for these problems. Supporters of liberal demo-cracy point to the centralized decision-making, suppressed public opinion and messianic ideology of Socialist and Communist systems as likely sources of the use of force and rely upon the social and political checks and balances of their own systems to prevent aggressive use of force. But the number of factors to be considered in such judgements is enormous and defies these oversimplified viewpoints. In general, the form of government is far too closely linked with other factors to be readily identified alone as either a restraint on or an encouragement to a state's use of force. Some forms of government, and some aspects of forms, appear to relate clearly to the use of force. It seems safe to say, for example, that Fascist and tribal governments that openly glorify war and the warrior cult will encourage the use of force. Quincy Wright, however, could not find statistical evidence to demonstrate that democracies were involved in war less often than autocracies.[2]

More specifically, certain legal and constitutional aspects of government, some explicit and some general, stand clearly as direct restraints on the state's use of force. Explicit legal and constitutional

[1] Quincy Wright, *A Study of War*, University of Chicago Press, Chicago, 1964 (abridged), pp. 161–2.
[2] Ibid., pp. 161–2.

factors usually take the form of written declarations in treaties, agreements or constitutions. Most of them are international in scope and so fall outside the bounds of the present chapter. One in particular, however, deserves mention here, and that is the famous Article 9 of the Japanese constitution which renounces Japan's rights to wage war and to maintain military forces. The United States imposed this article on Japan in 1947, but the Japanese have never renounced it, though renunciation would only require a two-thirds majority in their Diet. Their continued acceptance of the article, despite the removal of outside compulsion, makes Article 9 an essentially internal restraint. Although it has been weakened by a reinterpretation which allows self-defence forces, it still dominates the country's military policy. Japan's military spending is relatively small compared to that of other countries, and her armed forces are equipped wholly with defence-oriented weapons. Nonetheless, Japan's defence budget increased over threefold between 1960 and 1970, which indicates an increasing trend away from strict observance of Article 9.

The disarmament accepted by Germany following both World Wars in some ways resembles Japan's experience. For Germany, however, continued outside pressure played a much larger role. Both the German and the Japanese examples were dependent on foreign intervention, and neither case produced a stable or permanent situation. No major Power has yet spontaneously written a policy of unilateral disarmament into its own constitution or law, but precedents do exist. A Socialist government in Denmark approved and carried out almost total unilateral disarmament in 1926. It maintained this condition throughout the 1930s, and did not militarily resist the German invasion of 1940. The limited evidence on explicit legal and constitutional factors indicates that they act as strong, if unstable, direct anticipatory restraints. It seems unlikely that they would function as relative restraints.

General, legal and constitutional factors can be found in the formal political structures of some states where provision has been made for one part of the government to check or veto the actions of another part. Probably the clearest illustration is the division of powers between the Congress and the Executive in the United States. While the President holds most of the powers of initiative and is the commander-in-chief of the armed forces, the Congress retains control of the budget and of the power to declare war. This system, as demonstrated by the struggle over the war in Vietnam, can restrain the President's use of force. On 30 June 1970, the Senate passed the Cooper–Church amendment which barred further American military operations in Cambodia unless they had Congressional approval, and late in 1972 a strong movement in Congress expressed determination to cut off funds for the war. Senator Fulbright openly threatened the President with legislation to cut off funds unless the war was ended by 20 January 1973.[1] Congress's control over the power to declare war no longer carries much weight, but the power to withhold funds is decisive. In practice, however, it is a slow and cumbersome means of restraint. It requires that the President's use of force be extremely unpopular, and it leaves the enormous immediate power of the American military under his control. Although it is an impressive restraint in theory, in reality it operates only under very unusual circumstances.

Structural restraints in parliamentary systems like Britain's are even weaker than those in the American system. So long as the party in power has a majority in the House of Commons the Prime Minister has less to fear than his American counterpart. As shown by the Suez crisis of 1956, party loyalty tends to remain strong even when there is considerable disaffection among MPs over the use of force.[2] In a conflict, the Prime Minister's (or the President's) power to rally the nation to his cause is strong enough to override the danger of a party revolt in all but the most extreme cases. Only in the case of a minority or coalition government is the House of Commons likely to act as a direct restraint on the use of force. General, legal and constitutional factors, then, can act as both direct anticipatory and reactive restraints. But they are inefficient in the reactive role and probably much more influential in the anticipatory one.

Economic factors

Related to form of government is form of economy. Here Quincy Wright argues that states based on animal pasturage are more warlike than those based on agriculture, which in turn are more warlike than those based on commerce and industry.[3] But Wright's distinctions apply only to frequency of use of force, not to intensity, and in the economic realm intensity seems to be the more important factor. This is especially true of the last two centuries in which commercial

---

[1] *The Times*, 4 January 1973.
[2] L. D. Epstein, *British Politics in the Suez Crisis*, Pall Mall Press, London, 1964, p. 94.
[3] Q. Wright, op. cit., p. 165.

and industrial states have totally dominated the world. In this context, hairsplitting between Marxists and capitalists over which system indulges in force more frequently is unimportant compared with the relation between the economy and the intensity of force used or available for use.

The important factors in this regard are the size and technological sophistication of an economy. Large, highly sophisticated economies are capable of supporting an enormous range of options for using force that are unavailable to states with smaller, less sophisticated ones. The Soviet Union, for example, has far more options for force use in type, intensity and frequency than does Britain, because its economy is much larger, even if slightly less sophisticated than Britain's. The Vietnam War, and before that the many wars between European states and African and Asian peoples, provide dramatic illustrations of the disparity between different levels and sizes of economy in their ability to use force. Indeed, in terms of intensity the Vietnam War would outweigh hundreds of individual wars fought at the sword-and-spear level. At the levels of intensity now possible between large, advanced economies, any major use of force between them is unacceptable. In this sense, small and/or unsophisticated economies are a restraint on the state's use of force. But this statement must be qualified by the nagging suspicion that lower intensities are related to higher frequencies.

Certain other economic factors as well as form, size and technological sophistication might also influence the state's use of force. Access to resources is perhaps traditionally the most important of these. Economies that are self-sufficient in resources are less likely to generate pressures for expansion or colonialization than those which are deprived of resources. In this century, Japan up until 1945 is the most notable example of a resource-deprived economy generating frequent, high-intensity use of force. Since sophisticated economies require much larger quantities and many more types of resources than unsophisticated ones, they are more likely to use force for this reason. Other economic factors such as rate and stage of growth, dependency on trade, maintainance of colonies, level of external control and ownership, and type of production capability, might also be related to the state's use of force.

Military factors

Military factors are closely linked to economic ones, and military

172

capability, by definition, constitutes a fundamental direct restraint on a state's use of force. For example, an island state having only an army could not use force in its international relations unless it were invaded. In order to use force a state must control some form of military capability, and the specific form which this capability takes determines the options available to it in using force. All states can be placed on a spectrum which runs from 'no military capability to affect any other state' to 'the capability to destroy totally and rapidly all other states'. Their placing would depend on a formula which took into account their existing military capability in relation to their geographical location. The final list would also rate states according to their number of available options for using force. Britain would have fewer options than the US, Australia would have fewer than Britain, and Upper Volta fewer than Australia. The formula becomes much more complicated if potential as well as existing military capability is included. Almost all states have the capacity to increase enormously their existing military capability. Just how much and how quickly they can do this depends, among other things, on their size of population, natural resources, trained reserves, industrial capacity, political control, technological skill, internal communication and pre-planning for mobilization. For example, several states including Canada, Japan, West Germany, India, Israel, and Sweden have what is called the 'nuclear option' – that is, they have the resources and the skill to produce nuclear weapons at short notice but have so far decided not to. In addition, some states such as Israel are already mobilized to a considerable percentage of their total capability, whereas others, such as Japan, are scarcely mobilized at all. Military capability is the most important direct restraint on the state's ability to use force and can be effective as either an anticipatory or a reactive restraint. Its relationship to the frequency of use of force is obscure, with strong theoretical arguments for both minimum and maximum maintained capability as the best means of avoiding war. But its relationship to intensity is much clearer, and limits on capability are quite evidently restraints on possible intensity.

Another factor sometimes credited with affecting a state's propensity to use force is the way in which its armed services are organized. Long-term professional armies were traditionally thought to offer fewer restraints to use than short-term conscript armies recruited from the general population. Similarly, national militias, such as the one attached to the Chinese People's Liberation Army, enjoyed a long vogue as theoretically the best means of providing for national defence without a high risk of aggressive use of force by the government. Vestiges of this idea can still be seen in such forces as America's National Guard and Britain's Territorials. But the practicality of this approach to restraining the state's use of force depends heavily upon the prevailing military technology. In situations requiring a defence primarily on the ground against invading armies, militia or conscript armies are feasible. But if advanced military technology is the norm, such armies could not prevent unacceptable damage to the nation, and would be ill suited to operate the necessary military technology. They would also only suit régimes that had the strong general support of the population.

Social factors

'Social factors' is a catch-all category for the innumerable other characteristics of the state that might influence its use of force. Population characteristics, for example, are frequently associated with the state's use of force. Size has obvious links with military capability, but is not by itself clearly linked with frequency of use. Its significance varies according to other factors such as prevailing military technology, population density, and type of economy. Racial and cultural diversity might make use of force less likely if social cohesion were poor, or more likely if racial and cultural boundaries crossed state ones. Age structure might affect the state's inclination to use force according to whether young or old people were the majority. Even such relatively obscure factors as education, health, and the urban/rural living patterns of the population can be linked into the complex web of factors which may or may not influence the state's use of force.

Social factors such as the nature of élites and the prevailing social norms appear more directly related to the use of force. For example, ruling élites with a military heritage such as the European and Japanese aristocracies might be more likely to resort to force than élites based on trade and commerce. Indeed, the existence of *any* élite might imply a concentration of power that enables the use of force to take place. Evidence for this type of conjecture is extremely uncertain however, and again appears to depend on the cumulative effect of many interacting factors. Likewise, prevailing social norms can prove misleadingly simple. A truly pacifist society would be an impressive restraint on the state's use of force, but this has never existed. Dominant ideologies like Christianity have done little to restrain the use of force and have sometimes done much to encourage it. Communism has proved neither as internally peaceful as its supporters predicted, nor as externally aggressive as its enemies feared. Islam, once famous for its power to mobilize aggression, has been quiescent for many centuries. On a more specific level, authoritarian, father-centred family structures have been said to encourage the use of force by the state. Exhaustive psychological studies of leaders have tried to reconstruct the personal and social events which led them to initiate or not initiate a use of force. These necessarily link up with studies of role, and other governmental, economic, social and military factors.

Other social factors also demonstrate this interconnectedness in their function as restraints. Geography, for example, serves primarily to amplify or diminish the importance of other factors. Climate affects the national character and the type of economy. Territorial area affects population density and military thinking, while territorial characteristics influence availability of resources and vulnerability to land attack. Territorial location bears on relative cultural, political and military power, and has much to do with climate. Quincy Wright offers some evidence that the aggressiveness of a culture varies according to its age (the time since the last revolution),[1] and this may also be true of certain historical experiences like the total defeat in war suffered by Japan and Germany in 1945. Historical experience over a longer term may shape some cultures to be less belligerent than others. Belligerency may also be influenced by the degree of cultural, economic or political penetration of one state by another, and by the degree of social stability within the state.

Social instability might discourage the state's use of force in its international relations by causing it to turn its attentions inward or by weakening its military capability. Or it could encourage the use of force by prompting intervention from outside or by causing the leadership to create an external crisis in order to restore internal unity. Social stability and the role of the public as a restraint on the state's use of force will be explored in more detail below.

The public as a restraint

Compared with the characteristics of the state discussed above, the public frequently plays a highly visible and short-term role as a

[1] Ibid., pp. 163–4.

factor restraining the state's use of force. If the public are to be a restraint on a state's use of force, then they must either influence decision-makers against using force or undertake actions which actually limit the state's military capability. The public can influence a decision-maker in various ways. They can threaten or entice him with many kinds of action, including loss or renewal of his office through voting or revolution, praise and support for his actions, or criticism of and opposition to them. They can appeal to his conscience or morality as their representative; they can appeal to his intellect by presenting powerful ideas or arguments. Public opinion, or course, has always existed among populations, but only in the last few decades has it had general access to information on government actions through the news media, and day-to-day expressions of itself through regular polls. Even with these aids, however, public opinion is usually self-cancelling or not interested. To be effective, it must be united rather than diffuse, and actively rather than passively expressed. Achieving these conditions requires either organizations dedicated to mobilizing the public on particular issues or an issue of sufficient weight to cause spontaneous mobilization.

An organization concerned with mobilizing public opinion as a restraint on the state's use of force is faced with a formidable task. The decision-makers it must influence are usually few in number, high in status of office and consequently difficult to influence, and surrounded by the secrecy associated with national security. These decision-makers will invariably command far more expertise and information than is available to the organization, and will, by virtue of their status and resources, exercise much greater influence over public opinion. Unlike many other types of pressure groups, one which campaigns against force represents more a body of opinion and less an identifiable constituency whose interests will be adversely affected by a particular policy. Because of this, the interest of, for example, those campaigning for nuclear disarmament appears less legitimate to decision-makers than the interest of farmers concerned about agricultural tariffs.[1] On top of these difficulties, the organization must also face the huge task of informing, and gaining support from the public. It must usually operate with strictly limited resources, and must overcome public apathy and opposition pressure groups. Above all, it must convince people that they have a personal vested

[1] See L. W. Milbrath, 'Interest Groups and Foreign Policy', J. N. Rosenau (ed.), *Domestic Sources of Foreign Policy*, Macmillan, New York, 1967.

interest in controlling something as remote and yet as important as their government's use of force.

Public opinion can be mobilized against a state's use of force by an issue as well as by an organization. To take an unlikely example, if in 1962 the British government had sent a one-week ultimatum to France threatening to bomb Paris unless President de Gaulle changed his mind over enlarging the EEC, then there would in all probability have been an immediate and enormous mobilization of outraged public opinion in Britain. Huge demonstrations would have flooded the streets and very likely the trade unions and parts of the civil service and military would have threatened a general strike. A major political and constitutional crisis would have flared up, resulting in the fall of the responsible leaders within a matter of days, and the retraction of the ultimatum. In this scenario, public opinion would have led quickly to public and political action and resulted in a restraint on the state's use of force.

In general, governments do not flout their social and common-sense norms in the way described above. They try to keep public opinion on their side by justifying a use of force in terms of prevailing social norms. For example, the British government had little difficulty in persuading the vast majority of its people of the necessity to fight Nazi Germany in September 1939. Germany was well established as the aggressor, and the public largely favoured anti-Fascist views. Occasionally, however, governments alienate public opinion either by misjudging the social norm or by feeling strong enough to override it. More frequently, they find public opinion rising against them because a use of force is not turning out successfully or is expanding out of proportion to its original purpose. In all of these cases public opinion is much more likely to oppose a use of force which is remote from the immediate security of the home state.

Public opposition to the state's use of force takes a great variety of forms, which can be represented on a scale of intensity (see p. 178). The higher up the scale from (1) to (6) the public's opposition is, the more seriously the decision-maker should consider it. In this sense, a decision-maker can easily ignore public opinion on levels (1) to (3) if he is confident that it will stay on those levels. But to the extent that public opinion on levels (2) and (3) seems likely to foreshadow action on levels (4) to (6) the more difficult it becomes for him to ignore it. However, even a large-scale action on level (5) or (6) might not restrain an exceptionally strong and stubborn decision-maker from using force. Conversely, a decision-maker facing an imminent election might respond to a lower-level expression of public opinion than he otherwise would. Public opinion is most influential just before elections, but the changes made in response to it are often superficial and short lived. Many other factors, both internal and external, can influence the formation and effectiveness of public opinion/action, and consequently its operation is difficult to predict. One must also remember that public opposition to the use of force is seldom unanimous, and almost invariably accompanied by counter-vailing expressions of public support for the use, which may even be larger than the opposition. But the role of the public is usually visible and explicit, and one can therefore often analyse its effective-ness in particular cases. In the sections that follow, we will briefly examine public opposition to the state's use of force at each of the six levels on the scale of intensity presented below.

Level	Characteristics
(1) Negligible public opinion	– public opinion is uninformed, uninterested or unexpressed.
(2) Passive public opinion	– opinion polls, news media and a growing related literature express disapproval.
(3) Active public opinion	– formation and growth of interest and pressure groups accompanied by demonstrations, petitions, write-ins, active lobbying, increased publicity, and large amounts of relevant literature.
(4) Credible threats of public action	– groups and individuals pledge themselves to refuse conscription or war service, and *threaten* to withhold taxes, to initiate and support anti-war industrial action, to undertake action to disrupt directly military activities, and to undertake legal or illegal methods of changing the government.
(5) Moderate public action	– fulfilment of any or all threats made under (4) except illegal attempts to change the government.
(6) Extreme public action	– large-scale internal unrest varying from widespread rioting and disobedience to authority, to open revolution against the government.

Negligible and passive public opinion

Negligible public opinion is increasingly uncommon as a total response to the state's use of force. Rather, it tends to be the point from which opinion, both favourable and unfavourable, grows. It is still the norm, of course, in states where the public remain uninformed either because of lack of news media or because of strict control over what news is disseminated, or where fear of openly opposing government policy causes people to remain silent. It occurs even in more open and generally well-informed societies if the government successfully undertakes a small, covert or nearly covert use of force, as for example, the US involvement in Indochina in the late 1950s. But it no longer appears possible for government to use force openly without accounting for adverse public opinion.

Passive public opinion likewise tends to be a transitional step to higher levels. It does still occur, however, in the form of speculative journalistic and academic writings and certain types of opinion poll. The latter would be of the type that during the 1950s asked American citizens whether or not they favoured their government fully backing an invasion of mainland China led by Chiang Kai-shek. A substantial majority of opinion obtained in this way might influence a government that was trying to increase its popular support. But if opinion polls were the only indicator of public feeling on the issue, the government could safely assume that public interest (as opposed to opinion) was low. Opinion polls become more powerful when they are supported by actions indicating a high degree of public interest, or when they immediately precede an election. They work indirectly as either anticipatory or reactive restraints. They may also work against other more active types of public opposition to the use of force by revealing that a majority of the public is opposed or indifferent to the campaign of an active minority.

Active public opinion

Active public opinion is the most common level of public opposition to the state's use of force. We will look at two campaigns centred upon organizations whose goals were to achieve anticipatory restraints, and two issue-motivated campaigns directed towards achieving reactive restraints. One of the most obvious organizations to take the anticipatory role is an opposition party within the political structure. Although political parties do play this role, their

179

part is more appropriately considered in terms of the form of government. The most characteristic organizations found performing this function are those that make up the peace movement.

Perhaps the largest public-opinion-based peace organization ever created was the League of Nations Union (LNU) in Britain. It was politically non-partisan and between 1919 and 1939 attracted a million people into its ranks and spent well over half-a-million pounds. It had an impressive London headquarters, built up a national network of over 3,000 branches, and gathered 3,600 other organizations under its umbrella as corporate members. Every Prime Minister of the period except one (Ramsay MacDonald) accepted its Honorary Presidency, and social notables of all types gave it their support.

The LNU had the initial advantage of strong anti-war feelings among the public to work with. Since the First World War had been effectively promoted as the 'war to end war', and the League had been created to fulfil that promise, much of the public was favourably disposed towards it from the start. Partly because of this public attitude, all three political parties officially declared their support for the League. Superficially, the situation appeared ideal for the LNU, but in practice this was not the case. Although the Conservative Party supported the League verbally, its leaders were unenthusiastic about sacrificing British sovereignty to it and did little to encourage its growth and development. Since the Conservative Party dominated government for all but three of the years between 1922 and 1939, the LNU had to wield its influence against the background of an essentially unsympathetic set of decision-makers.

Among the many issues with which the LNU concerned itself, armaments and collective security ranked highest in importance. During the 1920s, disarmament was its main concern. It continually pressed for the fulfilment of the promises to negotiate a general disarmament plan which the Allies had made to Germany in 1919, but Conservative governments did not push the cause and it progressed with agonizing slowness. Conservative governments actually undertook a considerable amount of unilateral disarmament in the 1920s, but this was to keep down public spending and not an act of principle. It was also not in line with the LNU's desire for international disarmament by agreement. So long as an unsympathetic party held power, the LNU with all its supporters was utterly unable to influence the government to abandon its implements of force.

The advent of the minority Labour government in 1929 brought a brief respite to the LNU. Labour was sympathetic in its own right to most of the LNU's objectives and therefore did not need to be pressured. In its two years in office Labour concluded a multilateral naval arms agreement, and speeded up the preparations for the world disarmament conference. The LNU, along with the many other peace organizations of the time, embarked on a massive campaign in support of the world disarmament conference which was set to begin in 1932.

But by the time the conference met, Britain once again had a Conservative-dominated government unsympathetic to disarmament. The LNU, the rest of the peace movement, and many Labour, Co-operative, women's and religious organizations called for a bold British lead at the conference to achieve European disarmament down to the same level as Germany. Thousands of public meetings passed pro-conference resolutions, and well over two million people signed a petition supporting disarmament and the conference. But despite the unity of the peace movement's campaign and the enormous outpouring of public support for the conference, the government did not give a strong lead, and the conference withered away amidst technical complications and Franco-German rivalries. Left opinion strongly criticized the government's role in the conference, and even the LNU publicly stated that:

> Looked at in any aspect, the harvest of the first six months of the conference must be regarded as profoundly disappointing, and it is impossible to avoid the conclusion that the British government has done a great deal to make it so.[1]

With the failure of the disarmament campaign and the rise of threats to international security, the LNU sought a new way to refocus public opinion on the government. The Union's foremost aim now was that the government should organize international security through the League rather than by rearming for national self-defence. In order to bring public opinion to bear on the government, the LNU organized a coalition of thirty-eight national organizations committed to conducting a nation-wide 'Peace Ballot', or National Declaration. The idea of the Ballot was to take a national vote on questions relating to the League of Nations and armaments in the hope that a large-scale response would influence the government to follow the suggested policy.

An army of over 500,000 people took the Ballot door to door, the

[1] *Headway*, August 1932, LNU, London, p. 151.

size of this figure alone indicating the strength of feeling among the British public on the issues involved. By June 1935 their efforts had resulted in a vote far exceeding the organizers' expectations – over 11,500,000 people had voted in possibly the largest private referendum ever held. The respondents voted 96 per cent in favour of Britain remaining in the League, 91 per cent in favour of international disarmament, 83 per cent in favour of international abolition of military aircraft, 90 per cent in favour of international prohibition of private enterprise in the armaments industry, 87 per cent in favour of non-military international action against an aggressor state, and 59 per cent in favour of (20 per cent opposed to) international military action against an aggressor state.[1]

The government could hardly ignore such an enormous weight of opinion, and responded to it by emphasizing collective security and the League in its November 1935 election campaign. Yet the ballot boxes had scarcely been put away after a return of the government when the Hoare–Laval deal divulged its insincerity over collective security. The storm of public criticism that resulted was an impressive testimony of the impact of the Peace Ballot. But the flurry soon died, and in June 1936 the government ended its half-hearted sanctions against Italy, thereby signalling the death-knell of the League. So, despite the extraordinary achievement of the Peace Ballot in registering public opinion, the LNU's campaign to influence the government had failed. The Ballot's impact on the government was superficial and short lived, and the public's attention soon moved on to new events like the Spanish Civil War and the Abdication crisis in Britain. The LNU itself lost much of its momentum with the decline of the League. It suffered dwindling membership and mounted no further great campaigns.

The LNU's failure to achieve any of its major restraining goals stands as a significant example for this type of organization. Despite its large and prestigious membership, its efficient and relatively well-financed organization, its wide support among the public and its ability to mobilize that support visibly, the LNU could not influence the government to abandon either its right to, or its means of using, force. So long as the Conservative Party held power, the LNU was helpless, and when the Labour Party held power, it was superfluous.

One of the conclusions that can be drawn from the LNU's experience is that if organizations of this type want to see their

[1] Dame Adelaide Livingstone, *The Peace Ballot: The Official History*, Gollancz, London, 1935, p. 10.

programmes fulfilled, they should concentrate on converting a political party to their cause and then getting it elected. This was the approach envisaged by the founders of the Campaign for Nuclear Disarmament (CND) in 1958. CND decided to convert the Labour Party to unilateral nuclear disarmament, and paid no attention at all to the Conservative Party which, so far as unilateralism was concerned, was clearly a lost cause. The Labour Left wing was already largely sympathetic to unilateralism, so CND concentrated on increasing pressure for banning the bomb by making it a public issue. It organized public meetings, marches and demonstrations, turned out mountains of literature, and in every possible way dramatized the presence of the bomb and its danger to the British people. By 1960 the Campaign had successfully made unilateralism a popular issue, and in that year the Labour Party annual conference, in a victory for the Left wing, adopted it as Party policy. CND was jubilant. It had captured its political party and appeared only to need to get it elected to achieve its objective.

The victory was short lived, however, for in the following year the Labour Party annual conference reversed its decision. The fact that this reversal came in spite of increased public support for CND lends credence to the theory that Labour's brief romance with unilateralism had more to do with internal party politics than with a sincere response to the issue or to public opinion. That unilateralists were able to capture the Party at all probably reflected the unstable conditions caused by a decade out of office and the loss of three consecutive national elections.[1] The apparent ease and speed with which CND converted the Labour Party to unilateralism cannot therefore be taken as a typical example of a public pressure group working to influence a political party.

CND reached its peak in the year of its failure. In 1961 the Campaign's coffers bulged with £30,000, and its organizers could bring an army of 150,000 marchers into London. Opinion polls showed that 31 per cent of the population supported CND while 57 per cent supported banning the bomb.[2] In the same year its offspring, ally and rival, the Committee of 100, could mobilize 12,000 people to demonstrate against the bomb in Trafalgar Square despite the considerable risk of arrest and prosecution. But with the loss of

[1] Unilateralism was bound up in a struggle between Left and Right wings for control of the Labour Party. See Frank Parkin, *Middle Class Radicalism*, Manchester U.P., 1968.

[2] G. Thayer, *The British Political Fringe*, Blond, London, 1965, p. 167.

official Labour Party support and the achievement of bigness, CND began to decline. Increasing internal disunity sapped its strength, and the Test Ban Treaty of 1963 weakened its support by mollifying public fears. By the mid sixties most of the original leaders and marchers had deserted it.

CND and the LNU were the largest public-opinion-based organizations of their times. They were markedly different in almost every way, and yet the results of their efforts were strikingly similar. Despite their size, their ability to mobilize public opinion and their different tactical approaches, neither organization succeeded in convincing the state to abandon either any of its capabilities for using force or any of its rights to do so. Both of them accomplished admirable work in rousing and educating public opinion but as the best examples of their type they do not inspire much hope for the public-opinion-oriented peace movement as an indirect anticipatory restraint on the state's use of force.

There are many good contemporary examples of active public opinion aroused by a particular case of the state's use of force. These include the turmoil in France over the Algerian War; the debate in Britain over whether force should be used to prevent Rhodesia from unilaterally declaring independence; the reactions in the United States to the Bay of Pigs invasion, the US intervention in the Dominican Republic and the war in Vietnam; and the outcry in Britain over the Suez invasion of 1956. All of these cases illuminate interesting and significant points but space permits a glance at only two of them here.

Britain's participation in the attack on Egypt in October 1956 provides an example of a government successfully ignoring public opinion. Before the attack, public opinion polls showed that a significant plurality of the British people did not favour using force against Egypt. This plurality was maintained during the attack 1–2 (November) when 37 per cent thought that the government was right to take military action and 44 per cent thought that it was wrong. The Labour movement mounted a massive 'Law not War' campaign against Britain's action. Meetings and demonstrations were held all over the country, including a rally of 30,000 people in Trafalgar Square, which resulted in a crowd of 10,000 marching off to protest outside 10 Downing Street. But Labour specifically excluded the threat of a general strike from this campaign and so did not really challenge the government. Public opinion split along such heavily partisan lines that the government did not feel seriously threatened either from within its ranks or among its supporters. Only eight Conservative MPs abstained on the vote in the House and this number did not jeopardize the government's majority.[1] In this instance, then, decision-makers were not restrained by public opinion, by constitutional action or by military inadequacy. The norms they transgressed were primarily those of their political opponents and they were not threatened by public action. One therefore has to look for other restraints to explain fully the failure of the Suez intervention.

The longest running contemporary example of this type of public opinion was the movement in the United States against the war in Vietnam. Public opposition only became seriously aroused when President Johnson committed large numbers of American ground troops to the war in the summer of 1965. That event caused a merging of peace and civil rights organizations, which produced the nation-wide teach-ins, sit-ins, draft card burnings, public suicides by fire, and other protests of that year. The leaders of these demonstrations had no illusions as to their influence. In a telegram to Ho Chi Minh the Committee for a Sane Nuclear Policy urged Hanoi to respond to negotiation offers and bluntly stated: 'Demonstrations will continue but will not lead to US pullout.'[2] Opinion polls showed public support for the war declining steadily, and in 1967 opposition coalesced around Eugene McCarthy's primary campaign against President Johnson. Johnson was exceptionally sensitive to public opinion, and so came under increasing pressure from the dropping popularity polls and the strong showing by Senator McCarthy's anti-war campaign. In March 1968 Robert Kennedy added his weight to the primary campaign so threatening a major battle for Johnson over renomination. Public support for the US intervention had dropped from 61 per cent in August 1965 to 41 per cent in March 1968, while opposition over the same period had risen from 24 per cent to 49 per cent.[3] Similarly, Johnson's popular approval for the way he was handling his job was well below 40 per cent by March 1968. Under this mounting pressure of public disapproval Johnson announced that he would not seek re-election at the end of his term. His step-down was the biggest victory won by the anti-Vietnam war movement but it did not result in an end to the war.

[1] See L. D. Epstein, op. cit., p. 142.
[2] C. L. Cooper, *The Lost Crusade*, MacGibbon & Kee, London, 1970, p. 289.
[3] These are Gallup poll results for the question: 'In view of the developments since we entered the fighting in Vietnam, do you think the US made a mistake in sending troops to fight in Vietnam?'

Public opinion mobilized once more against the war in the massive 'moratorium' campaign of November 1969; and again in the wave of demonstrations against the invasion of Cambodia in April 1970; and yet again over the intensive bombing campaign late in 1972 which preceded the agreement ending the United States's direct involvement in the fighting. The exact role of public opinion in ending America's direct use of force in Vietnam is not yet clear, and the use of force itself may not yet be ended.[1] It seems likely that adverse public opinion encouraged the government to fight in the air rather than on the ground, and by proxy wherever possible, and that it made the government more cautious about intensifying the war. But these assumptions can also be interpreted in the light of external factors such as world opinion, military strategy, and fear of clashes with the USSR or China, and other internal factors such as the form of government and prevailing social norms. What is clear, however, is that even if public opinion was the main reason for America's withdrawal (and this seems unlikely), it took so long to work that its value as an indirect reactive restraint is questionable.

The Suez and Vietnam cases alone do not provide sufficient evidence for any concrete conclusions about the effectiveness of active public opinion as an indirect reactive restraint on the state's use of force. In reactive situations, and at the active public opinion level, countervailing opinion in support of the use of force appears to be an important factor. Opposing opinion at this level looks like a contributory, but not a decisive, factor in restraining the state's use of force.

Credible threats of public action

Credible threats of public action are usually made in the hope of achieving an indirect anticipatory restraint on the state's use of force. They mark a distinct departure from exercises in public opinion because they involve a commitment to oppose the state's use of force by undermining its military capability. This commitment, which is extreme by public opinion standards, tends to restrict this form of public opposition to relatively small organized groups. If large organized groups take it up, it is a sign of social instability.

Threatening to resist conscription or to refuse participation in any national war effort is one of the more common tactics of this type of opposition. It became prominent as part of the popular reaction

[1] Written in May 1973.

against the First World War and in Britain was led by the No More War Movement (NMWM). The NMWM wanted to recruit adherents to pacifism during peacetime and so create a standing army of war resisters which it hoped would deter the government from getting involved in any war. Members signed a detailed pledge renouncing all participation in war and committing themselves to work for total disarmament, the removal of all causes of war, and the establishment of a new social order based on co-operation. In the heady atmosphere of anti-war feeling following the First World War NMWM leaders thought that:

> Ten thousand converts would signify to the government that they must step with care, while a million would mean no less than the complete abolition of war.[1]

The NMWM itself, however, never achieved even the lower of those two figures in membership. Its combination of Socialism and pacifism restricted its popular appeal so that it was never able to build the broad social base necessary for a mass movement. By 1932 it was in a serious decline, and so never had a chance to test itself against the government.

Not until the middle 1930s did a mass pacifist organization develop. This was Canon Dick Sheppard's Peace Pledge Union (PPU). The PPU's pledge – 'We renounce war and never again, directly or indirectly, will we support or sanction another' – was much less complicated than the NMWM's, and so made the PPU attractive to a much larger segment of society. Dick Sheppard published his appeal in a letter to the papers in 1934. Initially he did not intend to found a new organization but the unexpectedly large response encouraged him and by 1935 the PPU had established branches all over Britain. By 1936 over 100,000 people had signed the pledge and by the eve of the Second World War over 130,000. The PPU took its purpose as being:

> to band all those pledged individuals together and thus make them strong enough, ultimately, to prevent any government from declaring a war.[2]

But even at their peak in 1939 these numbers did not prove sufficient either to deter the government from introducing conscription (which

---

[1] *No More War*, March 1926, NMWM, London, p. 1.
[2] M. Cardew, 'What the PPU Stands For', *Peace News*, 10 July 1937, PPU, London, p. 6.

187

both Baldwin and Chamberlain had promised they would not do), or to stop it from declaring war on Germany.

The example of the British pacifist movement between the two World Wars is an appropriate one for judging the effectiveness of pacifism as a restraint on a state's use of force. The interwar period was an especially fertile time for the growth of pacifism. Public revulsion against the horror and waste of the First World War ran high. Many people felt that the state could no longer be trusted with the right to war and these turned either to pacifism or to internationalism through the League of Nations. In addition, much publicity was given to the impossibility of defence against attack from the air and it was generally thought that a new war would see the use of poison gas on population centres. It was widely held that another war would bring about the complete destruction of European civilization.

It is within this context of exceptionally strong anti-war feeling that the pacifist movement must be considered. Although pacifist organizations mustered only about 150,000 declared adherents, public opinion polls in 1938 revealed a much larger group, nearly 18 per cent of the population, who said they would resist conscription in some measure.[1] Most of these, however, changed their sympathies with the rise of anti-Fascism in the late thirties. But even accounting for this change in fortunes, the interwar pacifist movement in Britain had as ideal a public environment as it is possible to imagine such a movement ever having. Despite this, its net achievement for twenty years' work was a mere threefold increase in the number of conscientious objectors (COs) from the First World War to the Second. Its inability under favourable conditions to create a significant internal restraint on the government's use of force casts doubt on the general utility of the threat of war resistance as a means to that end.

Another common threat of public action against the state's use of force is that of anti-war strikes by organized labour. Widespread strikes in key industries would rapidly impair a state's military capability and place it in danger of social upheaval. This is consequently a powerful threat, to be neither lightly used nor lightly received.

[1] C. Madge and T. Harrisson, *Britain by Mass Observation*, Penguin, Harmondsworth, 1939, pp. 47–8. Of the 460 people questioned, 10·25 per cent said they would give only qualified support to the government and 7·5 per cent would refuse all co-operation.

After the Second International's failure to fulfil its threat of labour anti-war action in 1914, the Independent Labour Party (ILP) in Britain was one of the few organizations that kept alive the idea of the general strike as labour's weapon against capitalist wars. Its patience was vindicated in 1919–20 by the Labour movement's action against Lloyd George's intervention in Russia. The government's support for counter-revolutionary forces was a direct affront to the Labour movement which had a deep emotional commitment to the Russian revolution. In June 1919 the Labour Party's annual conference called by a two-to-one vote for direct action to end Britain's intervention. A national 'Hands off Russia' committee was formed and a 'Resist the War Committee' collected 5,000 pledges from workers not to bear arms or manufacture or transport munitions.

Confrontation came in May 1920, when London dockers prevented a ship loaded with munitions from sailing because they believed it was going to Poland. By August Soviet successes against the Poles made British intervention appear imminent and the Labour movement came out in huge demonstrations against it. A joint resolution by the Trades Union Congress, the Labour Party and the Parliamentary Labour Party executives labelled war a crime against humanity and threatened to call out the workers *en masse* to prevent it. A Council of Action was set up with trade union and Labour Party support to implement this threat. The Council sent a delegation to see Lloyd George but obtained no satisfaction at all from him. Just as a direct clash between the government and the Labour movement seemed inevitable, the Poles stemmed the Soviet advance at the battle of the Vistula. This relieved the immediate pressure of the situation, and with Labour's threat caused the government to shelve quietly its intervention plans.[1] Because of the Polish victory, it is impossible to assess the exact extent to which Labour's threat restrained the use of force, but it seems evident that it was an important factor.

The anti-intervention campaign, in conjunction with the widespread disillusionment with war, gave the Labour movement fresh impetus to support the general strike as a method of preventing war. The ILP took a strong war-resistance stand throughout the 1920s, resolving against all war and advocating the general strike and resistance to conscription as the means to preserve peace. In 1926 an

[1] C. L. Mowat, *Britain Between the Wars, 1918–1940*, Metheun, London, 1968, pp. 41–2, 56.

189

ILP resolution was passed at the Labour Party conference, calling on the workers:

> to make clear to their government that they will meet any threat of war by organizing general resistance, including refusal to bear arms, to produce armaments or to render any material assistance.[1]

War resistance remained the heart of Labour's peace policy well into the 1930s.

Although the interwar period does not provide clear-cut evidence for the power of threatened Labour action as a restraint on the state's use of force, it does give some strong indications that such threats did affect government policy. This is particularly true in regard to Conservative and Liberal government's policy towards the Soviet Union. Strong groups within these parties were openly hostile to the USSR and their hostility made Anglo–Soviet relations one of the most contentious foreign policy issues of the period. Since the Labour movement looked upon the Soviet régime as part of the Socialist fraternity, it reacted strongly, as in 1919–20, to any hint of government action against it. Labour's move away from its anti-war position in the 1930s was primarily a response to the rising menace which Fascism posed to both Socialism and the USSR. So long as the government clearly directed its rearmament towards the Axis powers, Labour was bound to support it. If, however, the government had turned against the USSR in the 1930s, there is little doubt that it would have encountered serious Labour opposition. That the Conservative-dominated governments of the 1920s and 1930s kept their enmity towards the Soviet Union on a relatively passive level was in part due to their concern over the likelihood of such opposition. To this extent, the threat of Labour action was an effective anticipatory restraint on the use of force. It would probably also be effective as a reactive restraint.

Moderate public action

Most forms of moderate public action involve personal risk or discomfort and so require considerable personal commitment. Public action at the moderate level is therefore usually limited to a small minority of the population and only becomes widespread if there is

---

[1] *No More War*, January 1927, NMWM, London, p. 10.

severe social disunity. It almost always occurs as an attempt to produce a reactive restraint on the state's use of force.

Resistance to conscription is the most common form of moderate public action. For centuries a tiny minority of individuals has refused to undertake military service on the grounds that it contravened the dictates of their consciences. But the First World War generated politically motivated and organized resistance to conscription. When conscription came to Britain in 1916 it was met by a small, resolute organization called the No Conscription Fellowship (NCF). The NCF included many religious pacifists but these were outnumbered by Socialists who based their objection to conscription on political grounds. The NCF statement of faith committed its members specifically to 'deny the right of government to say "you shall bear arms"',[1] and the organization devoted itself to helping its 16,000 members face the severities of conscientious objection. But although their struggle won greater recognition for conscientious objectors' rights, and inspired subsequent efforts to mobilize pacifists politically in peacetime, it did not noticeably affect the government's war effort and was insignificant as a direct restraint.

Conscientious objectors in the Second World War likewise failed to produce a noticeable restraint. The interwar pacifist movement did not mobilize mass resistance against conscription and war but instead simply helped its members to resist individually. In the event, just over 60,000 people (fewer than 1 per cent of those enrolled in the services) declared themselves COs. The story for both World Wars in the US was similar to that in Britain, with a smaller number of resisters producing equally negligible direct restraining effects. In addition, the 60,000 young men who left the US to avoid being conscripted for the Vietnam War did not impair their country's military ability to prosecute that war. War resistance of this kind is seldom effective as a direct restraint simply because it is usually supported only by a small minority of the population. In theory, it is a powerful restraint but in practice it could only be effective if motivated by massive social discontent and loss of faith in the government.

Moderate public actions of other kinds are less common. Like resistance to conscription, they tend to be ineffective as direct restraints if they are limited to small groups, and only gain wide support, and thus effectiveness, in conditions of severe social and political unrest. Such conditions occurred in Russia in 1904–5 when

[1] *Troublesome People*, Central Board for COs, London, 1940, pp. 5–6.

public dissatisfaction with the humiliating performance of Russian forces against the Japanese strengthened the growing movements for drastic reform of government. In 1905 unrest resulted in strikes, demonstrations and mutinies which played a major part in causing the government to end the war. Troops were hastily brought back from the Far East in order to prop up the régime and suppress the dissidents. In such situations, however, the unrest and its causes are generally far more important than the restraint on the state's use of force and the moderate public actions are merely part of much larger social movements.

Extreme public action

The same line of argument applies even more strongly to cases of extreme public action. The relevant question under conditions such as in Russia during the revolution (1917–21) is not whether extreme public action is a restraint on a state's use of force, but whether a condition of internal unrest and violence is in itself likely to cause a use of force. Does it increase the likelihood of external intervention? Does it promote the risk of violence spilling over into neighbouring states? Does it strengthen or weaken the other factors which affect the state's use of force? These are far-reaching questions which carry the discussion well beyond the limits of the present chapter. Moreover, extreme public action is so dependent on special conditions of instability that it applies only to a small minority of situations. More important here, is whether or not public opposition to the use of force in stable states is an effective restraint.

Public opposition to the state's use of force, like the other individual factors we have examined, generally produces a restraint only in conjunction with other favourable factors. In particular, it requires a relatively open society with well-developed communications in order to operate on the lower levels. At the three public-opinion levels it appeared ineffective by itself as a short-term restraint but contributed to multi-factor restraints and had subtle and less calculable possibilities in the long-term formation of social norms. At the three public-action levels it had distinct possibilities as a direct restraint but depended on social instability for effectiveness, and consequently raised a wider set of issues. The effectiveness of the lower levels appeared to be enhanced by the threat of escalation to higher levels but this threat was difficult to make credible in socially stable situations.

192

Conclusions

Returning to the questions we began with, it is clear that there are a great many internal factors which might act as restraints on the state's use of force. Indeed, almost every aspect of the state relates to the question to some degree. Likewise, it is not difficult to suggest the way in which these various factors work to produce a restraint. Where problems arise, however, are in assessing the effectiveness of restraints and in predicting their operation. Rarely does a single factor such as total lack of military capability emerge as a complete, identifiable restraint. Restraints are nearly always partial in effect, obscure in operation and the result of complex interactions among many factors both internal and external. Detailed historical studies suggest some of this complexity but as yet social science has only just begun to make progress with statistical correlation between characteristics of the state and its use of force. A few factors such as population size are readily quantifiable but many, like social stability, are not. Moreover, the tangle of unique, interreacting factors relevant to any particular case has so far defied systematic generalization. Only where the restraints are reactive, direct, short-term or highly visible can one safely assess the specific effectiveness of particular factors and attempt prediction of their operation. Where restraints are anticipatory, indirect, long-term or obscure, analysis and prediction of their specific effects are much more difficult.

8 Force and International Law

> The Law is the true embodiment
> Of everything that's excellent.
> It has no kind of fault or flaw,
> And I, my Lords, embody the Law.
>
> – The Lord Chancellor in Sir W. S. Gilbert, *Iolanthe.*

States, not unlike Gilbert's Lord Chancellor, often make their own laws. In one breath, governments extol the virtue of an international system ordered by the rule of law; in the next, national force directs and protects national interest. The smoke having cleared, the troops withdrawn, the *fait accompli* presented to the other states, these 'Lord Chancellors' can only conclude that what they do *is* law, if there be law at all. While negotiations between the Soviet Union and the United States for a treaty to ensure the mutual and balanced reduction of forces between them suggest that law can order the very instruments of force, no one has forgotten the Czechoslovakian or the Cuban crises. Moreover, no government neglects its military forces entirely even while admitting the relevance of international law.

That is not to say that the use of force is necessarily inconsistent with international law. The United Nations Charter, for example, specifies in Article 42 that the Security Council 'may take such action by air, sea or land forces as may be necessary to maintain or restore international peace and security'. In the light of the legal obligations enumerated in the Charter, few would deem to be illegal the military action of the United Nations Force in Korea in 1950–3. Some might argue that the authority of the law derives from the forces which guarantee its observance. But most would agree that the unauthorized use of force threatens the development of a strong international legal order.

Indeed, the nexus between force and international law can be viewed from different perspectives. It is possible to isolate those

194

rules governing the use of force – where force is both prohibited and permitted – and to give a descriptive account of these. Having tentatively established what the rules are, it is helpful to consider the separate role played by force in their implementation as well as the possibility of force being used by states to defy the law. It may be advantageous to identify three separate sets of questions.

The most obvious set of questions concerns the *content* of international law with respect to the use of force. The law can be studied in terms of what it says. The questions that can be asked will be practical in the sense that they look for an authoritative policy. The answers, however, are frequently contentious. What is the legal status of war and what are its rules? Is a treaty valid if it has been imposed by force? Can a state have recourse to force in self-defence? Does a state ever have a legal right to intervene with force in the affairs of another state?

A second set of questions examines the *nature* of law. This discussion is recognizable by its terms: 'concept', 'idea', 'pure theory'; and these questions will all be looking for principles. By abstracting law in this way, we may ask about the possible place of force in the notion of law. Must law be backed by force or sanctions? Is it force that makes law binding? Can legal rules by their relationship to force be distinguished from other norms, such as moral rules? With respect to the above questions, are the situations of international law and municipal law very different?

The third set of questions focuses on the political context in which international law must *function*. The emphasis is more on how the law works than on what the law is. These questions are more sociological: they concentrate on the legal order rather than on the laws themselves but they are nonetheless real in explaining how force relates to law. Are states ruled by a law of power or the power of law? Does the balance of forces affect the making of the law? Do states obey international law and are their policies determined by the content of the law or the alignment of force? Again, does the fabric of the international system make the situation any different for international law from what it is for municipal law?

The content of international law[1]

All members shall refrain in their international relations from the threat or use of force against the territorial integrity or

[1] For a more detailed account of what follows see either: I. Brownlie,

political independence of any state, or in any other manner inconsistent with the purposes of the United Nations.

– Article 2(4), UN Charter

The concern of international law with rules governing force is hardly new; the first systematic treatise on the law of nations, *De Jure Belli ac Pacis* (1625) by Hugo Grotius, was essentially a study of the laws of war. Further, while in addition to legal defences, Grotius's contemporaries benefited from the time necessary to mount an armed attack, the rules for the use of force take on added meaning in modern society where the decision to use force and its effective deployment can occur simultaneously. Political considerations aside, there is considerable legal expression about when force is prohibited, when force is permitted, and how force is to be controlled.

The rules of war

With respect to the 'rules of war', international law is very much like the annoying grandmother who, no longer able to tell her own children how to behave, insists on telling her children's children what to do. Ironically, even where states repudiate law by choosing war, the law still says something about the way in which their armies can fight. There are still rules of the game. If it is somewhat macabre to think of American soldiers in Vietnam carrying wallet-size cards outlining the rules, it is nonetheless true. Classes on relevant international law form part of the basic training for armed forces in many countries of the world. Soldiers are instructed to 'fight nicely' in addition to such varied topics as treatment of prisoners and lawful and unlawful ways of killing combatants.

To be sure, there is no complete agreement on these rules but there has been some attempt to overcome this problem through codification, as in the Hague Conventions of 1899 and 1907, and the Geneva Conventions of 1929 and 1949. Sometimes it is the scope of a particular law which is in question. For example, where it is generally recognized that the use of poisonous and asphyxiating gas is prohibited by the Geneva Protocol of 1925, it is uncertain whether in view of the fall-out they create, nuclear weapons are thereby outlawed. The 1961 General Assembly Resolution on the Prohibition of Nuclear Weapons clearly stated that the use of such weapons

International Law and the Use of Force by States, Clarendon Press, Oxford, 1963; L. Oppenheim, *International Law*, *II*, Longmans, London, 1952; or J. Stone, *Legal Controls of International Conflicts*, Stevens, London, 1959.

'was contrary to the spirit, letter and aims of the United Nations and, as such, was a direct violation of the Charter'.[1] However, the legal standing of such resolutions, aside from possible evidence of customary law, is questionable.

In any event, the problem of prosecuting violators of the rules of war has raised several interesting problems of jurisdiction. The right of a state to try its own civilians has long been recognized; the United States, for example, held well-publicized proceedings for several high-ranking American military officials for alleged violations committed during fighting in Vietnam. But to deny a state the right to prosecute the nationals of an enemy country could permit a number of guilty men to avoid punishment. Fear of such injustice in the light of offences committed in the Second World War led to the Agreement for the Prosecution and Punishment of the Major War Criminals of the European Axis concluded on 18 August 1945. Under this agreement, an International Military Tribunal was established which subsequently delivered convictions for 'Crimes against Peace', 'War Crimes', and 'Crimes against Humanity'. Again, whatever the initial legality of such actions, the decisions of the International Military Tribunal create important precedents for international customary law.

War and international law

The question arises: When are the rules of war applicable, what stage in the fighting between states constitutes war in a legal sense? A United States Circuit Court of Appeals considered this problem in the *New York Life Ins. Co.* v. *Bennion* case.[2] Captain Bennion was killed in the Japanese attack at Pearl Harbor on 7 December 1941. His life insurance policy specifically excluded from its coverage death resulting from 'war or any act incident thereto'. The Court was therefore asked to decide whether or not the United States was at war with Japan during the Pearl Harbor attack. It was reported that 250–300 Japanese bombing planes participated in the raid resulting in 3,435 American casualties, severe damage to or the loss of 8 battleships, 3 light cruisers, 3 destroyers, 3 other vessels, 188 planes, in addition to damage to land bases. Japanese losses included 100

---

[1] Cited in *Everyman's United Nations*, UN Publication, New York, 1968, p. 50.

[2] United States Circuit Court of Appeals, Tenth Circuit, 1946, 158 F.2d 260.

casualties, 29 planes, and 5 midget submarines. However, at the time of the attack the United States was in fact conducting a peace conference with envoys of the Japanese government.

The attack began at 7.30 a.m. Honolulu time (1.30 p.m. Washington time) and Japan broke off diplomatic relations one hour later through a message delivered to the US State Department in Washington. At approximately 10.30 a.m. (Honolulu time), the Japanese Imperial Headquarters announced that war had been in progress since 'dawn' (7.30 a.m.) and confirmed this position in a communication to the United States Embassy at Tokyo eight hours later. The US Congress did not declare war until the next day at 4.10 p.m. (Washington time).

At issue in this case was whether or not a war to be recognized as such by a court of law must be formally declared. In reaching their decision, the majority of the Court concurred in the view that:

> When one sovereign nation attacks another with premeditated and deliberate intent to wage war against it, and that nation resists the attacks with all the force at its command, we have war in the grim sense of reality. It is war in the only sense that men know and understand it. Mankind goes no further in his definitive search – he does not stand on ceremony or wait for technical niceties. To say that courts must shut their eyes to realities and wait for formalities, is to cut off their power to reason with concrete facts.

It must be pointed out that the decision in *New York Life Ins. Co. v. Bennion* is by no means definitive. Precedents can be cited for the view that war does not begin until officially declared – even in American courts and with reference to the attack on Pearl Harbor. As might be expected, the number of cases which have arisen from undeclared wars is considerable. The United States alone has participated in six major undeclared wars (Naval War with France, 1798–1800; First Barbary War, 1801–5; Second Barbary War, 1815; Mexican Border War, 1914–17; Korean War, 1950–3; and Vietnamese War, 1961–73), while of the five declared wars (War of 1812; Mexican War, 1846–8; Spanish–American War, 1898; First World War, 1917–18; and Second World War, 1941–5), four were declared as such after the fighting had begun. Among the non-American examples of undeclared war, hostilities between Italy and Abyssinia in 1935, Japan and China in 1937, Germany and Poland in 1939, and the USSR and Finland also in 1939 are notorious.

On the commencement of war, Grotius's position was uncompli-
cated if somewhat idealistic: 'That a war may be lawful . . . it should
be publicly declared.'[1] The problem was reconsidered at the 1907
Hague Conference and an attempt was made to codify state practice
in the Hague Convention Relative to the Opening of Hostilities. The
signatories agreed that 'hostilities between them must not commence
without a previous and unequivocal warning, which shall take the
form either of a declaration of war, giving reasons, or of an ultimatum with a conditional declaration of war'.[2] The degree of
formality attached to such declarations has varied in practice
throughout history and at present much of the pre-war ritual has
been eliminated, probably for very practical reasons. However, the
fact that forty-seven declarations of war were made in the First
World War alone suggests that chivalry in the twentieth century is
not completely dead.

Nevertheless, while it may be legally forbidden to go to war without a prior declaration of intent, there is a long record of state
practice to the contrary. States continue to tone down their involvement by cloaking their action in euphemisms like 'armed conflict'.
Although none of the parties involved in the fighting in Vietnam
issued a declaration of war, war existed nevertheless at least to the
extent that obligations under the rules of war were admitted. Here
the discriminatory treatment of prisoners by South Vietnam illustrates the legal enigma that customary practice can present. Saigon
recognized North Vietnam as a belligerent and held North Vietnamese prisoners in accordance with the rules set out by the Geneva
Conventions; the Vietcong, on the other hand, were viewed merely
as traitors and their treatment was governed by the criminal code of
the South Vietnamese municipal law. Courts, as we have seen, will
often reject a narrow or technical definition of war for the purpose
of considering claims. Once at war, declared or otherwise, states
clearly are bound by the rules; however it managed to be at war,
there is no excuse for a state to ignore those rules.

The rules of war come after the fact of war; their purpose is to
avoid needless suffering. While the need for such rules has been
recognized for centuries, the status of war itself has changed considerably in the last hundred years. Prior to this century, war was

---

[1] Hugo Grotius, *De Jure Belli ac Pacis*, Clarendon Press, Oxford, 1925,
p. 633.
[2] James Brown Scott, *The Hague Conventions and Declarations of 1899
and 1907*, O.U.P., New York, 1915, p. 96.

totally compatible with international law though a distinction was sometimes made between 'just' and 'unjust' wars. Until 1928, efforts like the Hague Conventions and the League Covenant attempted more to restrict than to prohibit war. However, on the 27 August 1928, the Kellogg–Briand Pact (General Treaty for the Renunciation of War) was concluded by which the signatories agreed to 'condemn recourse to war for the solution of international controversies and renounce it as an instrument of national policy in their relations with one another'.[1]

The Kellogg–Briand Pact may permit the use of force short of war. Peru, for example, deemed her action consistent with the Treaty's commitments when she invaded Colombian territory in 1932. Further, a lack of sanctions may limit the Treaty's political significance. However, inasmuch as there are no provisions for abrogating or terminating the Treaty and no evidence in state behaviour of an intent to do so, the Kellogg–Briand Pact remains valid law.

The standing of war in international law is undermined further by the United Nations Charter. Article 2(4) of the Charter broadens the scope of the Kellogg–Briand Treaty by prohibiting not *war* but more generally *force*. In addition, the threat of force as well as its use is forbidden. Article 2(6) makes these provisions applicable to non-member as well as to member states. Moreover, where problems of political effectiveness accrue to the Charter as well, the creation of a permanent organization ensures at least an audience to hear complaints of violation.

On the other hand, states are free to use force in dealing with domestic problems since Article 2(4) refers to relations with another 'state'. It is in any event highly unlikely that a state would consent to restrictions on its ability to keep internal order. Rebellions and civil wars pose particular problems of interpretation; however, once the conflict is recognized as an international one, the norms clearly apply. It would be very difficult for Pakistan legally to justify the use of force in Bangladesh as an instance of internal policing.

Self-defence and intervention

There are important exceptions to the general prohibition of the use of force under the Charter. First, states, like individuals in domestic society, may use force in self-defence. Article 51 provides that

---

[1] Text in J. W. Wheeler-Bennett, *Information on the Renunciation of War*, Unwin, London, 1928, pp. 188–9.

'Nothing in the present Charter shall impair the inherent right of individual or collective self-defence.' Similar reservations to the Kellogg–Briand Pact were made in an exchange of notes among signatories. The French government wrote to the United States:

> Nothing in the new treaty restrains or compromises in any matter whatsoever the right of self-defence. Each nation in this respect will always remain free to defend its territory against attack or invasion; it alone is competent to decide whether circumstances require recourse to war in self-defence.[1]

What the right of self-defence entails is less certain than that the right exists. The widely accepted formula of American Secretary of State Daniel Webster outlined in the 1837 *Caroline* case includes two rules: (1) the need must be immediate; (2) the action taken must be proportionate. Taking these principles in the light of the Charter, it is generally agreed that while the state may determine such a need in the first instance, its decision is subject to review by the Security Council.

It is a contentious point whether a state must actually suffer physical attack in order to justify force on the grounds of self-defence. Clearly, advanced weapons technology suggests that an initial strike could be fatal, with no chance of defence after the attack. For such reasons, Article 51 has been broadly interpreted by some to include the right of *anticipatory* self-defence where it can be shown that danger is imminent. Although never argued as such by the American government, several writers justify United States action in the Cuba missile crisis as anticipatory self-defence. More explicitly, the British Prime Minister relied on the doctrine of self-defence to vindicate sinking the French fleet off Oran in 1940, rather than allowing the ships to fall into German hands for future use against the British. Likewise, Pakistan defended sending troops into Kashmir in 1948 on this basis before the UN Security Council.

Forceful intervention in the sense of 'dictatorial interference' may be permissible in other circumstances as well. Treaty obligations sometimes confer rights to such intervention in the affairs of a protected state, or a state which has willingly restricted its territorial sovereignty. In 1906, under provisions of the 1903 Treaty of Havana, the United States intervened to restore order in Cuba. Similarly, for the purpose of maintaining peace, the Security Council can order

---

[1] Ibid., p. 151.

collective intervention including force under Article 42 of the Charter.

The legality of force used as a reprisal is less certain. A reprisal is the illegal use of force but in reply to the previous illegal act of another state. Reprisals are a way of taking the law into one's own hands in a kind of 'eye for an eye' fashion. The use of reprisals dates back to antiquity and until the nineteenth century it was not uncommon for states to commission private individuals to exercise the right of self-help in this fashion. The general practice has since been for state forces alone to take such measures. The legality of reprisals was restricted by the Geneva Convention of 1949 and probably denied by Article 2(4) of the Charter. However, recent practice has indicated if not a *de jure* at least a *de facto* recognition of these actions. Some Israeli raids into Arab territories have received formal condemnation, others have not. There is indication that reprisals fulfilling certain requirements will be condoned: first, the action taken must be proportional; this principle was cited in the 1928 *Naulilaa* case between Germany and Portugal where a tribunal ruled that an invasion of Portuguese territory was not justified by the shooting of three German soldiers near the border. Second, other peaceful means of settlement, such as negotiations, must first be exhausted. And third, reprisals must cease when reparation is made.

A final way in which international law permits the use of force is for the collective enforcement of all Security Council decisions. The Security Council can, for example, take whatever measures it deems necessary to enforce a decision of the International Court of Justice under Article 94 of the Charter. A Security Council decision to use force would then be binding according to Article 25. Although such a decision has not yet been made, the Security Council did invoke Article 39 to authorize the use of force after the invasion of South Korea in 1950. In this respect, the law of the Charter is considerably more comprehensive than the League Covenant which allowed individual members the right to decide in each instance whether a violation of the Covenant had been committed.

Legal effects of a treaty imposed by force

In addition to regulating the use of force by states, international law has had to consider the legal effects of results brought about by forceful means. Is, for example, a treaty binding if it has been imposed under duress? This problem is complicated by the fact that it is often difficult to say when force has been used to secure accept-ance of a treaty. When it comes to treaty-making, states can exert different kinds of power which are often out of proportion to their military strength. However, even in the case where a treaty is clearly the outcome of a military victory, the status of such a treaty is not always certain if for no other reason than that the law in this respect seems at present to be changing.

There has long been a consensus that force applied to the person of any of the representatives concluding a treaty invalidates the treaty for the states concerned. However, where force is directed against a state generally, in order to obtain the acceptance of treaty conditions, the legal consequences are less definite. In contrast to the private law of most municipal systems where duress vitiates a con-tract, the customary international practice had been to recognize treaties even where they had been dictated by forceful means. In the last half century, however, this position has frequently been rejected both in principle and in practice. The prohibitions on force, most particularly those of the Charter, make it difficult to rationalize ends achieved by forceful means. Frequently cited as a move in this direction is the Stimson Doctrine of 1932 in which the American Secretary of State addressed China and Japan on the point that the United States 'does not intend to recognize any situation, treaty or agreement which may be brought about by means contrary to the covenants and obligations of the Pact of Paris of 27 August 1928'.[1] In considering a case involving the acquisition of Czechoslovakian territory by Germany in 1938, a Netherlands court applied this principle when it held that the provisions of the 1938 Treaty of Berlin 'must be regarded as null and void, as they were brought about under unlawful duress exercised upon Czechoslovakia'.[2]

The problem of the legal effects of a treaty imposed by force was again taken up at the Vienna conference of 1969 which produced the Vienna Convention on the Law of Treaties. The Convention is not yet binding since it lacks the thirty-five ratifications necessary for it to enter into force. Nor is the Convention merely a restatement of customary practice; it admits to going beyond codification to the 'progressive development' of international law. Nevertheless it was adopted nearly unanimously and ought to be considered in any

[1] US Department of State, *Papers Relating to the Foreign Relations of the United States*, III, 1932, Government Printing Office, Washington, 1948, p. 8.
[2] Cited in J. E. S. Fawcett, *Law of Nations*, Penguin, Harmondsworth, 1971, p. 110.

general statement about the law of treaties. The invalidating effect on a treaty of coercing a state representative is provided for in Article 51 of the Convention. Article 52 draws attention to more recent developments concerning rules regulating the use of force by acknowledging that: 'A treaty is void if its conclusion has been procured by the threat or use of force in violation of the principles of international law embodied in the Charter of the United Nations.'

Ironically, many of the treaties which we today look to for the stability of the international system were themselves imposed by force or at least by a military victor. Indeed, one international lawyer has insisted that treaties of coercion must be valid or 'there would be no end to the struggle of nations and a secured state of peace could never be expected.'[1] It is interesting, then, that whatever their departure from earlier practice, the provisions of the Vienna Convention were they to come into force would not have a retroactive effect.

How effective are the rules governing the use of force?

On the basis of day-to-day newspaper reading, the rules governing the use of force do not appear particularly effective. It is difficult to think of a soldier who has just seen his best friend killed or a state facing possible annihilation as being particularly concerned with rules which must be followed. But put in the perspective of history, the constraints operating on the use of force ought to be recognized. As Professor Hinsley aptly concludes:

> When one realizes the great rapidity and the enormous extent of the increase in men's knowledge and organization of power during the first fifty years of this century, and when one realises also the complications and opportunities thrown up by the circumstances in which those things grew, then the surprising thing is not that there were such violent wars and tyrannies in that period. It is that the wars and tyrannies were not more frequent and more violent even than they were.[2]

It is difficult to say exactly what part law has played in containing force but it would be more difficult to deny altogether law's role in

[1] J. C. Bluntschli, *Das moderne Volkerrecht*, 1868, cited in Julius Stone, op. cit., pp. xxxi–xxxii.
[2] F. H. Hinsley, *Power and the Pursuit of Peace*, C.U.P., Cambridge, 1963, p. 280.

this respect. Certainly a descriptive account of what the rules are is not enough. Just as important is an analysis of the nature of law generally and the way in which it functions internationally.

The nature of international law

> I know not whether Laws be right,
> Or whether Laws be wrong;
> All that we know who lie in gaol
> Is that the wall is strong.
> – Oscar Wilde, *The Ballad of Reading Gaol.*

Gaol walls and bobbies' truncheons are the terms by which the public often recognizes the law. The view that law seeks order and that order depends on force and authority is widely held. Like the 'bad guys' in the 'Westerns', we find it difficult to distinguish in 'Johnny Law' the law from its enforcer. The reliance of law on force can be traced back to mythology where Zeus, the supreme law-giver, could always count on a few well-placed thunderbolts to make good his will. Yet international society has neither gaol nor sheriff and for this reason many question whether international law can be thought of as law properly so-called.[1]

Force and the validity of international law

John Austin provoked the controversy of whether international law is true law, that is, law in the same sense as municipal law. In his lectures on jurisprudence, first published in 1832, Austin insists that every law properly so-called is a general command, subject to an evil in case of disobedience, and emanating from a sovereign. As a result, he excludes from the body of proper law those 'laws by metaphor',[2] like laws of science and laws of a game, and those laws by 'analogy',[3] which reflect a general opinion of an indeterminate body, like rules of behaviour. The latter category of law 'improperly

---

[1] Among the best general readings on the nature of law are: H. L. A. Hart, *The Concept of Law*, Clarendon Press, Oxford, 1961; H. Kelsen, *Pure Theory of Law*, University of California Press, Berkeley, 1967; and D. Lloyd, *The Idea of Law*, Penguin, Harmondsworth, 1970.

[2] John Austin, *The Providence of Jurisprudence Determined*, Noonday Press, New York, 1954, p. 122.

[3] Ibid., p. 154.

called' includes, then, customary law, an acknowledged source of international law. Austin's position on customary law is explicit:

> Now, till they become the grounds of judicial decisions upon cases, and are clothed with legal sanctions by the sovereign one in number, the customs are merely rules set by opinions of the governed, and sanctioned or enforced morally: though, when they become the reasons of judicial decisions upon cases, and are clothed with legal sanctions by the sovereign one or number, the customs are rules of positive morality.[1]

International law, according to Austin, is guilty on two counts; lacking the legitimate authority of a sovereign, and the essential feature of guaranteeing forceful punishment for violation, it is at best a positive morality.

Of course, implicit in Austin's argument is the view that what international law lacks, municipal law has. It remained for his critics to posit that much of what is accepted as valid law in domestic society would also fail to satisfy Austin's criterion. H. L. A. Hart, for example, argues that the theory of law as a sovereign's coercive orders is lacking for three reasons. First, even those orders entailing penalty for disobedience differ from, say, a 'gunman's threat' in that they apply to those who enact the orders as well as to others. Second, certain laws which confer powers can only in the most nonsensical way be thought of as backed by threats. Third, some laws differ by way of origin in that not all laws are prescriptive; some laws owe their authority to a gradually developed status achieved through repeated practice. These 'customary rules' were nonetheless law. As a result, Hart bemoans the absence of the 'idea of a rule' in Austin's theory. Hart admits that such an idea is not an easy one, but he insists that the problem can be alleviated by distinguishing two classes of rules. Hart thus denotes: 'primary rules', by which 'human beings are required to do or abstain from certain actions, whether they wish to or not';[2] and 'secondary rules' which confer powers by determining the incidence and controlling the operation of the primary rules.[3] Law, Hart maintains, exists in a combination of these two types.

Force and different kinds of law

The importance of Professor Hart's analysis is that it differentiates

[1] Ibid., pp. 163–4.   [2] H. L. A. Hart, op. cit., pp. 78–9.   [3] Ibid., p. 79.

kinds or categories of law. It is impossible to generalize, as Austin has done, about a single source of validity for all the legal norms collectively thought of as law. Generally, the relationship between force and the nature of the law will depend upon which law we refer to. Lawyers are quick to draw a distinction between kinds of law in domestic society, that is, to see very differently the criminal law and the law of torts. The dissimilarity in nature between constitutional law and the law of property is stressed for the law student in his curriculum. The citizen, as well, knows that contingent on whether he is illegally parked, in breach of contract, or has killed someone, his case will go to a different court concerned with different legal consequences; again, a different law may apply if the citizen be a member of the military rather than a civilian. These discrepancies in the nature of laws are particularly acute, and therefore analogous to law at the international level, in those domestic societies which reflect a composite of radically different legal cultures. For example, modern Chinese law is an outgrowth of both *li*, a social order based on spiritual myth, and *fa*, a system of punishment and control for those whom *li* fails to govern. Force is integral to the nature of *fa* and irrelevant to the validity of *li*.

We need not trace anthropological origins here to appreciate the differences between kinds of law. The problem is that whereas the public draws these distinctions with respect to its own municipal law, there is a dangerous tendency to generalize about all law at the international level as one kind. The International Court of Justice, on the other hand, carefully distinguishes different sources of international law in Article 38 of its Statute, as well as between particular law, which is valid for a few states only, and more general international law.

According to this view, is there a real difference between international and municipal laws? In the past, a good deal of time has been spent arguing about whether international and municipal laws are two distinct systems or essentially one and the same. The dualists argue that the sources, substance, and relations regulated are in each instance different and that there are, therefore, two distinct systems. The monists, on the other hand, deny the differences stressed by the dualists and insist that the authority of all law is hierarchical but derives from a single rule. However, neither view does justice to what is in fact the pluralistic nature of law; to the fact that the differences among municipal laws are in certain instances greater than the differences between similar kinds of law at either the municipal or international spheres. The dissimilarity in nature at the domestic plane between the criminal law and the law of contract is probably greater than between the law of contract and treaty law, for example, although these differences are nonetheless real. Indeed, international and municipal are merely terms of convenience denoting levels of activity in which laws function.

Force and legal obligation

We can imagine someone about to quench his thirst with a pint of beer suddenly being told by a policeman that a law forbids him from enjoying himself in such a way. He might naturally ask, 'What law?' Now his sense of obligation and his reaction might differ depending upon whether the law be scientific, moral, or legal. If the policeman pointed out that the man in question had been running for some time and that it was a law of science that in such a condition, drinking would make him sick, the man would be 'obligated' by that law because he could not be otherwise. If the policeman insisted that morality would not condone drinking, the thirsty man might then consider what he *ought* to do. But were the policeman to cite a parliamentary statute forbidding drinking in this situation, his presence might take on a whole new meaning for the man holding the beer.

States get thirsty too and the question must be asked whether, aside from the validity of the legal restraints they face, states can be said to have any legal obligations even if they need not fear the enforcement of such obligations. It is, for example, the actual conduct of nations which leads Hans Morgenthau to question the relevance of a binding character in his appraisal of international law:

> If rules of international law are consistently violated and the violations are accepted as a matter of course by all subjects of the law – if, therefore, the legal rights are treated by those who ought to enforce them as though they did not exist – the question arises: Do they still exist as binding legal rules?[1]

However, Morgenthau ignores the valid distinction between obligation and observance. Our scientific laws like 'all people must eat' are inevitably observed but give no rise to legal obligations. At the

[1] H. Morgenthau, *Politics Among Nations*, 4th edn., Knopf, New York, 1967, p. 271.

same time, the many who ignored the rules of Prohibition in America were nonetheless bound by law to do otherwise.

But just as the 'force' of violation cannot deny a legal obligation, it is difficult to deem law as binding because it is backed by force. Austin tried to describe the obligation of law in terms of the likelihood of evil or punishment in the event of the law being broken. This cannot be the case; were it so, it would mean that by getting away with a crime, one would escape from one's legal obligation as well.

It has been suggested that 'the ultimate basis of the obligation to obey the law cannot be anything but moral.'[1] The implication is that law is necessary for man and society to fulfil their potential and that there is a 'natural' law which makes this command. But as Hart has pointed out, much of law is morally neutral and often the moral thing to do is to break the law.

In the last analysis, law must be binding by definition; you cannot have a law that is not binding. Legal obligation, as Professor C. A. W. Manning explains,[2] derives from the status which is the very nature of law. Just as all circles are circular, all laws have binding force. To create legal obligations, a law need only be proper.[3]

Force and the sanctions of international law

Aside from whether laws are right or wrong and whether they are valid, we must ask about the strength of the 'gaol walls' – the legal sanctions. We have argued that much law is *valid* without the backing of force but this is not the same as saying that law is *possible* without a system of sanctions. Now it must be asked: first, 'Is international law backed by the force of sanctions and, if so, what might their nature be?' and, second, 'To what extent does physical coercion ensure legal compliance?'

It would be possible to think that since the international community lacks a central government it must necessarily be a lawless society. However, sanctions have long been a part of international law under a system of self-help rather than central administration.

[1] J. L. Brierly, *The Law of Nations*, 6th edn., Clarendon Press, Oxford, 1963, p. 56.

[2] C. A. W. Manning, *The Nature of International Society*, Bell, London, 1962, p. 106.

[3] As has already been suggested, different kinds of laws will be 'proper' for very different reasons.

Moreover, the issue is not simply one of the strongest states being able to help themselves the most. Rules applying to these sanctions have been discussed earlier along with other rules governing the use of force but it is worth making a distinction here. While there are different categories of laws, there are as well different kinds of force. Diplomatic force and economic force cannot be ignored at the international level. There is the sanction of military might which favours the great Powers and by which, for example, the United States enforced what it deemed to be its legal commitments in South-East Asia during the 1960s and early 1970s. Nonetheless, the nature of contemporary international society also affords smaller states a force for sanctioning their legal rights. The competition among the powerful states and the sensitivity of their governments to popular criticism both at home and abroad make it very difficult for these Powers to use physical force against a weaker state. Perhaps for this reason, Britain has taken its fishing dispute with Iceland to the International Court although Iceland's defences would be hardly adequate were Britain militarily to contest Iceland's legal claim.

Beyond the nature of force available as sanctions, we may question the relevance of force to legal compliance. There are several compelling arguments against the need for sanctions. There is the moral argument that the use of force is immoral. Therefore, the moralists would insist that a law backed by force offends morality. But since law is not morality, the argument here is that moral law, and not the law of nations, condemns the use of force.

A stronger argument against the need for sanctions, and one that holds true for certain *kinds* of law, is the consensual argument. According to this view, the plea for force misunderstands the function of law. States obey, not law which they are forced to observe, but law to which they consent. The important point, then, is that law to which states consent exists in its own right whether or not it is obeyed. Legal coercion is incidental and not essential to its existence.

On the other hand, it can be argued that the sanction of force is important in maintaining social cohesion. Emile Durkheim, who classified laws by the sanctions they impose, stressed the important psychological effect of backing law with force. Here he even admitted that sanctions serving as an outlet for vengeance are helpful in preserving social equilibrium. The distinction necessarily to be made is that while the issue of sanctions is tangential to the question of the law's authority, force is yet a means for translating law into effective action.

Many categories of law are not backed by force and yet remain proper law. The kinds of sanctions have varied, as well, from internal pressures to external threats of military violence. Yet societies have needed sanctions thus far – if only for the psychological effect that Durkheim describes. The need for force is at best a relative one; the difference in crime rates of the average American city of 500,000 and of Edinburgh cannot be attributed to the effectiveness of the respective police forces alone.[1] The law's observance can be imputed to many things, not least among them habit and the long-term expectation of profit from stability. Whereas the validity of law has many sources, the final justification for sanctions must always be a sociological one.

The function of international law

> Laws were like cobwebs;
> where the small flies were caught,
> and the great break through.
> – Francis Bacon, *Apothegms.*

To abstract law as we have done, to talk of law as if it were distinct from its social milieu, may be to miss the point. Law exists in and for the society that creates it. Where there is no society, there cannot be law.

Furthermore, the nature of international society suggests tangible problems with which the law must cope. Law, quite properly, is the concern of lawyers while politics occupies politicians. In international relations, rightly or wrongly, it is often the politicians who make the decisions. To describe a particular situation at the international level simply in legal terms may be to distort the picture, at least for the student of international relations. Nor in this picture can we ignore force external to the law, or certainly the threat of force which seems omnipresent.

Finally, it is not enough to say what the law is and why it cannot be otherwise; something must be said of the way in which the law functions in its political context. We want to treat law not only as an idea but as a social phenomenon as well. Questions can be asked about 'when' and 'why' the law succeeds and the same questions

---

[1] This point is made by M. Banton, 'Law Enforcement and Social Control', V. Aubert (ed.), *Sociology of Law*, Penguin, Harmondsworth, 1969, p. 127.

raised about the law's failures. It is in this more sociological light that we must now consider the relationship of force and international law.[1] Whereas we have been discussing force in terms of the rules governing its use and the extent to which force can be seen as an internal feature of the legal system, we now speak of force outside and in conflict with the law.

While the United Nations General Assembly recently listened to varied proposals and panaceas for dealing with the problem of containing force in international relations, there was a persistent tendency among the broader audience of the world community to discount the discussion as political rhetoric. Positive expectations were kept to a minimum. Reflecting on the past record, an editorial in *The Times* pessimistically observed: 'It is as if the imperfections of the UN as a peace-making body somehow proved the futility of the UN as an aspiration.'[2] This pessimism is attributable to a general scepticism that has accompanied the development of the international legal order: world law and world organization were no match for the predominance of force which characterized contemporary international society.

For some the disenchantment lies in the frequent failures of existing legal arrangements for international order. They react to a particular violation going unchallenged as when the United States admitted breaking the law in the U-2 incident of early 1960. Yet for others there is a more permanent and perhaps, therefore, more critical cause for contempt. This group expresses the conviction that at present, the plight of international law is inevitable; that the failure of the legal system is immutably rooted in the nature of the society to which it applies. To these critics, inadequate protection from terrorism and futile attempts to maintain peaceful order in the Middle East reflect more accurately than the law what is the fabric of contemporary international relations.

In international society what governs: is it the power of law or the law of power? Can nations pick and choose their laws? How much do governments share with the eighteenth-century Englishmen of whom Mandeville said, 'Their Laws and Cloaths were equally/ Objects of Mutability.'

[1] General readings in this respect include: C. de Visscher, *Theory and Reality in Public International Law*, Princeton U.P., Princeton, 1968; L. Henkin, *How Nations Behave*, Praeger, New York, 1968; and M. Kaplan and N. Katzenbach, *The Political Foundations of International Law*, Wiley, New York, 1961.
[2] Editorial, *The Times*, 25 October 1970, p. 12.

Is international law dominated by force?

One of the more persistent criticisms of international law is that it is a law dominated by power. The contention is that international law exists for and is determined by the will of the stronger nations. As a spokesman summarizes this view:

> Whether or not an attempt will be made to enforce international law and whether or not the attempt will be successful do not depend primarily upon legal considerations and the disinterested operation of law-enforcing mechanisms. Both attempt and success depend upon political considerations and the actual distribution of power in a particular case.[1]

The implication is that a state behaves in accordance with its national interest always, with a view only to limitations in its power to realize that interest; when this behaviour accords with international legal norms, it is coincidence, not purpose. From this assumption it might be inferred that among the strongest states, a virtual invulnerability and manipulative power exists with regard to the law. It is this explanation which was offered when the Soviet Union invaded Czechoslovakia in 1968, allegedly an infraction of international law under the Charter.

Yet it can first be said that these violations are more the exception than the rule. There is a misconception on the public's part that international law, as pictured by the media, is generally disobeyed. But the fact is that newspapers learned long ago that bad news sells better than good news. In what amounts to unreported good news, one finds the most powerful of nations yielding to everyday short-term inconvenience in matters such as diplomatic immunities, for the long-term advantage of international order and stability.

However, we have been arguing that simply to generalize about the law in this way is self-defeating. In order to do justice to the complexity of law, the way in which force relates to law must be made more specific. There are, first, distinctions pertaining to kinds of law. For some kinds of law, what might be called the legal 'givens' or systemic law, the question of forceful violation or domination is irrelevant; the legal principles applied by a judge at the International Court, the evolving case law of judicial precedent, even the rules by which a treaty acquires legal standing, are proper law and, although usually of limited interest other than to lawyers, the law in this

---

[1] H. Morgenthau, op. cit., p. 282.

respect is unaffected by force. Second, for much of law, the likelihood of forceful interference, if not impossible, is yet improbable. This law reflects a strong common interest among the parties to it as in the case of the law regulating the international mail service. Professor Georg Schwarzenberger speaks of this type of law as 'community law' or the 'law of co-ordination' since it 'serves the purpose of assisting in the maintenance and continuous integration of the community and the protection of the group against abnormal aberrations on the part of its members'.[1] In all fairness, the distinction Professor Schwarzenberger makes is less concerned with the nature of the law than with the nature of the social arrangement which the law hopes to regulate. However, it can be seen that laws of a certain nature will be more or less likely to lend themselves to communal interests.

Schwarzenberger identifies two further kinds of law: 'society law' or 'law of power' 'which is characterized by gross disparities in rights and duties'[2] and, somewhere in between, the 'law of reciprocity' for which 'both sides are content if they are convinced that they have received more than, or at least as much as, they have given'.[3] It is in the former class of law, society law, and to a certain extent the law of reciprocity, as well, that the influence of force is felt by international law.

These distinctions are meant to be loose. Seen over a period of time and allowing for the different legal personalities involved, each category of law will suggest different legal arrangements. But while it is worth noting that some law will be little affected by state power, part of the law or at least the effectiveness of that part will be influenced by force in a very real sense.

However, the likelihood of forceful interference will depend not only on the general nature of the society and its law, but as well on the nature of the conflict in any given situation. In one instance the United States is willing to defend its legal rights under the Charter with nuclear weapons as when the Soviet Union moved missiles into Cuba in 1962; yet depending on the circumstance, American reaction

---

[1] G. Schwarzenberger, 'The Three Types of Law', *Current Legal Problems, 1949*, p. 108. Like Schwarzenberger, Stanley Hoffman divides law into three similar categories which he calls 'the law of the political framework', 'the law of reciprocity', and 'the law of community'; see S. Hoffman, 'International Systems and International Law', *World Politics*, XIV, pp. 205–37. Compare the three kinds of law in L. Oppenheim, *International Law*, I, Longmans, London, 1947, pp. 4–5.

[2] Schwarzenberger, ibid., p. 107. [3] Ibid., p. 110.

to alleged Soviet violations of international law can be quite different. When in 1951 a US aircraft was intercepted in Hungarian airspace, the American government protested against Soviet involvement which the US believed to be contrary to international law by asking that the case be brought to the International Court of Justice. When the Soviet Union refused to accept the Court's jurisdiction, the case was removed from the Court list and the matter effectively ended. Why, then, in both instances of reputed legal infraction involving the same governments did force play a drastically different role?

Many critics differentiate between 'political' and 'legal' disputes, insisting that force will predominate with respect to the former. The inclination here is to accept Dr. Rosalyn Higgins's distinction that such usage of terms is incorrect, that the words 'political' and 'legal' describe the *methods* used for settling disputes, and that all disputes between states are political but that those involving a legal decision-making process can be identified.[1]

There is, however, an important distinction between a routine conflict in which a state concerned merely wants something and a vital dispute in which a state claims something as its own or believes its honour to be at stake. Clearly where primary interests are involved, the state, not unlike the individual, may be willing to fight for what it believes to be its right and the law will necessarily take a back seat to force. Again, the distinction between a dispute and a routine conflict is a relative one; 'at any moment a minor detail, charged with accidental significance, may become the subject of political dispute that defies settlement by pre-established norm.'[2] What can best be hoped for in such circumstances is that law, while not determining action may at least have a tempering effect.

Admitting that force will dominate law in the sense that sometimes force will be used to breach the law is not tantamount to saying that the strongest states (strength being measured in terms of military might) will necessarily prevail in those instances. States rely on different kinds of power. The power of a state can be described in terms of a nation's physical strength and resources; but a state also has power in the sense that it is able to achieve what it desires. Power in this second instance need not necessarily be correlated with a state's power in the first sense. A reality of contemporary

---

[1] R. Higgins, 'Policy Considerations and the International Judicial Process', *International and Comparative Law Quarterly*, XVII, January 1968, p. 74.
[2] P. Corbett, *Law in Diplomacy*, Princeton U.P., Princeton, 1959, p. 277.

international relations is that the great Powers often cannot afford to alienate the smaller states. As might possibly have been the case in the Middle East, a small state can choose to ignore a ceasefire order assuming that the major Powers, who could contain whatever force is employed, will be reluctant to take sides in the issue. Putting the dichotomy of power more succinctly: the United States always had the force to obliterate North Vietnam but the option was never a practical one; instead the two sides met as political equals at Paris in order to reach an agreement.

The final qualification to the view that 'laws grind the poor and rich men rule the law' is a highly speculative one. It is worth considering, if law was not admitted at the international level, would states be more or less vulnerable to the interplay of forces? Even if a certain state in a certain circumstance can influence the effectiveness of a certain kind of law, would that state have been less likely to get its way in the absence of that law? Certainly in practice, few of the small or new states are willing to abandon the law's protection by denying altogether its validity.[1]

Force and international law-making

While law once made often has a will of its own, the making of law is essentially a political process. Although legislation at the international level is a highly decentralized procedure, it is expected that if not naked force, certainly the *power* of states will be reflected in the law. Rights earlier guaranteed by certain privileged states and defended by force are now accepted customary law. This evolution is clearly seen in American influence on the laws of neutrality and British practice adopted by the law of the sea. More recently, as international law turns to areas of a highly specialized and technical character, as in the cases of outer space and certain rights to natural resources, relatively few countries are in a position to address themselves to certain nonetheless pressing issues. For the moment this minority of governments alone will be affected both in terms of rights and obligations, but the rules they choose to follow will inevitably be deemed to be important precedents, as well.

---

[1] See, for example, Shihata to the effect: 'In their writings, scholars from new states may be critical of some of the old rules of international law, but none among them are known to be against the whole system or its judicial machinery', 'The Attitude of New States Toward the International Court of Justice', *International Organization*, XIX, p. 213.

However, even where international law is consciously legislated it is usually a far cry from being imposed. For a state to be bound by a treaty, it must consent to its being so obligated. Furthermore, whereas any law is likely to favour some party to it, the privilege is probably one of detail since there is beforehand a general agreement to the overall objectives of that law. Finally, as has already been pointed out, in any political process, legislation not excluded, a state's power to get what it wants need not be proportionate to its force on hand.

On the other hand, national force has a real and perhaps positive role to play in changing the law. Again, law by its nature is a conservative influence and legal change, even at the domestic level, rarely keeps pace with the rapid changes taking place in society. For international law because of its decentralized character the problem of change is particularly acute. This problem should not be exaggerated -- as Kaplan and Katzenbach point out: 'At any given time there is some consensus as to the rules applicable and their interpretation, and considerable good faith in their honest execution. . . . By comparison, the area in which change is desired . . . is relatively small.'[1] But the need for change is nonetheless real. Methods for peaceful change do exist internationally – both direct, treaty negotiation and legislation, for example, and indirect, in the way by which state practice becomes customary law – yet these alternatives are not always adequate. Therefore, it must be admitted that in certain circumstances force may be the only means by which a state can achieve change, albeit unlawful, which it deems to be just. Judging by a principle of effectiveness, there can be little doubt now of Bulgaria changing the law by unilaterally declaring independence in October 1908 in defiance of Article 1 of the Treaty of Berlin, 1878. Similarly, it may become increasingly difficult to obtain from Israel the territory which is being held in contravention to the law of the Charter as a result of the six-day war in 1967. Moreover, inducing a state to take the law in its own hands in this way is the principle *allegans contraria non audienda est* by which a state can lose a legal right by failing consistently to defend that right. In the *Case Concerning the Temple of Preah Vihear*, the International Court of Justice ruled that Thailand was now precluded from proper legal rights denied her in a treaty with Cambodia by having for a time not defended those rights.

[1] M. Kaplan and N. Katzenbach, op. cit., p. 21.

Force versus law observance

Still it would be no small forensic achievement to prove at the international level the absence of the rule of law in the sense of legal compliance having simply admitted a role of force in the making, amending, and enforcing of certain laws. Having previously argued that much of the law's observance is not determined by considerations of force, it is worth considering a few final points about why states use force to violate law. As argued above, states may break what they deem to be unjust law with the hopes of changing that particular law and without denying the validity of remaining law. Law is not morality and, according to a state's ethics, breaking the law may be the moral thing to do. The law, as well, may be uncertain or disputed, and states may be reluctant to *appear* to favour a specific precedent. In the 'cod war', Iceland and Britain each insisted that the other's action was illegal despite the fact that these claims naturally contradicted each other.

Finally, just as the individual who pleads guilty but asks for clemency on the grounds that he was forced to act as he did – be it by his health, his financial plight, or his wife – so too states have commitments and are subject to domestic pressures of varying degree. Subsequently, in simple cost-effect terms, for the state and the individual what can be gained by a certain violation compared to the risks involved may prove too great a temptation.

In certain instances, forceful breach of the law if not permissible is at least understandable. Moreover, when we speak of these violations we are taking note of the exceptions to the rule. For at the international level, most laws are generally observed by governments, by foreign ministries, and by more private interests who continue to justify their action in terms of the law.

International law versus municipal law

With respect to these questions of a more sociological character, something should be said about the international and municipal laws analogy. Those who argue that international law is dominated by force usually would contrast the international situation with what they believe to be a well-controlled domestic order. However, it is arguable that municipal law contends with the considerable influence of force as well. When the level of forceful interference reaches certain proportions, the situation is spoken of in terms of civil war; but more limited forceful inervention may be admitted without threatening the fabric or at least the validity of the law in question. Just as law in Northern Ireland functions simultaneously with IRA destruction, it is to state the facts to say that many individual crimes of violence go unpunished.

The content of municipal law is likewise vulnerable. The general comment that law protects the interests of the powerful was first observed long ago before international law was thought of in terms of written rules. Even in democratic societies, legislation by majority may not always protect the interests of the minority. Further, while the machinery for legal change may be better developed domestically, powerful lobbies often dictate what changes there should be.

Contrasting the domestic situation with the international, existing differences between certain social phenomena should not be minimized. The level and nature of force likely to be used and its purposes may be quite different. As yet, domestic law has not had to contend with nuclear weapons. But the complexity of municipal law, not unlike international law, in part stems from the fact that force affects different kinds of law very differently.

Law can be thought of in many ways: in terms of rules, of principles, and of effectiveness in the social order which it attempts to regulate. More importantly, law can be thought of in terms of laws. Such a classification, though neither exact nor complete, helps to explain the complex interplay between law and force at the international level.

9 War and Social Change

The preceding chapters in this book have gone some way towards explaining how the facts of political life, both domestic and international, influence and may restrain the decision to use force in international relations. Despite these and other influences, real or perceived, contemporary history reveals that even in the age of nuclear weapons the decision to use force is still frequently made. This being so, an important question still remains: when states use force in pursuit of political objectives, what kinds of consequences attend that act? Quite clearly, some consequences are anticipated; 'loss of face', breaking of diplomatic relations, sanctions or some such response may have to be considered. However, in the last analysis, when the risks and stakes are evaluated, these consequences are held to be 'worth it' in face of the perceived gains. Nevertheless, decision-makers, being merely mortal, lack the gift of prescience for there are, to be sure, certain things that cannot be predicted given limited information. Nowhere is this more evident than when states resort to war. British troops leaving to aid Belgium in 1914 fully expected to be 'home by Christmas'. The war that began in 1914 ended four years later, with a death toll reckoned in millions. Furthermore, as we shall see, British society was altered by the war in ways that could not have been forseen at its outset.

Reiterating, states resort to force in pursuit of political objectives when the anticipated gains are adjudged to outweigh the forseeable costs. In this sense, war is quite evidently an instrument of change; it is employed to bring about a state of affairs that is judged to be desirable, or to prevent the imposition of unwanted change. Alternatively, we could discuss changes that result from the use of force which are neither anticipated nor particularly desirable. Within this category could be included the alteration of borders and, consequent upon that, the large-scale resettlement of population. But, in the final analysis, states can, and do, deny responsibility or turn a blind eye to problems of this nature on the grounds that they are not the state's concern. Yet war can promote changes that are undesirable or unplanned (or both) within the social and political systems of the state itself and these types of changes will be the primary focus in what follows. This is, of course, not to deny the importance of other types of upheaval that attend war; restricting the analysis to internal changes is important in view of the fact that they are of primary importance to the society and the state and have consequences for them. Apart from the main issue of inconvenience or embarrassment, the changes consequent upon the use of force have implications for the future international role of the state.

What do we mean when we speak of internal changes that are unplanned or undesirable? Consider the following examples. Almost 2,000 years ago Livy described in considerable detail the war between Rome and Carthage and in doing so discussed issues relevant to the point of discussion. For example, following two heavy defeats by Carthaginian forces at Lake Trasimene and in Umbria, the mood in Rome as described by Livy was one of doubt and uncertainty:

> The report of this new defeat affected people in various ways; some, having a greater cause for sickness at heart, found it a small thing compared with what had gone before; others could not weigh the gravity of what had happened as an isolated event, but only in the context of circumstances: a sick body is more sensitive to the least pain than a healthy one and in the same way the seriousness of any reverse for their suffering and afflicted country must, they felt, be weighed not by its intrinsic magnitude but against their present weakness which could not endure any additional burden. The government accordingly had recourse to the appointment of a dictator, a remedy which for many years had been neither wanted nor applied.[1]

More recently, the popular interpretation of the First World War was that *inter alia* it precipitated Kerensky's liberal revolution and later the Bolshevik *putsch* in Russia, when 'the peasants voted with their feet' and abandoned the war effort. Whilst certain sections of Russian society deemed revolution desirable the Russian monarchy certainly did not. Similarly, in Britain it is said that the war gave the vote to women, despite the recorded evidence that the campaign for women's suffrage had originated in the early nineteenth century.

[1] Livy, *The War With Hannibal* (trans. A. de Sellincourt), Penguin, Harmondsworth, 1972, p. 102.

221

The American sociologist, William Fielding Ogburn was prompted in 1948 to ask 'Are our wars good times?'[1] and, in relation to the American experience in the First and Second World Wars, answered his question in the affirmative. On the basis of a comparison of statistics for births, deaths, divorces, homicides, employment and similar indices, Ogburn felt confident enough to reach the conclusion that American wartime experiences were sufficiently similar to the peak years of the business cycle in the period 1925–9 to be called 'good times'. It must be added, however, that the analysis was restricted largely to statistical comparisons although Ogburn conceded that certain factors such as fear and distress were incalculable.

Doubtless other examples could be found, but these will suffice to make the point at issue. In these few cases war has been held to be, explicitly or otherwise, intimately related to changes that vary both in nature and scope. In the cases cited war is linked to dictatorship, revolution, democracy and economic and social prosperity. What follows is a review of some of the issues implicit in a discussion of war and its relation to social change. Specifically, the types of questions to be reviewed include: Is war necessary to obtain certain kinds of change? Are types of change related to types of war? Does it make any difference whether the war is being won or lost? Is there a causal relation or is war merely a catalyst? Is it simply that the war acts as a barrier to perspective, clouding the long view and leading to a confusion of precedence and causality? But before we become involved in these questions we need to clarify essential terms.

Force, violence, and war: their relationship to social change

A major problem of human society concerns the proper distribution of roles and the structure of relationships. Most people try to find an equilibrium which will satisfy their immediate and long-term requirements without too much effort or trouble. The same axiom holds true in relation to states, for they also seek a delicately balanced relationship between their aspirations and their means, their hopes and their fears, and in trying to establish a suitable balance they employ a range of devices. Generally speaking, they prefer pacific means yet they prepare the means of force in case 'normal' diplomacy fails. Logically, there is a clear distinction between pacific and warlike instruments and the growth of world law is, in

---

[1] *Scientific Monthly*, LXVII, 1, July 1948.

flection of the efforts made to draw distinctions
nd peace as separate forms of activity. Trying to
rically the distinction between pacific and warlike
wever, far from simple, especially in modern times. The
raphernalia in former times, with the social conventions
ed the first shot of battle and the transition from a state of
a state of war, indicate that at certain times in history the
tion has been fairly easily made. Yet in the modern world,
cterized by the fact of nuclear deterrence, the symbolic use of
e clouds the clarity of definition. Is the stationing of troops along
sensitive border the actual use of force or simply a display to indicate that if undesired activity continues then force will actually be
used? Or, where force is actually used in the sense that soldiers kill
and are killed, is this a skirmish or is it a war? On the face of it, this
appears to be a discussion of semantics but it is more than this; it
reflects the need to draw key distinctions if we are to proceed on the
basis of a proper definition of what we mean by war, and how we
distinguish it from the generic term 'force'. Nor is this an end in
itself; we are seeking to understand why limited uses of force do not
lead to consequences which we normally associate with war.

At this point we can clarify the analysis by dealing with the
conceptual problem concerning force as a threat rather than as
actual use. In conventional force terms, the consequences we associate with the symbolic use of force are more akin to low-level uses
rather than to war (although this does not mean that a subsequent
increase to a higher level is prohibited). Thus, for the purposes of
what follows we may confine threats of force to the part of the
category called low-level force. As far as nuclear threats are concerned, these are qualitatively different from both conventional
threats and conventional warfare; if nuclear threats lead to nuclear
warfare, then the consequences are quite clear and sufficiently
different to constitute a different category.

The major conceptual issue, then, is to decide how we distinguish
war from force. We could evade the problem of definition and argue
that whilst we cannot define a war, we know one when we see one,
and we could find examples sufficient to verify this position. We
generally acknowledge that the large-scale uses of force that characterize the years 1914–18 and 1939–45 were wars and we describe
them as such. But if we consider the use of force by Britain in Ulster
and by the United States in the Dominican Republic in 1965, whilst
we know that force was used, we hardly classify it as war, but rather

as intervention, peace-keeping, 'a police action', or some such term. Intuitively we know that one was 'bigger' than the other and it is the concept of size that enables us to make a phenomenological distinction; all war is force but not all force is war. There is also a semantic point; 'war' has been used as a label to describe various phenomena or situations which, though they may be rightly described as conflicts, may not be correctly described as wars. For example, the labels 'Cold War', 'cod war', or 'the war of the sexes' each describe different types of conflict, which may be violent. But in these cases the term war is used in a sense distinct from that used in the present chapter. That is not to say that these other types of conflict are without consequence, but rather that the study of these consequences is beyond our present scope.

The fundamental distinction between war and peace needs to be recognized when we define what we are to mean by war. Consider, for example, the definition of war given by Quincy Wright:

> War in the ordinary sense is a conflict among political groups, especially sovereign states, carried on by armed forces of considerable magnitude for a considerable period of time. In this sense it is not sharply distinguished from peace.[1]

By the currently accepted standards of definition in social science this appears to be rather loose; what does Wright mean by a 'considerable magnitude' and a 'considerable period of time'? The answer is, it all depends on who is waging war, for there is no absolute definition of war, at least not in sociological terms, and Wright recognizes this by adding the proviso that war cannot be sharply distinguished from peace. At this point we may clarify the idea, used previously, of low-level military force. Given the incremental changes that mark a gradual movement away from one situation and towards another, it is quite evident that some decisions mark the end of one phase and the beginnings of another. However, the transition stage may be identifiable only *ex post facto*. That is, whether a distinction or decision is critical will depend on subsequent events. In relation to the Vietnam conflict, the decision to send more than 500,000 troops in support of American aims appears to have been a critical decision but the extent of its 'criticalness' assumes importance only in the context of a longer view. Clearly, scale is an important factor but whether force is low-level will depend upon the

[1] Entry on 'War', *International Encyclopaedia of Social Sciences*, VIII, 1968, p. 453.

extent to which high-level force is subsequently used. The term is essentially relative, as is Quincy Wright's definition of war.

Scale is important but the factor of scale is not simply quantitative; it is argued that once a key threshold has been reached, quantitative increases in force lead to qualitative changes. That is, once force is committed in such amounts or for such a long period of time, then qualitative changes take place in the domestic system of the state that is using force. What form these changes are likely to take is what concerns us. If we again consider the American venture in Vietnam in the 1960s the qualitative aspect of the definition becomes clearer. Initially, the American commitment was at a low level. By 1965, with more than half a million troops in Vietnam and a rising number of combat deaths, the by now large-scale conflict was promoting nation-wide debate within the United States regarding the stakes and risks that the venture entailed, the costs and the alternative uses to which the finance expended in war could be channelled. By virtue of the scope and duration of such conflicts it is argued that they are likely to have widespread consequences for the state that commits these forces, be they social, political, economic, or otherwise. These types of changes within the system may be generally referred to as social change. That is to say social is used in a particular maximal sense and refers to an aggregate change in the larger system which comprises other partial groups. By contrast, specific terms such as 'political' and 'economic', important as they are, refer to specific groups or subsystems. Generally, in what follows, when we refer to social changes we are referring to economic, political and other changes that significantly affect the behaviour of the system at large.

War and society in history

The question of the relationship between war and society is not particularly novel. Indeed, it has been a major preoccupation of moral and political philosophers since the time of Ancient Greece in the West, not to mention Islamic and Oriental cultures. Generally speaking, we may divide those who have discussed this issue into two groups: those who argue that war is somehow necessary or desirable in relation to the spiritual and/or material development of man, and those who argue that it is not. To give a detailed, comprehensive account of this controversial debate here is beyond both our scope and limited space, but a brief review by reference to prominent positions is in order. A convenient starting point is a discussion of the views of Heraclitus of Ephesus. Writing in pre-Socratic Greece, Heraclitus clearly stated his position: war, he contended, was the father of all and without it civilization, as he knew it, would perish. Thus, he went on, Homer was quite wrong in wishing to see the end of strife and war, for their complete disappearance would mean that not only war but 'all things would pass away'.

Heraclitus was quite emphatic: 'We must know that war is common to all and strife is justice.'[1] Nearer our own day G. W. F. Hegel, though he did not go so far as Heraclitus in supporting the view that war was the father of everything, contended that war was necessary to the prolonged existence of the state. (Why the 'state' is chosen by Hegel in preference to, say, the city, the church or the civilization is one of the enigmas of his philosophy; there is no logical reason why he should have limited his analysis to the state *per se*.) This element of Hegel's philosophy has been responsible for a good deal of controversy among those who maintain that Hegel justifies both war and the totalitarian state.[2] Yet Hegel did not glorify force for its own sake; he specifically rejected the notion that the state itself was to be organized solely on the basis of force, and not, as Hegel preferred, by a fundamental sense of order.[3] Nor did he argue that war, once begun, should be allowed to continue uncontrolled. War was, for Hegel, only a passing state of affairs and ought to be limited to the extent that it did not interfere with daily life: 'War ought not to be waged against domestic institutions, against the family and private life, or against persons in their private capacity.'[4] Yet when he comes to discuss war itself, Hegel is quite clear that it is not an accidental occurrence; accidents happen to accidental phenomena, but war is not one of them. For Hegel,

> War has the higher significance that by its agency . . . the ethical health of peoples is preserved in their indifference to the stability of finite institutions; just as the blowing of the winds preserves the sea from foulness which would be the result of a prolonged calm, so also corruption in nations would be the product of prolonged let alone 'perpetual' peace.[5]

War was the reification of 'the state' in Hegel's philosophical system.

---

[1] Quoted by Bertrand Russell, *History of Western Philosophy*, Allen & Unwin, London, 1946, p. 60.

[2] See, for example, B. Russell, ibid., p. 711.

[3] G. W. F. Hegel, *Philosophy of Right* (trans. T. M. Knox), Clarendon Press, Oxford, 1952, p. 282.

[4] Ibid., p. 215.   [5] Ibid., p. 209.

Hegel's use of the wind analogy becan[...] sed in the later years of the nineteenth century when war [...] orated into the system of Social Darwinism. The enorm[...] y of Darwin's *The Origin of Species* led to its permeatio[...] ls of thought, not least in social relations and politics. T[...] of the fittest' provided a justification for war in the [...] m of Social Darwinism and Spencer's widely accep[...] of progress. Steinmetz's conception of war is eminently [...] is context; echoing Hegel he observed:

> War is an institution ordained by God, [...] e nations in its balance. . . . Its dread hammer is [...] men into cohesive states and nowhere but in s[...] human nature adequately develop its capacity. [...] only alternative is degeneration.[1]

Ratzenhofer and Treitschke, an Austrian sociologist and German historian respectively, similarly considered war as an essential aid to progress. Nor was the sentiment necessarily shared only by those of Germanic origin. The French theological philosopher Renan had argued in 1871 that 'war was the cut of the whip which prevents a country from going to sleep',[2] whilst Bernhardi[3] contended that war was 'a biological necessity'. This position is currently represented by Mao who has argued that war is like a breeze, serving to waken populations. Nietzsche, it should be added, seemed to glory in war for its own sake, at least in his earlier works.

Needless to say, this position, which praised the supposed utility of war, did not go unchallenged. St. Augustine saw in war the embodiment of Original Sin and subsequently the view that war was a hindrance to progress gained widespread support. Seventeenth- and eighteenth-century plans for world peace reflect these views, as for example, Penn's and Kant's formulae for lasting peace (to which Hegel contemptuously referred).[4] Again in the nineteenth century, the Utilitarian and liberal economists and philosophers showed their disapproval (absolute or qualified) of war as an

---

[1] Quoted by Q. Wright, *International Encyclopaedia of the Social Sciences*, XVI, p. 453.

[2] Q. Wright, ibid.

[3] Quoted by C. E. M. Joad, *Why War?*, Penguin, Harmondsworth, 1939, p. 76.

[4] See F. H. Hinsley, *Power and the Pursuit of Peace*, C.U.P., Cambridge, 1963.

institution; Bentham, for example, argued that only as a choice between evils might war be necessary. James Mill's views were clear:

> To what baneful quarter are we to look for the cause of misery and stagnation which appear so general in human affairs? War! is the answer. There is no other cause. This is the pestilential wind that blasts the prosperity of nations. . . . Not only is the progression of the country stopped . . . but inroads are almost always made upon the part of the annual produce previously devoted to reproduction. The condition of the country therefore goes backward.[1]

In defence of his thesis Mill invoked the argument of Vauban, the French fortress builder, who had explained the comparative backwardness of France as being solely due to war.[2] Mill's son, John Stuart Mill, maintained that only one thing was worse than war and that was a failure to resort to war in the face of a just cause. In these terms he defended the American Civil War as a means to an end of injustice.

The confrontation between progress and war played a key role in the philosophy of Auguste Comte. Comte envisaged progress as being the necessary transition of society through three stages; the theological stage of progress lasted until the fifteenth century and was replaced by a metaphysical stage lasting until the mid nineteenth century, when it was superseded by the positivist stage. Trained as a scientist, Comte believed that scientific thought was the key to progress and, as a means to peace, he saw the union of an international, scientific meritocracy as the first step. In an age of industrialization Comte saw the means to unite states and peoples; the common, scientific interests of factory owners and managers would, he argued, begin to develop into a world community. War, he argued, would prevent this natural progression, for through the institution of war industrial development and intercourse would be retarded and, logically, so would world peace. In positing that war and industrial progress were diametrically opposed Comte was proved wrong by subsequent events, though why he was wrong need not concern us here. What is relevant here is that Comte's position is directly refuted by Sombart.

---

[1] James Mill, *Commerce Defended*, 2nd edn., 1808, pp. 119–20. Quoted in Edmund Silberner, *The Problem of War in Nineteenth Century Economic Thought*, Princeton U.P., Princeton, 1946, p. 42.
[2] Silberner, ibid.

Werner Sombart, a German economist, published in 1913 *Krieg und Kapitalismus*,[1] a study of the relationship between capitalism and war. The significance of Sombart's contribution is that whereas most of the philosophical discussions of war had centred on the discussion of whether war was 'good' or 'bad' in a spiritual or ethical sense, Sombart argued that the fact of war altered the fundamental structure of society which, in turn, influenced material, rather than spiritual, development. Initially, Sombart saw the frequency of European wars as being related to the development of capitalism, but instead of asking 'How far is war a consequence of capitalism' he asked, 'How far is capitalism a result of war?' Whilst he acknowledged that, from one viewpoint, war might destroy the seeds of capitalism by virtue of the force of absolute annihilation and transference of the means of financial control away from entrepreneurs and into the hands of the state, Sombart's thesis was that the incidence of war effectively acted as a stimulus to capitalist development. In order to fight a war the state must organize an army – this is Sombart's initial premise and the analysis that follows from this point is completely dependent, that is, the need for an army is an independent variable. The origin of a modern-style army, says Sombart, is uncertain but by Cromwellian times in England the martial style was in evidence, for the Puritan virtues were absorbed and formed the basis for martial virtues. 'This', for Sombart, 'is the decisive change which armies undergo from the sixteenth to the eighteenth centuries; in this period the free mercenary became the exercised, disciplined parade soldier, regimented with the birch.'[2] The demands made by the army upon the society it is to represent are the links with capitalist development.

Initially, the army has to be financed through income from colonies, taxes and loans. The consequence of this transfer of wealth is to pave the way for capital formation, the commercialization of economic life (with, as an example, the formation of stock exchanges) and the government practice of issuing subsidies. Once formed and financed, the army has to be armed, and this is the next step. The need for armaments, said Sombart, leads to the creation of military arsenals, necessarily larger and more concentrated than the workshops of craftsmen gunsmiths. Furthermore, the production and use of arms on such a large scale led to a standardization of weapon sizes, bores and, hence, standardized methods of production, which set the

[1] Duncker and Humboldt, Munich, 1913.
[2] Sombart, ibid., p. 30.

precedent for standardization of methods outside military workshops. The longer-term effects were to produce a concentration of manufacturing and a specialized division of labour. Also, since kings and princes needed to be self-sufficient in armaments, they wished to build their own factories – and did so. Subsequently, the demand for bronze cannon led to a rise in the price of copper and other metals, thus stimulating mining industries. The expertise gained in cannon making also facilitated the training of workers in the machine tool industry.

Apart from the demand for armaments, the demand for other supplies compounded the disruptive effects already caused by this new style of warfare. The state took over provisioning, absolving the individual in the army of the duty to do so himself, and this demand for goods necessitated a demand for ships in which they could be carried. Not only this, agriculture itself was stimulated in order to meet the demands of a growing market. Where there were garrisons, urbanization followed and created local mass markets. Entrepreneurs were stimulated by the desire to feed these growing markets and, when they did so, their accumulated profits formed a basis for capital accumulation.

In shipbuilding Sombart saw another stimulus to industrial development; the demand for ships to carry the food and provisions itself stimulated further demands. In support of this argument Sombart presents data from shipbuilding; in the period between 1620–30 and 1749 (during which the Thirty Years War and its aftermath afflicted Europe) the merchant marine of Britain increased by almost six times whilst the navy increased by almost nine times. In consequence, forests were depleted and the search for alternative fuels began, with the result that the coal industry flourished and paved the way for the Industrial Revolution.

Such was Sombart's thesis and anyone familiar with the elements of economics will recognize in it the chain of events akin to the multiplier; a single disruptive injection unfolds to produce large-scale changes. What, in effect, constitutes a refutation of the Sombart thesis appeared in 1950 with the publication of *War and Human Progress*[1] by the Harvard historian John Nef. Nef agreed that within the limits that Sombart had set his thesis was sound, but he questioned whether these limits were proper. 'What makes Sombart's thesis false is the limits he imposed on the subject', but fundamental

[1] John U. Nef, *War and Human Progress*, Harvard U.P., Cambridge, Mass., 1950.

problems had been ignored, wrote Nef. 'How important was the demand for new arms as compared with other, new, non-military demands, in changing the forms of industrialization, in encouraging the progress of capitalistic mining and manufacturing? What effects did fighting with the new weapons have on industrial development?'[1] These are, for Nef, the real questions to be answered and it is his contention that the large plant was not a creation of modern war, nor did war invariably lead to such a conclusion, as the continuing domestic manufacture of gunpowder in France demonstrated.

Furthermore, evidence is provided to show that the demand for private arsenals by dukes and kings did not necessarily lead to their construction; during the early seventeenth century, the only large-scale arsenal in Europe was at Suhl, in Germany, the products of which were widely distributed throughout Europe, and not until 1648 were similar factories built. Nef also provides evidence to show that the coal, alum and salt industries were characterized by 'capitalist' methods of production and that they developed independently of warfare. Moreover, during the reigns of Elizabeth and James I, times of relative peace, England developed her heavy industry.

Contrary to Sombart's assertion that war is itself a stimulus, the English experience of comparative calm whilst Europe was at war suggests that the very immunity from war stimulated industry, albeit due, in part, to the fact that competitors were handicapped. In the latter half of the sixteenth century and the first part of the seventeenth, the English and Dutch textile industries proceeded apace. Similarly, the English sugar industry grew most rapidly when, during the 1560s, the industry of the Spanish Netherlands was destroyed. Whilst most English sugar came from Antwerp before 1560, following the sack of Antwerp the English industry grew. The same is true of the iron industry, which grew rapidly in Sweden and England as the rest of Europe was at war. But the gains did not necessarily outweigh the losses; in 1640 the European output of iron was apparently no larger than it had been in 1530. Only the pattern of production had changed, with England and Sweden the leading producers, and if the demand for cannon is sufficient to explain the Swedish boom, it is not sufficient to explain the English growth; at this time cannon never became the largest item of production of the Weald iron industry.[2]

Evidence from ship construction too casts doubt on the Sombart

[1] Ibid., p. 66.   [2] Nef, ibid., p. 81.

thesis, for in the English case the desire to increase the size of the navy was made manifest during the reigns of Elizabeth and James I for trading purposes and not necessarily for warfare. Even in finance and commerce,

> It was not in France, Spain, Italy or Germany but in the states of Northern Europe – above all in England, the most peaceful state in the period 1558–1640 – that the private merchant gained an independence, an economic security from princely rule, and a consequent influence in government which were novel.[1]

Nef's refutation has been reviewed only very briefly here; anyone seeking a more detailed understanding of the historical and material development of warfare ought to consult it more fully. Yet from what has been said it is sufficient to cast serious doubt on Sombart's thesis and to render it controversial.

Yet what is the point of this historical discussion? Referring back to Hegel we find a defence of war in the abstract. What events subsequently proved to be the case was that warfare in defence or furtherance of the state was, implicitly, to alter the nature of the relationships within the state itself. This partly accounts for the current misinterpretations of Hegel's 'theory of war' – Hegel could not have defended war as we now know it, as a review of his precise call for limits to warfare make clear; on the basis of what Hegel wrote we must assume that he would have condemned, say, aerial bombing. In a longer perspective, as Nef's review of history shows, besides changing the nature of the state, warfare changes cultural values and, subsequently, intellectual and other values. War inevitably changes the nature of society – and with it, in turn, the nature of war. Thus, whilst the philosophical debate concerning the nature of war continued, it was reinforced by arguments focused upon the precise role of war. On this point both Nef and Sombart were agreed: war is significant as an agent of change – the precise point at issue concerned the real nature of war in the process of change. To ascertain with greater precision the role of war we need to look at particular cases, and this is our next task.

War as an instrument of change: three case studies

The three cases under scrutiny represent examples of what we may term three types of war: a civil war, a large-scale interstate war and

---

[1] Ibid., p. 100.

a war of national liberation (or a war of counter-insurgency). Whilst they represent different types of war they also illustrate the way warfare has developed in the last century: the American Civil War represents the 'classic' civil war of the nineteenth century; the First World War represents the total war of mass societies in armed conflict; and the Algerian War represents the war of national liberation that has been a conspicuous feature of the international system since 1945.

Furthermore, if these cases represent the changing nature of war they also typify the extent to which different changes are made manifest by different wars. Thus, British participation in the war of 1914–18 had the effect of extending the scope of democracy within Britain, as well as radically altering the relationship between state and society. Conversely, the experience of the French in the Algerian War of 1954–62 is sufficient to demonstrate that if war can extend the scope of democracy in some cases, in others it can severely strain the democratic system, perhaps even destroy it. Such was the case in France in 1958; the revolt of a significant part of the army was sufficient to threaten the constitutional system and lead to a major constitutional and political crisis. The precise role of the war, as compared to the influence of background factors, will be a major focus in what follows.

Yet if the French and British cases show the extent to which war influences different types of change in democratic practices ('progress' in one case and 'crisis' in the other) the case of the American Civil War is more perplexing. In one sense the role of the war in the economic development of the United States (which will be our major emphasis) is now less clear than it was previously. As we shall see, recent evidence seems to question prevailing interpretations. Given these simple pointers to aid the interpretation of each case, we can proceed to examine the cases in some detail. In a final section we will consider the implications of our findings.

Britain in the First World War

It is beyond our scope to give a detailed account of British involvement in the First World War, but it is possible to map the effect of the war on British society by reference to two important areas of reform; the extension of the franchise to women and the extension of government control of and intervention in society.

Britain declared war on Imperial Germany on 4 August 1914

following the German violation of Belgian neutrality. When the British Expeditionary Force left for the Continent it was fully expected that it would be home, triumphant, by Christmas. At home, the slogan 'business as usual' was coined by Churchill and it came to characterize the prevailing mood. Yet on the outbreak of war there was a call for volunteers to join the armed forces and by the end of September 750,000 had come forward. The mobile war that was envisaged came to nothing and by Christmas the British forces were enmeshed in the trench warfare of the Western Front. Consequently, and in conjunction with the enormous casualties suffered in the trenches, the call for volunteers persisted and men were leaving industry at the rate of 125,000 a month until June 1915.

As the pattern of warfare emerged after a few months, industry in Britain had to be reorganized and, with the manpower shortage, women began to fill the vacancies in industry and commerce. The effect of this was to provide an enormous boost to the campaign for women's suffrage – a campaign clearly in evidence as early as 1832, when Orator Hunt put the case for universal suffrage during the Commons debates on the Reform Bill. Throughout the nineteenth century the campaign gained momentum and in the years that preceded the outbreak of war in 1914 certain sections of the movement, under the leadership of the Pankhursts, became increasingly militant. The death of Emily Davison, who threw herself in front of the King's horse during the 1913 Derby, showed that at least a few were prepared to die for the cause. Large-scale demonstrations were held in London and the provinces, but with the coming of war a truce was declared. However, by July 1915 Christabel Pankhurst was again leading London demonstrations demanding for women 'the right to serve'. The war gave them ample opportunity to participate, even more so after the introduction of conscription in January 1916.

We must not, however, form the mistaken impression that, simply because of the war, women suddenly began to work. The major change was to move women into strategic occupations, munitions and transport, and out of domestic service. That is, women moved into occupations that had previously been the sole preserve of men. The number of women in manufacturing industry increased by 800,000 to 2·9 million.[1] Almost 200,000 women entered government service, half a million took clerical jobs and many worked on the

[1] Report of the Committee on Women in Industry, 1919, Parliamentary Papers (1919), XXXI, Cmnd. 135.

land.[1] The war changed the pattern of female employment; women were now conspicuously employed and seen to be doing responsible jobs. More important, 'middle-class women rallied to the call of duty and this could not pass unnoticed in homes which took for granted and therefore failed to notice the various occupations of the women of the working classes.'[2] Again, the war provided the opportunity to register the claim for a vote in view of the fact that, due to wartime disruption, the reform of the electoral register became a necessity, thus giving women the chance to press a claim for registration at a time of unavoidable disruption. The settlement of the issue came in 1917 with the report of the Special Speaker's Conference, which recommended that the issue of the women's suffrage be left to a free vote. As a result, the vote was extended to women on 6 February 1918, but initially only under stringent qualifying conditions and only to women over thirty years old.

If the war extended the scope of British democracy it also altered the guidelines on which that democracy ran; the war destroyed the basic tenets of *laissez faire* that had been the principle of state management before 1914 and necessitated the introduction of the rudiments of state control. Although this was done reluctantly by the government, it was subsequently unable to prevent the extension of state control. In three areas this pressure for novel government intervention manifested itself: the shortage of munitions, the spiral of prices due to profiteering and the shortage of foods caused by the wartime interruption of trade. The trench and bombardment warfare necessitated demands being made both for women to take the place of men and for the industrial system to produce more shells. Despite government directives to increase supply, shortages persisted and in consequence the government, under the provisions of the Defence of the Realm Act (DORA), set up several committees to investigate the problem of munitions. As a result, by March 1915 the Army Council and the Admiralty were empowered to occupy premises and utilize them for housing essential workmen, to requisition output and regulate the operations of factories. In April 1915 the Munitions of War Committee was established and later became the Ministry of Munitions, the first achievement of which was the War Munitions Act of July 1915. Under the terms of the Act, the government was

---

[1] A. J. P. Taylor, *English History, 1914–1945*, Penguin, Harmondsworth, 1970, p. 68.
[2] Constance Rover, *Women's Suffrage in Party Politics in Britain, 1866–1914*, Routledge & Kegan Paul, London, 1967, p. 206.

empowered to limit profits and attempt the settlement of industrial disputes which were held to hinder essential production. Such was the scope of the government powers that by March 1918 the government owned 250 quarries and mines and was in effective control of 20,000 other establishments.[1]

As far as the problem of prices was concerned, it was the subject of heated Commons debates, especially in 1915, with Asquith and Runciman hard put to defend *laissez faire*. Such was the campaign, however, that by the year's end the government had requisitioned shipping space and, after a widespread campaign against high rents, pegged rents at the 1914 level. The problem was compounded by the shortage of food. Yet, as late as 1916, there was still no means of food control other than for sugar, of which more than half of the pre-war British consumption had come from Austria–Hungary. In the latter half of June there was some anxiety about food shortages being deliberately created so as to raise prices, which led to the establishment of a committee to inquire into profiteering. As a result of these investigations the Food Department of the Board of Trade was established and, following the fall of the Asquith government, in December 1916, it was elevated to the status of the Ministry of Food.

The resumption of German submarine warfare in October 1916 led to the setting up of a commission to look into the supply of wheat and flour, to purchase, sell and control the delivery of flour on the government's behalf and to take steps necessary to ensure an adequate supply. However, the shortages persisted and rationing by compulsion was introduced in January 1918, with rigid controls on sugar. Public fears led to panic buying up of available supplies and inevitably this led to general rationing, first in London and then, from April 1918, throughout the country.

The War thus marked a clear turning point in terms of the intervention of the government into affairs it had previously reserved to the natural forces of the market. In the circumstances there seemed little alternative and ideological differences were of little consequence as the situation persisted. The facts of the transformation were clearly evident; as the government itself observed, 'the war has brought a transformation of the social and administrative structure of the state, much of which is bound to be permanent.'[2] Furthermore,

[1] A. Marwick, *Britain in the Century of Total War*, Penguin, Harmondsworth, 1970, p. 74. This book has been an especially valuable source of information relating to this particular section.

[2] Report of the War Cabinet for 1918, Parliamentary Papers (1919), XXX, Cmnd. 325, p. 214.

a prominent English historian has remarked of this transformation:

> The state established a hold over its citizens which, though relaxed in peacetime, was never to be removed, and which the Second World War was again to improve. The history of the English state and the English people merged for the first time.[1]

The Algerian War, 1954–62

What was to become the French war in Algeria began in the early hours of 1 November 1954 when a series of shootings and bombings occurred throughout Algeria. The immediate French response, not unnaturally, was to see these events merely as outbursts of anti-French feelings in Algeria. The official French reaction was therefore prompt and unequivocal; on 5 November the French Prime Minister, Pierre Mendès-France, firmly stated that Algeria was and would remain a part of France and that his government would tolerate no compromise with sedition. Within Algeria the French troops, numbering 60,000, were concentrated in the mountain areas with a view to apprehending the terrorists, who were assumed to be members of the Movement for the Triumph of Democratic Liberties. In fact the bombings were the work of the Revolutionary Committee for Unity and Action, which subsequently became the National Liberation Front (NLF). Since the major French preoccupations in the Maghreb at this time were concerned with the colonial campaigns in Tunisia and Morocco it is plausible to assume that the initial French view of the developing situation in Algeria was essentially one of limited control. However, as troops returned from Indochina and autonomy was granted in Tunisia, Algeria assumed greater significance. Thus, by mid 1955 the French forces in Algeria numbered 100,000. By August 1955 a State of Emergency was applied to the whole of Algeria, reinforcing emergency powers granted earlier to local officials, whilst at the same time it was announced that the conscripts who had entered the forces in 1954 would have their period of service extended.

Initially the terrorist activity was on a small scale but as it increased in scale, so did the French commitment to Algeria. Thus, despite allied pressure, France withdrew troops from NATO (as well as from metropolitan France and French West Africa) and sent them to Algeria. In April 1956 it was decreed that conscripts would

---

[1] A. J. P. Taylor, op. cit., p. 26.

be used in Algeria and that up to 200,000 reservists could be called up for the same purpose. The aim of French policy at this point was to establish a firm and large commitment in Algeria; after the defeat at Dien Bien Phu in Indochina in March 1954 and the granting of independence to Morocco and Tunisia, in February of 1956, the message was quite clear – France was not prepared to grant independence to Algeria. The sending of conscripts to Algeria, a move that, in the case of Indochina, had been fiercely opposed, provided further evidence of the French resolve.

The FLN were also reorganized in the latter half of 1956 but a good deal of harm was done to the FLN organization when in October 1956 Ben Bella and several other political leaders within the FLN were captured by the French whilst on their way to Morocco. Moreover, the stronghold of the FLN in Algiers, the Casbah, was neutralized in February 1957 when General Massu, with French paratroops, destroyed the FLN network by entering the area to break up the highly organized FLN network. Despite sporadic bombings within densely populated areas, the FLN was in an inferior position in 1957. However, so successful was the French strategy that by the end of 1957 there was talk in France of a devolution of power to a limited extent to Algeria. Thus, in the autumn a plan for some devolution of power to the Algerians was debated in the French National Assembly. The plan, or *loi cadre*, involved the continuation of Algeria as part of France but made provision for a series of federated territories each administering its own affairs and with provision for a system of electoral assembly that could lead to eventual Muslim control. In fact the plan was rejected by the National Assembly. It was, however, put before the Assembly again in January 1958 by the government of Felix Gaillard (which had come to power in November). By April, the Gaillard government had fallen from power when its Algerian policy came under fire in the wake of the Sakhiet incident. This occurred on 8 February 1958 when French aircraft bombed the Tunisian border village of Sakhiet, killing seventy-nine people and injuring more than one hundred. Given that the Tunisian and Moroccan border areas were used as sanctuaries by the Algerian guerrillas, the significant factor in relation to the Sakhiet incident was that it was carried out without ministerial consent.

Despite his fall from power, Gaillard was asked by President Coty to form an interim government until such time as a new government, led by Pierre Pflimlin, could be approved by the National Assembly.

The proposed appointment of Pfimlin precipitated demonstrations in Algiers on the part of the European settlers (*colons*) who feared that Pfimlin might negotiate with the Algerians, thus jeopardizing the position of the *colons*. By 12 May (the day before the National Assembly was to debate the appointment of Pfimlin) there were calls for a general strike in Algiers in protest. In this situation, with street demonstrations being held, General Massu called Gaillard and asked for instructions but was told that no authority could be granted since he (Gaillard) was no longer in power. At the same time, Pfimlin argued that he had no constitutional power since no confirmation of his appointment had been forthcoming. In this impasse, Massu assumed personal control in Algiers and became a central figure in a plot to return General de Gaulle, former leader of the Free French and the Assembly of the French People (RPF), to power. On 14 May President Coty broadcast to the army an appeal for loyalty. In Paris the newly approved Pfimlin was granted emergency powers for a period of three months and promptly proscribed a number of Right-wing groups in France. Five days later de Gaulle gave a press conference which in turn precipitated Left-wing strikes.

In this situation, the military leaders in Algiers threatened to invade France and install de Gaulle. Thus, on 24 May paratroops from Algeria landed in Corsica and took control of the capital, Ajaccio. On 27 May de Gaulle issued a statement to the effect that he had begun normal procedures to establish a republican government. In due course de Gaulle's assumption of power was legitimized at the ballot box; in September 80 per cent of those voting approved the plan for a new constitution and after a period as Prime Minister de Gaulle assumed the office of President in January 1959. The significance of all this is, briefly, that the policy that developed in relation to Algeria was sufficient to bring together two forces which contributed to the end of the Fourth Republic.

The representation of parties in the Fourth Republic was such that coalition governments became the norm rather than the exception. However, these coalitions were distinguished by, first, a minimal consensus and, second, essentially negative government. That is, few, if any, of the coalition partners were able to push through policy but they could, singly or together, prevent policy from being made by threatening to resign and bring down the government. Thus, between 1946 and 1958 more than a score of governments fell from power. Moreover, this system of rapid changeover inevitably produced periods in which there was an impasse in government whilst the search for coalition partners went on. Such a situation developed in 1958. In this situation, aptly described as *immobilisme*, the autonomous groups in Algiers precipitated a crisis of authority. Thus, the *colons* and the army determined to make a stand on the Algerian issue to prevent the total disintegration of the French empire – or so they believed. The net result was a constitutional crisis of the first order. This was, however, only the first stage. Whilst de Gaulle was supported by the Right on the assumption that he would not preside over the dissolution of the French empire, it became increasingly clear that his policy towards Algeria was more and more conciliatory.

Moreover, the Algerian War was becoming a cause of political conflict at home. In the early months of 1960 trades unionists and students struck in protest against the war, to be followed by the teachers' union, which advocated unconditional negotiations with the FLN. A good deal of opposition to the war centred upon the conscription issue and in September 1960 the 'Manifesto of 121' was issued. Signed by writers, intellectuals, civil servants and teachers, the manifesto questioned the duty of conscripts to serve in Algeria. Furthermore, in this atmosphere of intense vocal and highly publicized dissent, the government had frequent recourse to its emergency powers, which gave it the right to seize books, films and newspapers.[1]

In this atmosphere, French policy towards Algeria became increasingly conciliatory and, despite another Right-wing revolt in Algiers, moved on to a negotiated settlement at Evian, the result of which was an independent Algeria. The significance of the Algerian War should be fairly evident: the issue of French policy in the Algerian conflict led to the development of a situation in which the fundamental weaknesses of the Fourth Republic, a defective world view and domestic *immobilisme*, coincided to precipitate a major crisis. In this sense, the Algerian War was clearly instrumental in fundamentally altering the French perspective in political affairs.

The American Civil War

The origins of the American Civil War lie in the developing conflict between the northern industrial states and the southern agricultural

[1] On this point, see Martin Harrison, 'Government and Press in France during the Algerian War', *The American Political Science Review*, LXIII, 2, June 1964.

states over the issue of slavery. This is a conventional view. It is, however, a questionable assumption since slavery was only one of several issues which separated the northern and southern states in the middle years of the nineteenth century. Before the slavery issue became prominent, the question of the future nature of the developing United States was a source of political conflict. In the early 1850s the United States was industrializing only slowly, but by 1860 northern manufacturing was forging rapidly ahead. Technical innovations, for example, the sewing machine and the vulcanization of rubber, together with the rapid development of basic industries such as iron-making, paved the way for rapid growth. By contrast, the southern states were primarily agricultural, relying on the plantation (and hence, slave) system to produce cotton and tobacco, with this agricultural specialization being reflected in the low proportion of manufacturing done in the south, that is, less than one tenth. Furthermore, the majority of the southern trade with Europe (mainly cotton exports) was routed via northern ports. Thus growing southern dependence on the north led to a growing resentment among southerners, many of whom sought to establish their own independent trade links with Europe.

More importantly, the agricultural south still adhered to the basic tenets of Jefferson's conception of agricultural democracy as the ideal form of political organization in the United States. Consequently, among influential slave-owners in the south the northern drift to industrialization was perceived as a reactionary trend and, moreover, with the growing dependence of south on north, the theory of a northern conspiracy radically to alter the social fabric of the south gained currency. It was in the context of this growing conflict that the issue of slavery gained added importance. The issue came to a head in 1854 with the issue of the Kansas-Nebraska Bill, the core of which gave to the new territories (that is, the status accorded to the new lands before statehood) the right to decide for themselves whether or not they should be free or slave-states. After long debate the Bill was enacted by Congress, but the political stances adopted during its passage led to the sharpening of the north-south conflict. By 1856 the new Republican Party appeared to fight in the Presidential election on the platform of 'free soil', and whilst the stance did not favour the abolition of the institution of slavery, it did seek to contain it in the south. The Democrats sought a compromise with a view to reserving to the states themselves the right to decide the slavery issue and, although the Democratic candidate was elected to the Presidency, the predominantly Democratic south saw the rise of Republicanism as a growing threat.

Meanwhile, the verdict in the case of Dred Scott was being appealed against before the Supreme Court, fanning the flames of the conflict. Scott, a slave, was taken by his owner into free territory and claimed the rights of a free man. When these rights were denied he sought legal remedy. By the time the case reached the Supreme Court the issue assumed major importance and became the source of political dissent within the court. Republican gains in the elections of 1858 and the abortive attempt by John Brown to begin an armed insurrection at Harper's Ferry were seen in the south as evidence of a growing northern determination to use force to resolve the conflict.

Such was the developing conflict. By the time of Lincoln's election to the Presidency in 1860, pledged to the maintenance of the Union, the state of South Carolina summoned a state convention to decide on its future course of action. The convention favoured secession from the Union and five other states followed suit within six weeks. The immediate cause of the outbreak of fighting was the move by Lincoln to provision a garrison near Charleston, in South Carolina. When this move was made the garrison, Fort Sumter, was attacked by southern forces and surrendered. Thus, in April 1861, Lincoln called for a force of 75,000 volunteers to put down an insurrection in the southern states. In fact, the war that began in 1861 lasted until 1865, during which time the by now separate economies of the north and south were sufficiently reorganized to be able to support a war of movement and campaign. The precise extent of the war effort is difficult to ascertain owing to the paucity of information, but the war settled, for four years, into a war between a northern, industrial population of 22 millions, supporting an army of more than 2 millions, and a southern, agricultural population of more than 9 millions (with eleven states finally adopting the secessionist position), supporting an army of less than one million.

Strictly speaking, the American Civil War is not our major concern, but the issues that surround its interpretation are germane to the present analysis and it is especially valuable as a case study on these grounds alone.

The traditional interpretation of the effects of the war was that, by virtue of the demands it made upon the two systems, it inevitably led to the growth of the United States as a major industrial power and, equally inevitably, doomed the south to submission. Clearly recognizable in this interpretation is a thesis similar to that propounded by

Sombart in different historical circumstances. The demand for guns, ammunition, cannon, shoes and uniforms was held to provide the stimulus to northern industry and, in view of the more favourable circumstances in which these demands could be fulfilled, helped ensure a northern victory. Secondly, and consequent upon the shift towards industrial growth, it was held that the decline of Jeffersonian democracy paved the way for the transformation of political life to the extent that 'big business' was highly favoured and, in turn, American power assured.

Such is the thesis generally supported by Beard, Schlesinger and Hofstadter, among others. Beard's characterization of the war may be recognized simply by reference to his description of it as 'the Second American Revolution'. The war, for Beard, 'was a social war, ending in the unquestioned establishment of a new power in the government, making vast changes in the arrangements of classes, in the accumulation and distribution of wealth, in the course of industrial development and in the Constitution from the Fathers'.[1] Yet if this was the final result of the war, Beard was quite clear what role the war had played in bringing about this state of affairs: 'the physical combat that punctuated the conflict merely hastened the inevitable.'[2] Similarly, Schlesinger conceived the war as a catalyst which helped to accelerate existing trends: 'On these tender growths, the Civil War had the effect of a hothouse . . . nearly every branch of industry grew lustily.'[3] For Hofstadter, 'the growing demand for farm machinery as well as the demands for the "sinews of war" led to American industrial expansion . . . of necessity, iron, coal and copper production expanded.'[4]

This dominant thesis was challenged in 1961 when, at the centenary of the start of the war, a prominent American economic historian asked 'Did the Civil War retard industrialization?'[5] Whilst Cochran's analysis, which attempted to demonstrate that in certain fields (for example, the production of pig iron and the extraction of copper) the war actually halted or slowed down the rate of progress, was subsequently challenged on methodological grounds, it was sufficiently

[1] C. A. Beard, *The Rise of American Civilisation*, MacMillan, New York, 1927, p. 53.

[2] Ibid., p. 54.

[3] A. M. Schlesinger and A. C. Hockett, *Land of the Free*, New York, 1944, p. 345.

[4] R. Hofstadter, et al., *The United States*, Prentice Hall, Englewood Cliffs, N.J., 1957.

[5] T. C. Cochran, *Mississippi Valley Historical Review*, XLVIII, p. 197.

provocative that it opened up a field of debate that continues. Subsequently, evidence has been produced to support both positions. Engerman,[1] for example, cites evidence to suggest that the demand for small arms accounted for only 1 per cent of total iron output in the period 1861–5 and that this was more than offset by increased railway production. Similarly, the war may have been responsible for the relative decline of the Massachusetts shoe industry, which was cut off from access to its southern market. Again, a recorded decline in wheat output tends to cast doubt on the thesis that as food output grew, then so did the output of farm machinery.

What this recent reinterpretation of the standard assessments of the impact of the Civil War demonstrates is that these interpretations may be only partially correct. To be sure we can say that American society was changed by the war but to what extent was the war responsible? Could it be that the supremacy of the north would have been guaranteed anyhow, given the relative size of the combatants and their degrees of economic specialization? Or alternatively, we might be able to contrast the impact of economic as compared to political factors. However, the essential feature of this case, as compared to the other two cases studied, is that, given the prevailing state of the conflict before it developed into armed conflict, it appears that the combatants were developing separate economies and practices. The war itself seems to have acted as a catalyst by hastening the advent of northern supremacy, so that the relative influence of the war is measurable in relation to a prevailing state of conflict.

Conclusion

Given the nature of these three cases, what kinds of inferences, if any, can we draw from them that might help us assess the role of war in the process of social change? Initially, if we make use of two simple variables, time and commitment (that is, the extent to which resources are expended in armed conflict), both of which can be measured on a simple scale, then we can conceive of at least four possible situations involving the use of force:

(1) Short time and small commitment.
(2) Short time and large commitment.

[1] S. Engerman, 'Economic impact of the Civil War', R. Andreano (ed.), *The Economic Impact of the Civil War*, 2nd edn., Schenkman, Cambridge, Mass., 1967.

(3) Long time and small commitment.
(4) Long time and large commitment.

On the basis of a simple review of these four situations, certain simple hypotheses spring to mind. For example, one might reasonably expect to find a greater probability of social change in the type (4) case, where there is a large commitment of resources spread over a long period of time: one would expect that the longer the conflict endures, with no sign of a declining commitment, then the more likely is it that existing patterns of social behaviour will be unable to cope with these high demands. That is, if the commitment is sustained, at whatever cost, then we may say that the war is in pursuit of the survival goals of the system, which are at stake in the conflict. Into this category we may place the example of Great Britain in the First World War; as the limits of the normal system were reached (that is, the shortage of men), then the system was changed (to include women, in many cases for the first time), so as to provide sufficient resources to win the war. If type (4) is an extreme type, then so is (1). Here we might expect to find little, if any, social change resulting from the use of force. Furthermore, we need not characterize this situation as a war situation, but rather as a situation where force is used only within the normal limits of the system. The case of Anguilla springs to mind in this regard; the sending of British troops to Anguilla was a negligible drain on the British armed forces since only a few soldiers were sent to do fairly routine tasks, with no special requirements. The effects upon the British system of sending troops to Anguilla were negligible.

Cases (2) and (3) represent interim cases or transition stages between the two extremes. Thus we might usefully classify the British forces in Ulster as belonging to case (3), and the American intervention into the Dominican Republic in 1965 as something approximating to a case (2) situation. However, given this initial classification, it does not account for obvious differences in apparently similar cases. For example, we might describe the French commitment to Algeria as being similar to the British case in the First World War in that both might properly be classified as examples of type (4). There are, however, quite apparent differences. Whilst the British case, generally speaking, led to a 'closing of ranks' for the duration of the conflict, the French case did not. To explain the difference between them we have to refer to the nature of the war and relate it to the prevailing conditions at home. If the war is 'popular'

– in the strictly limited sense that people think that it is worth fighting, say, in defence of liberty, opposition to Nazism or any other tyranny – then the greater is the probability that people will 'get on with the job' and tolerate conditions they would not normally tolerate in peacetime. To cite another example, the shift-work system in the Second World War was hardly popular, but it was tolerated on the simple grounds that it was necessary. In such cases, any changes are likely to take place within a consensus framework; that is, give the situation, people will tolerate rather than enter into conflict.

This may be contrasted with the situation where the utility of the war is questionable on the grounds of efficacy, morality or justice. Thus, for example, in regard to the French conflict in Algeria, as the conflict wore on the methods being used came into question. Hence, there were conflicts in France regarding the morality of the torture methods used in Algeria, conflicts over the sending of conscripts to fight in a colonial war (witness, for example, the conflicts that followed the 'Manifesto of 121' and the Right-wing counter-manifesto) or conflicts over the suspension of civil liberties (for example, seizure of books or newspapers). In this situation, where the fundamental war aims are brought into question, it is more probable that people will dissent rather than tolerate. On this point the experience of the United States in Vietnam is also indicative of this situation. As the conflict wore on, with few perceived gains, the strategy and tactics of the war came under increasing criticism. For example, the defoliation of forests, the high-altitude bombing of settlements, uncontrolled killings and extension of the war into adjacent areas was increasingly criticized on moral and political grounds. Furthermore, the criticism manifested itself in widespread demonstrations – although whether this is in itself significant is another issue.

Related to this situation is that which may be characterized by a simple win-lose dichotomy. Thus, other things being equal, one might expect to find more widespread social change, characterized by conflict, where the war is quite evidently being lost. Conversely, one might find less social change where the war is being won.

The issue of what precisely constitutes change must, of necessity, be discussed in relative terms. To take an example that is not clear-cut, is a street demonstration a symptom of a change or is it a cause of change? When one observes a street demonstration in a situation where it is not a normal event (for example, Red Square, Moscow) then this may be symptomatic of a change in the system. However, where demonstrations are an accepted form of protest, then, by demonstrating, demonstrators may help set in train a process of change.

By a circuitous route, we come back to where we started, with Livy arguing that the effect of the war will depend upon the body it afflicts. This ought not to be construed as stating that we have advanced little since Livy. Rather it highlights the problems inherent in the social sciences; given the nature of human relationships, we cannot confidently state that 'A will lead to B'. What we can do is say that, given certain factors, some things are more probable than others. Thus, there is no simple answer to the question: Does war lead to social change? What we can say is that certain types of changes follow certain types of wars in certain types of states. Of course, we could argue that all cases are unique – as they are – and eschew generalization; but in some situations particular instances illustrate remarkable similarities.

Be that as it may, the evidence from history and from more recent cases suggests that the use of force is a double-edged tool; on the one hand, force has a clear role as an instrument of change. On the other hand, the use of force may also lead to situations where change is neither planned nor wanted.

Index

DATE DUE